ECONOMIC ISSUES, PROBLEMS AND PERSPECTIVES

THE FUTURE OF REAL ESTATE

ECONOMIC ISSUES, PROBLEMS AND PERSPECTIVES

Additional books and e-books in this series can be found on Nova's website under the Series tab.

ECONOMIC ISSUES, PROBLEMS AND PERSPECTIVES

THE FUTURE OF REAL ESTATE

JAN VEUGER
EDITOR

nova
science publishers
New York

Library of Congress Cataloging-in-Publication Data

ISBN: 978-1-53619-414-2

Published by Nova Science Publishers, Inc. † New York

CONTENTS

PREFACE

***Jan Veuger**, PhD**
Saxion University of Applied Sciences, The Netherlands

The future of real estate? Whoever knows, may say what it looks like. No one can really predict how the real estate market will develop. However, we can look at patterns, how they might develop and thus give a direction to the future of real estate. This book wants to contribute to that.

COVID-19 has had a considerable influence on society and real estate in particular in the recent period. We are surprised by a development that we have not seen coming and that has a considerable influence on living, working and shopping. The various manifestations of lockdowns around the world have been gradually phased out and reset in 2020. This has a structural impact on living, working and shopping and therefore has a direct impact on the use of property. In view of the fact that COVID-19 will be present in many respects as long as there is no or sufficient vaccination or effective medicine available (yet), this means that COVID-19 will have a significant impact on real estate and urban developments. Perhaps if we look back later on this period and any new lockdowns, this

* Corresponding Author's E-mail: j.veuger@saxion.nl.

pandemic will prove to have been the starting point for drastic property changes.

Many were surprised by the empty shelves in supermarkets during the first days of the pandemic. The supply chains were running at full speed, but a large part of the retail sector came to a standstill or switched to online. Multi-channel has now really proven itself and COVID-19 has abruptly increased the demands on 'last mile' logistics spaces. Much more will change in the area of supply chains. Moreover, in the light of increasing trade tensions, there is a trend of onshoring and it is clear that logistics and warehousing will become increasingly important. Public space is also in the spotlight. The importance of parks and greenery was great during the lockdown. Guaranteed distance on streets and squares will remain the focus of attention in the coming period. Space is scarce. We need terraces in order to realize some turnover. And the fact that the car is currently considered a safe means of transport - what does that mean in terms of traffic pressure?

A number of real estate experts in the world at various universities have each looked at developments affecting the future from their own perspective and share that knowledge with everyone. Topics covered in this book are: (1) Blockchain and Real Estate in The Netherlands: a Database exploring 2015-2018 and Extrapolation to the Future, (2) Principle of Substitution in the face of COVID-19 Pandemic: An Application to Tenant's Choice in Commercial Real Estate Markets. (3) Selected Aspects of Slovenian Legislation on Lease of Agricultural Land and Forests, (4) Land Value Capture's Potential in Norwegian Projects, (5) Environmental Stress and Contemporary Understanding of Human-built Environment relations: Study Case on Zero-waste City Ljubljana, (6) Property development viability and community spirit – rethinking the safety angle, (7) Implementation of Land Policy at Local Level, and impacts of the Functioning of the Real Property Market, (8) Work From Hotels: is Hybrid the Future and (9) Real Estate as a Service. The following summaries can be drawn from these contributions.

1. The way in which Blockchain and real estate will develop in the coming years are not the only obvious. The true meaning of the blockchain technology for real estate still needs to be investigated. I am still curious to understand and clarify the value of Blockchain for real estate processes. Doubt continues to exist and is therefore a feeding ground for further research, because we do not know what we have not seen (Jan Veuger).
2. The principle of substitution is an important concept in economics and valuation of real estate. The principle postulates that the upper limit of the market value will be set by the cost of acquiring a similar substitute property. This means that no investor will be willing to pay more for an investment property than the amount it would cost to build or buy a similar one. However, most studies on the application of this principle are focused on assessment of value and less on tenants' choice. The recent COVID-19 pandemic, which has resulted in a barrage of scholarly articles on its impact to various sectors of the economy, provides an opportunity for the investigation of the principle of substitution from the tenant's perspective. While most studies have focused on the investors' side, as it relates to vacancies and loss of business, little attention is being paid to the behavioural changes amongst tenants as clients of these services. As explained within the concept of the principle of substitution, tenants are trading-down (especially in the residential market) or being forced to work from home, in essence abandoning commercial space. Thus the question that emerges is: what is the future of real estate in a post COVID-19 environment? The paper undertakes a detailed analytical review of emerging literature on measures to combat COVID-19 (such as social distancing, working from home, etc) in relation to levels of rentals and vacancies in residential and commercial real estate rental markets. The paper then goes further to investigate these dynamics within the Zambian context (Ephraim Kabunda Munshifwa, Niraj Jain, Anthony Mushinge and Roy Alexander Chileshe).

3. The article presents the legal provisions on the lease of agricultural land and forests in Slovenia, as well as some of the issues arising from the current Agricultural Land Act (ZKZ) and Forest Act (ZG). These two laws feature several specific limitations in leasing out farmland, some of which have been kept from the socialist times of former Yugoslavia. Under the ZKZ, a landowner who wishes to lease out agricultural or forest land must first publish their intent and wait for applicants. Each agricultural lease agreement must be approved by the relevant administrative unit and entered in the land register. Moreover, the law grants pre-emption rights to certain persons (existing tenant, tenants or owners of neighbouring plots, etc.). The long and complicated procedure, as well as the inability to freely choose the tenant result in a large majority of landowners leasing out their agricultural land without the mandatory procedure, although court practice considers such agreements null and void. This often leaves tenants without the legal protection intended for them by law (e.g., minimum lease duration). Nevertheless, even tenants with contracts that have not been approved have the possibility of registering actual use of agricultural land, which is a requirement for direct payments to farmers under the EU's common agricultural policy. Because the Farmland and Forest Fund of the Republic of Slovenia, which manages publicly owned farmland and forests, is virtually the only one to fully comply with the provisions of the ZKZ, the authors propose removing some of the limitations. While the obligation of publishing a lease offer may be appropriate for publicly owned land, it is a disproportionate intervention in the property rights of private landowners. Moreover, the pre-emption rights have proved problematic, since they allow existing tenants on state- and municipality-owned agricultural land to extend their leases indefinitely, and they also limit the right of private landowners to freely choose their tenants (Marijanan Kunc, Boštjan Aver and Alenka Temeljotov Salaj).

4. The potential for implementing Land Value Capture (LVC) strategies in Norway was the object of research. In order to evaluate such a potential, case studies have been oriented both to look at a re-zoning's effect on real estate value and to understand how private infrastructure contributions are gathered in Norway today. Methodology used is a literature review for establishing knowledge regarding LVC instruments, an analytical study regarding relevant Norwegian legislation for private infrastructure contributions, and a case study. The results show that several professionals, mainly real estate developers and academics, have been consulted regarding the matter throughout the work, as well as basic estimations and calculations have been carried out in the study. The land value of the properties assessed in the case study, which are a subject for re-zoning and a new local plan, turned out to be highly dependent of the utilization degree. The implications show a possibility to develop a new system for gathering private infrastructure contributions in Norway, based on replacing both development agreements and the infrastructure work up duty with a re-zoning fee, that captures plan made values, where the revenues shall be spent on nearby, necessary infrastructure measures (Alexander Bergsland Finsnes and Alenka Temeljotov Salaj).
5. In this research, we systematically review the impact that research on environmental stress, i.e., poor housing and neighbourhood quality, has had on the current understanding of the relationship between humans and the environment. It is shown that poor quality housing, high noise levels, lack of natural light in the house, poorer physical quality of neighbourhoods, living in low-income neighbourhoods, etc. are associated with increased physiological and psychological stress. We believe that built environmental relationships are closely related to attitudes towards waste in the neighbourhood. We focus on transforming our society so that all unnecessary waste is disposed of and everything that is produced can be reused, repaired, composted, or returned to the system. In a

growing number of regions, local groups of individuals, businesses and municipalities are taking significant steps to eliminate waste in our society. We highlight the case study: Zero Waste City Ljubljana, which is the first European capital to be on the way to Zero Waste. We confirmed the hypotheses that there is a strong sustainable interaction between the psychological processes underlying human behaviour and the built environment and that among sustainable construction environmental factors waste management expresses these interactions at night. We believe that the positive effects of research can only be achieved with sustainable interactions between the psychological processes underlying human behaviour and the built environment (Bojan Grum and Darja Kobal Grum).

6. In the spirit of Jardina's (2019) eloquent argumentation, humans are tribal creatures, when push comes to shove. We cannot ignore deeper instincts programmed into us, despite our cognitively developed brain functions. In a crisis situation, cognitive higher level "learnt" behavior is forgotten, and replaced by simpler neural processes. So the thin crust of altruism disappears; instead, we just favor our own kin, or reasonable similarity, the very least. By implication, what by today's standards is "racism", becomes the norm, as with all animals including humans. From a public choice perspective, the logical assertion [sic] would then be that, if we really live in a "racist" reality, as so often heard, we would need representatives of this "silent majority" of "racist" communities to decide about how we develop our built environments – and not just physically, but socially too (Tom Kauko).
7. The central question of the research was whether land policy impacts the operation of the real property market at local level in Slovenia, specifically in the City Municipality of Nova Gorica (MONG). The research found that land policy is an important integral part of the social and economic system and the spatial planning policy; and it should function in conformity with other policies. When defining the land policy, its principles, objectives

and instruments need to be taken into account. However, in this respect, it is required to make an analysis of the situation and trends in the areas of spatial planning, land transactions and land management. The research presents the results of the analysis of several spatial planning and real property market aspects over the period of the last 13 years in the MONG and its surrounding area of Gorica. They confirmed the research dilemma (Božena Lipej and Nastja Mihelj).

8. Already before but especially during the Covid-19 pandemic, working remotely and working from home increased. However, not every knowledge workers can and wants to work from home. Before the crisis, e.g., business travellers, independent professionals, small business, freelancers already looked for flexible workspace. This group has now been joined by those who look for an alternative to working from home. This provides opportunities for coworking spaces and organisations that traditionally are not focussed on providing workplace: hotels. Besides hospitality, they may also offer workplaces: hybrid hospitality. This chapter discusses what options there are in the market regarding alternative workplaces. It examines coworking spaces, working-from-hotels, and hybrid hospitality. Furthermore, the chapter discusses what hybrid means, as it may be diversification of the offer, using existing rooms for another purpose, and intensifying space use by enabling an easy conversion of a room depending on the function needed. Furthermore, the chapter discusses the hybrid trend for hotels is there to stay (Hester van Sprang and Brenda Groen).
9. When looking at the expertise in the RICS Research Group and Development in The Netherlands and a holistic approach to the possible relevant developments in the field of the built environment - whether or not influenced by COVID-19 - an integral approach is of great importance for the raison d'être of real estate. A long-term approach to real estate will increasingly play a role in which the boundaries between construction and

management of the built environment are blurred, but where there is still a long way to go to bring service to a higher level. We therefore look from three different perspectives by experts from this group at (1) Corona crisi accelerates the green blue revolution in real estate (2) Perspectives of Urban Mixed Use in Post-Corona Central Urban Areas and (3) cooperation in new coalitions (Jan Veuger, Joris Winters, Herman Kok and Paul Wessels).

In: The Future of Real Estate
Editor: Jan Veuger

ISBN: 978-1-53619-414-2

Chapter 1

Blockchain and Real Estate in the Netherlands: A Database Exploring 2015-2018 and Extrapolation to the Future

***Jan Veuger**, PhD**

Professor Blockchain, Saxion University of Applied Sciences, Schools of Finance & Accounting, Creative Technology and School of Governance, Law and Urban Development in the Netherlands

Abstract

The Foundation for International Blockchain and Real Estate Expertise (FIBREE) was founded in Amsterdam in 2018 with the aim of bringing together real estate professionals and blockchain specialists from all over the world to exchange expertise. FIBREE is aware of the current hype about blockchain technology, which does not always contribute to getting to know it better. FIBREE's mission is to help create a realistic

* Corresponding Author's E-mail: j.veuger@saxion.nl.

expectation pattern that will allow the real estate market, step by step, to discover and exploit the true potential of blockchain technology. By bringing together the expertise of pioneers in this field and sharing knowledge and insights already gained, FIBREE wants to make an important contribution to the adoption and implementation of this technology in the real estate market in the coming years. On the MIPIM Proptech Paris July 1-2 we presented a first Industry Report 2019 that gives an indication of development of Blockchain and real estate from research of FIBREE worldwide. This article provides an overview and analysis of all relevant scientific publications in the Netherlands, and does so within a context of a first small international exploration of international research, experts and products.

Keywords: blockchain, real estate, database, research, products, experts

Introduction

There are some arguments for development the foundation as an international platform of professionals for professionals which is objective, neutral and integrity as core values. There is a growing network of 2.000+ professionals who share an interest in blockchain & real estate with partnerships with relevant professional business organizations and -platforms. FIBREE works in a decentralized structure: participants set the agenda via regional representatives. Together they create a realistic perspective on the applicability of blockchain in the real estate industry. In this article we look at a study that was carried out in 2018 to give an idea of the state of affairs regarding blockchain in real estate across 5 continents and 63 regions to the extent that this was public at the end of 2018.

1. Covering and Regional Chairs

FIBREE has been developing a global network since the beginning of 2018 to facilitate a global network on the current situation regarding blockchain and real estate on three different perspectives: research, experts and products. In total we are working on covering 63 regions and 5 continents: Eurasia (consisting of the continents of Asia and Europe), Africa, America (North and South America), Antarctica and Australia. On the reference date 31 December 2018, 24 regions - 38% of the target number of 63 regions - are represented in this study, in which Europe is strongly represented with 14 regions or 58% of the participating regions.

Table 1. Covering country, continent and region

Target Country	Continent	Region
Austria	Europe	Vienna
Austria	Europe	Graz
Brazil	America	Sao Paulo
Croatia	Europe	Zagreb
Georgia	Europe	Tibilisi
Germany	Europe	Berlin
Germany	Europe	Stuttgart
Germany	Europe	Frankfurt
India	Asia/Pacific	Bangalore
Israel	Middle East	Tel Aviv
Italy	Europe	Milano
Netherlands	Europe	Amsterdam/Enschede
Poland	Europe	Warsaw
Slovenia	Europe	Ljubliana
Switzerland	Europe	Zug
Taiwan	Asia/Pacific	Taipeh
TheNetherlands	Europe	Amsterdam
United Kingdom	Europe	London
USA	America	New York
USA	America	North America
USA	America	Seattle
USA	America	Chicago
USA	America	New York
USA	America	Silicon Valley

2. Methodology Worldwide and the Netherlands Specific

We asked everybody at the Regionals Chairs (RC) to collect data with the info of (1) which blockchain and real estate product-suppliers or initiatives do you see, (2) which research-output on blockchain and real estate do you have and know and (3) who are the experts with which specific expertise in the field of Blockchain and real estate that you see?

Table 2. Overview of libraries of universities (of applied sciences) in the Netherlands with a real estate course or subject related thereto

University	City	Source	Hits
Amsterdam School of Real Estate	Amsterdam	Public	5
Delft University of Technology	Delft	Public	25
Eindhoven University of Technology	Eindhoven	Public	80
Fontys University of Applied Sciences	Eindhoven	Not public	0
Hanze University of Applied Sciences	Groningen	Not public	0
Maastricht University	Maastricht	Not public	0
Radboud University	Nijmegen	Not public	0
Rotterdam University of Applied Sciences	Rotterdam	Part Public	95
Saxion University of Applied Sciences	Enschede	Public	23
Tias Business School	Tilburg	Public	491
University of Groningen	Groningen	Public	24
Unvirsity of Amsterdam	Amsterdam	Public	47
Univirsity of Twente	Enschede	Public	10
Utrecht University	Utrecht	Not Public	0
Wageningen University & Research	Wageningen	Public	29
Total Dutch universities			829

The research looked for the combination of blockchain and real estate in the output of the various universities for research. The data collection started in mid-2018 and in particular for the 24 regions in the month of December 2018. In January and February 2019, the analyses were carried out centrally and in co-ordination, with some checks being carried out at the RC. The data collection does not include the announcements and reports of seminars, conferences and meetings, as well as duplications in professional journals. It has also been observed with some regularity that publications were no longer available in the libraries and gave an error message. The data collection for research in the Netherlands took place at all universities (of applied sciences) to which a real estate course is linked or related. In the public or non-public libraries, the data collection took place whereby it should be noted that much was public, but not everything.

3. Conclusion Research The Netherlands

The database of the Netherlands has a scale of 131 virtually one hundred percent score on the parts author, title, company name or university, research - product - expert, level, subject, country, publication year, keyword and link. The accrued database thus amounts to 16% (n = 130 ^{829}) of the hits found that have been stripped of regular announcements of seminars, master classes, press releases, news items, opinions, columns and the like. Within the database, a distinction has been made between General or Real Estate because a number of articles do contain material about Blockchain and real estate, but most of them are about Blockchain in general. From this perspective, 59% (n = 77 ^{130}) are fully focused on real estate and blockchain.

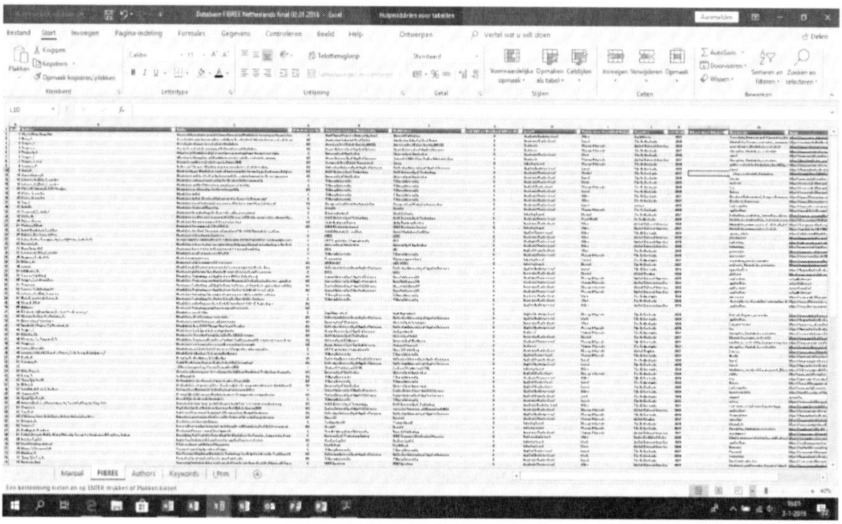

Figure 1. Example of the database Research the Netherlands.

If we fully analyze the database that has been built up, the following figures will be published on numbers of publications in company name or (applied) university, numbers or publications levels, number of publications by Topic, number of publications by country, publication year, keywords and most common authors.

3.1. Company Name or University

Of all 131 publications, a total of 82 universities in the Netherlands, with several producing only one or two publications. When these are excluded from the analysis, it appears that much can be traced back to the libraries of Tilburg University (24 publications), Rotterdam University of Applied Science (18 publications), followed by Saxion University of Applied Sciences (7 publications) and Hanze University of Applied Sciences (7 publications) and University of Amsterdam (7 publications). As far as is known now, there is no PhD research in the Netherlands in the area of Blockchain and Real Estate.

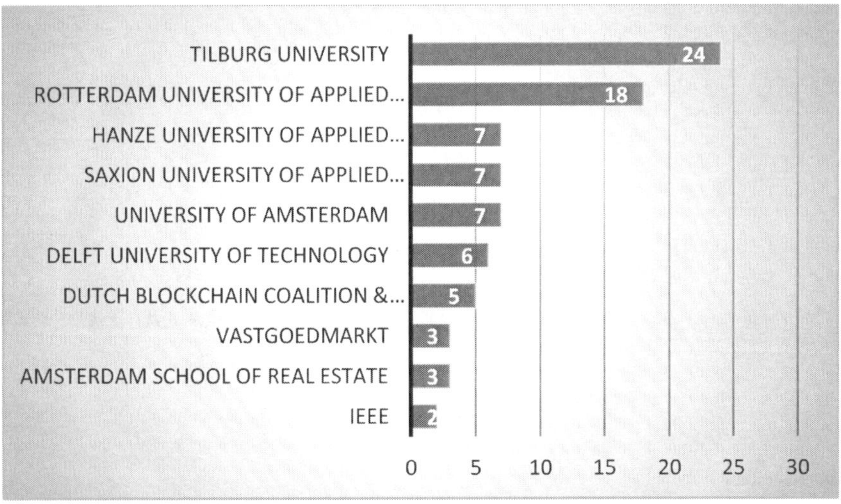

Figure 2. Number of publications in company or (applied) university.

3.2. Levels

The level of publications is high, especially at the academic master level (n = 64 [130]), followed by industry-based (n = 30 [130]), applied bachelor's (n = 21 [130]) and master's level (n = 10 [130]). This means that the academic level is high and the industry is also explicitly present in the field of publications.

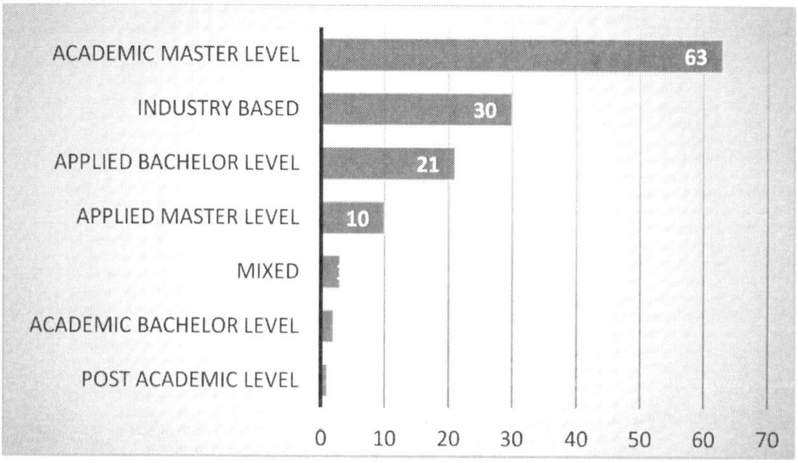

Figure 3. Number of publications per Level.

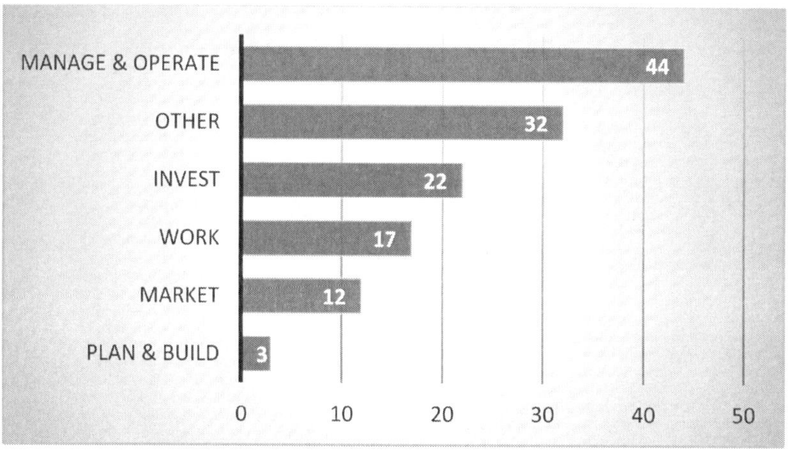

Figure 4. Number of publications per Topic.

3.3. Topics

The topics are mainly in themes such as Manage and Operate, Invest and Work, together a share of 65% (n = 84 [130]). The topics of the publications are in sequential numbers: Manage & Operate 35% (n = 45 [130]), Other 25% (n = 32 [130]), Invest 17% (n = 22 [130]), Work 13% (n = 17 [130]), Market 9% (n = 12 [130]) and Plan & Build 2% (n = 3 [130]).

3.4. Countries

The Netherlands is strongly represented in the number of publications, but in view of the demarcation of the working area of universities and applied universities in the Netherlands, this is not a special feature. However, the influence of the United Kingdom and United States of America compared to all other countries in the table below is clearly visible in this database. This means that they are also in this research area on this research area in the Dutch database.

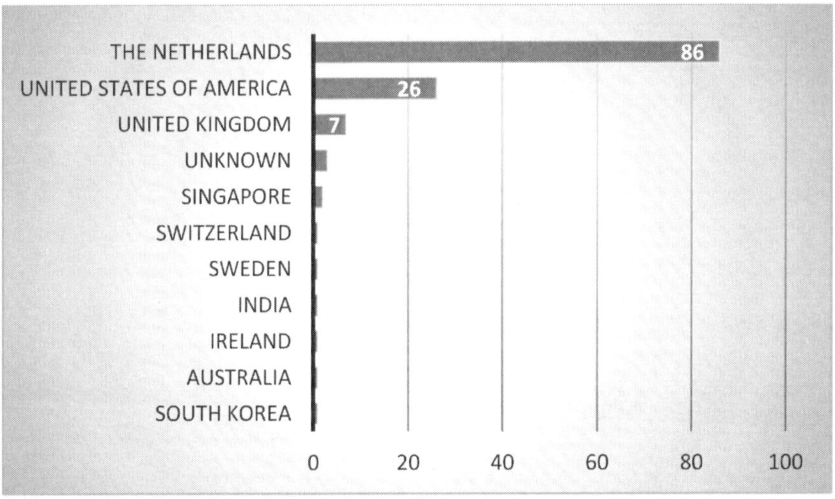

Figure 5. Number of publications per Country.

3.5. Publication Year

When we look at the years in which the publications took place, in 2018 the number of explosives has risen in relation to the previous year 2015-2017. This study shows that 55% (n = 72 [130]) of the publications appeared in 2018 compared to 36% (n = 47 [130]) in 2017 and 4% (n = 5 [130]) in 2016 and 1% (n = 1 [130]) in 2015. At the start of 2019, a number of (4%) publications are already visible (n = 5 [130]). The attention in publications about Blockchain and real estate has mainly developed in 2017 and will continue in 2018. Given the upward trend, it is interesting for a follow-up study into how 2019 will develop in this area.

3.6. Keywords in a Word Cloud

The 130 databases from which this research is based have been added as far as possible. When these are included in a word cloud and the most common words in size of the word become visible, the following figure and image will appear. This shows that besides blockchain, technology, estate and disruption, the words governance, public, energy, economic, management, invest, finance and registry are very common.

3.7. Most Common Authors

The database shows that the most common authors are Veuger and co-authors 10% (n = 15 130), Tjong Tjin Tai 5% (n = 7 130), Lafarre and van der Elst 3% (n = 4 130) and Dutch Blockchain Coalition and Dutch Digital Delta together are 4% (n = 5 130). A substantive analysis of these authors shows that their focus is on vision, agenda, organization meetings, notaries, contracts. Legal business application possibilities in general to real estate and blockchain. Specifically, this can be described per author in alphabetical order as follows.

The Dutch Blockchain Coalition (DBC) and Dutch Digital Delta, two affiliated organizations, mainly published their mission and vision (Blockchain for Good, the vision and mission of the DBC, 2018), the knowledge and innovation agenda (Knowledge and Innovation). Agenda ICT 2016-2019, 2017) in anticipation of further elaboration of its plans in the Legacy Coalition (2017) and Smart contracts as a specific application of Blockchain technology in 2017-2018. The Dutch Blockchain Coalition is a public-private partnership of partners from financial services such as banks and insurance companies, the logistics, energy, security and ICT sectors, ministries, the knowledge world, supervisory parties such as the

Netherlands Authority for the Financial Markets (AFM)) and the Royal Dutch Notarial Association (KNB) and organizations such as TNO, NWO and ECP | Platform for the Information Society. The coalition is an initiative of the Ministry of Economic Affairs and Climate. Dutch digital delta is the meeting place to connect and create. It is a national platform, intended for everyone involved in technological innovation.

Figure 6. Keywords in a cloud.

All publications of dr. A.J.F. Lafarre LLM MSc (professor of law Tilburg University with the expertise on Corporate Governance, Law & Economics and Shareholder Meetings (AGMs)) en prof. dr. C.F. van der Elst (professor of law and management of Tilburg University with the expertise Business transactions; Corporate governance; Enterprises; Law and economics; Legal persons law) were published in 2018 and are mainly about the organization around the application of Blockchain for meetings: *Blockchain and smartcontracting for the shareholder community* 2018),

Blockchain and the 21th century annual general meeting (2018), *Blockchain maakt vergaderen efficiënt* [Blockchain makes meetings efficient] (2018) en Blockchain *for corporate governance and shareholder activism* (2018).

Publications of Prof. T.F.E. Tjon Tjin Tai (Private Law professor at Tilburg University with Private law, Law of civil law, and IT law) mainly has Invest topics with attention to notary, contracts and law: The blockchain as an alternative to the notarial practice (2018), The reasonable third and Blockchain (2015), Formalization of contract law for smart contracts (2017), Legal aspects of blockchain and smart contracts (2017), Legal Issues or Blockchain and contract (2017), Smart contracts and the law (2018) and The reasonable third party and the Blockchain (2018).

In 2017 the research *A viable real estate economy with disruption and blockchain* has done by dr. ing. J. Veuger MRE FRICS (professor Blockchain of the School of Finance & Accounting, School of Creative Technology and School of Governance, Law and Urban Development of the Saxion University Enschede and therefore from 2012-2019 professor Real Estate Hanze University) which submitted other new publications and presentations: *A viable real estate economy with disruption and Blockchain* as a book (2017), *Attention to disruption and Blockchain creates a viable real estate economy* in the Journal of USA-China Public Administration (2017), *Blockchain: kantelpunt in de vastgoedsector* [Blockchain: turning point in the real estate sector] (Vastgoedmarkt 2017), *Blockchain: vertrouwen in een wendbare vastgoedeconomie* [Blockchain: confidence in a maneuverable real estate economy] (VastgoedJournaal 2017), *Een wendbare vastgoedeconomie met disruptie en Blockchain* [An agile real estate economy with disruption and Blockchain] (Real Estate in Control, Reasult, 2017), *Noordelijk Vastgoedcongres 2017: disruptie, blokchain en vastgoed* [North Real Estate Congress: disruption, blockchain and real estate] (2017) en *The true meaning of the Blockchain technology for real estate still needs to be investigated* (International Journal of Engineering and Sciences, 2017). In 2018 is the before mention research presented on the American Real Estate Society (ARES) Congress 2018 with the title *A real game changer in real estate: blockchain* (2018) - Manuscript Prize

Competition in category Property/Assetmanagement American Real Estate Society (ARES) 2018 - and on Barometer Maatschappelijk Vastgoedcongres [Barometer Social Real Estate Congress] 2018 in de publication *Barometer public real estate: special issue 2018.* In 2018 is also the article *Trust in a viable real estate economy with disruption and blockchain* published in the Journal Facilities, subject area Property Management & Build Environment. The fulltext of this document has been downloaded almost 2.000 times since 2018. In May 2019 the scientific peer reviewed book Blockchain Technology and Applications appeared by Jan Veuger as editor of 8 chapters and (co)writer of three articles: Blockchain technology looking for a problem in real estate (Bronckers and Veuger, 2019), Influence of blockchain applications and digitalization on real estate (Veuger, 2019) and Start up GetaBrick in real estate (Hulsebos and Veuger, 2019). A publication of Nova Science Publishers New York is announced in May 2019 but has supposed to published in 2021.

Conclusion

Conclusion 1

Never before has an investigation been conducted on such a scale about the state of affairs of publicly available information about blockchain in combination with real estate. However, it should be noted that this is a snapshot on 31 December 2018 and is not necessarily exhaustive. This research should therefore also be seen as a first step for further (annual) research.

Conclusion 2

A follow-up study is necessary for further complementation and the best possible completeness of the database and the development and sharing of knowledge in the field of research, experts and products. The system and methodology of this study has shown that this method can provide the right information and can therefore be used to further broaden the scope of the study worldwide.

Conclusion 3

Finding innovative configurations for business models for the real estate sector is not easy when using blockchain technology. A distinction can be made between three platform generations: (1) Bitcoin, (2) blockchain platforms and (3) network of allowed participants. The first variant is not suitable for the real estate sector due to the fact that it is not possible to exchange assets other than token and currency than, for example, contracts. The second generation platform is mainly focused on improving exchange opportunities. This has led, among other things, to the development of smart contracts in an Ethereum network that is aimed at a global and public network where all transactions are visible. The third generation platform is accessible to admitted participants and they are therefore the only ones who have insight into this network. Corda (www.corda.net) is an example of this.

Conclusion 4

Limited research has been done into the influence of blockchain technology in the real estate sector (Veuger 2018, Veuger 2019). Studies by Dijkstra (2017) and Gout (2017) provide an initial exploration (Veuger 2017). Dijkstra (2017) concluded that blockchain can add five values to real estate management (1) a building passport, (2) alternative financing options, (3) trading real estate via the blockchain, (4) smart leases and (5) sustainability applications. Gout (2017) concluded that a possible application of blockchain technology could be used when setting up Marketplace funding.

Conclusion 5

The real estate chain is a highly fragmented chain with many information exchanges between a large number of involved parties, as well as traditionally many data silos and a large diversity in standards and used software protocols. The real estate chain can be roughly divided into 5 information domains (Bronckers 2018), with the identity of the building or building part as connecting factor. If the various actors are then also projected, it should not come as a surprise that tedious communication and information exchange is among the top complaints. And that is exactly where blockchain shines, as we just discussed in being able to trust that everyone has the same information. In other words, many use cases are conceivable, but who will allow parties to not only communicate better, but also make them want to communicate?

The real estate column lists various national or international, established or new standardisation initiatives, such as Oscre[1], Redex[2], Vastgoedtaxonomie[3], BIMchain[4], NEN[5], ISO[6], et cetera. These standards provide uniform definitions, data, protocols or IDs within the scope of the specific field of application, which is often still a silo. In other industries, such as the automotive[7] or the international transport industry[8], the same issue is at hand. Broad consortia are now established to settle barriers, since they want to take maximum advantage of the blockchain potential. Why should this be different for the real estate column? Is it not time that parties who consider themselves trend setters to unify and take the initiative? As history as taught us, new technology for a broadly applicable administrative foundation can lead to revolutionary business models. L'Histoire se repète. Will time tell? (Bronckers and Veuger 2018).

---

[1] http://www.oscre.org/oscreblockchaininitiative.
[2] www.redex.nl.
[3] Website SBR Banken.
[4] www.bimchain.io.
[5] Website smartindustries/NEN.
[6] Website ISO.
[7] www.dlt.mobi.
[8] www.bita.studio.

Conclusion 6

The way in which disruption, Blockchain and real estate will develop in the coming years are not the only obvious characteristics of a particular era, but also its social impact and user behaviour. This also applies to how this real estate transition can best be tracked, guided and utilized in society at the international, national and regional level. Disruptive organizations clearly respond to the viability of the (built) environment and therefore determine competitive strength. This affects the current and future valuation of real estate. The value of the possible applications of Blockchain in real estate processes is reflected in more effective and efficient transactions, increasing transparency, a better foundation for investment and new development for the mortgage market. All of this will then grow into more trust in fundamental elements of an economy: land and real estate and from the 'internet of things' to an 'economy of things'.

Looking at the impact of Blockchain on real estate, we can draw a number of conclusions. First of all, the relationship between Blockchain and real estate has not yet been proven in practice. It is expected to develop further in the form of registering transaction processes and the DNA passport of a real estate object. Secondly, completeness and transparency are the basic ingredients for trust in the system. Third, real estate wants to remain viable. For this reason, taking the offense is necessary for real estate and management to connect with social demand. Behaviour also leads to new earnings models of the social and economic spin-off of disruptive real estate. If the Dutch real estate sector embraces Blockchain and is able to realize innovations, then there are opportunities for real estate entrepreneurs to exploit the disruptive character to provide those new services.

Artificial intelligence through algorithmizing of Blockchain will increasingly play a role in the taking of decisions by learning organizations. It is good to realize that (thinking) processes and decisions are being outsourced by algorithms. This artificial intelligence cannot combine hard and soft factors to make considerations. The question is whether we will use the big-data models correctly and not inadvertently bring about inequality, discrimination and less vigilance. That technology develops faster than the adaptability of people is also not new: the parachute was invented only after the first plane flew. Ethics for individuals and organizations remain important for judging and utilizing data.

Changes in value concepts affect the valuation of real estate and the thinking about it. The orientation of changing users and owners of real estate affects innovativeness, values and flexibility in managing that property. Orientation on disruption must be seen as proof that the real estate world is able to actually innovate the accumulated assets and consolidate this. The financial and real estate markets are markets that exaggerate through irrational behaviour. Fear of 'eat or be eaten' determines people's behaviour. Financial and thus real estate markets are always unstable and must always be regulated by people and organizations.

The question that remains is whether it is important to look at disruptive innovations in existing markets or newcomers in the real estate market and Blockchain. The question is whether Blockchain is only a technological disruption, or a real game changer, and whether the entire value chain of the real estate market will embrace it. No two disruptions are the same. Trust in Blockchain is a prerequisite for guiding the predictable form of that disruption where start-up companies use new technology to offer cheaper and inferior alternatives to real estate in the market (Veuger 2017).

Conclusion 7

Blockchain could have a huge impact on the value chain in our society. Examples are efficiency, transparency, ownership, value (transfer), automation and service provision. When we want to understand the world of blockchain, we need to understand the innovation of the currency Bitcoin in 2009 that is built on underlying technology called Blockchain. Bitcoin is a combination of four individual elements: (1) cryptography, (2) a peer-to-peer network, (3) an open source protocol and (4) a shared ledger. This makes it a phenomenon that people are enthusiastic about. The internet already makes it possible to transfer information quickly, cheaply without paper and without intermediaries being involved. Blockchain gives the same benefits for transferring values. Internet is used to transfer word and image, blockchain for transactions. Blockchain is a combination of two elements: a shared and distributed ledger with synchronized data spread over multiple sites, countries and/or institutions and a cryptography: digital token with a monetary value. This book provides an overview of the latest developments on blockchain technology and its applications with the following themes and with the assistance of experts from Austria, Brazil, China, Croatia, Georgia, Germany, Italy, Netherlands, Slovenia, Spain and Switzerland: (1) Blockchain and the Agenda 2030 by Danielle Mendes Thame Denny, (2) Application of Blockchain Technology in the Field of E-Government Services by Jiarui Zhang, (3) Can the Cybersecurity of Smart Building be Improved Using Blockchain Technology? by Ben van Lier, (4) Infuence of Blockchain Applications and Digitalization on real estate by Jan Veuger, (5) Blockchain: Technology Looking For a Problem in Real Estate? by Jo Bronckers and Jan Veuger et al., (6) Start up 'Get a Brick' in Real Estate by Wendel Hulsebos and Jan Veuger, (7) Blockchain: An Efficiency Solution For Housing Associations? by Michel Vonk, (8) Blockchain Applications in Support of the Energy Transition by Mieke Oostra and Jelle Rijpma, and (9) Many Keys of Blockchain for Real Estate by Esther Dekker (Veuger et al., 2019).

Conclusion 8

A question that remains is to continue to look at existing markets or to disruptive innovation newcomers in the blockchain market. The question is whether blockchain is only a technological disruption or a real game changer and whether the entire value chain of the market is going to embrace this. Confidence in blockchain is therefore a precondition for guiding that disruption where (new) companies use new technology to offer cheaper and superior alternatives in the market. But the big question is how quickly blockchain will develop as well as all its applications. (Veuger et al., 2019).

Overall Conclusion

The way in which blockchain and real estate will develop in the coming years are not the only obvious. The true meaning of the blockchain technology for real estate still needs to be investigated. I am still curious to understand and clarify the value of Blockchain for real estate processes. Doubt continues to exist and is therefore a feeding ground for further research, because we do not know what we have not seen.

References

Anand, S. (2018), International Property Report: Europe: Test of Blockchain for Real Estate Is Readied. *Wall Street Journal.* https://www.wsj.com/articles/a-pioneer-in-real-estate-blockchain-emerges- in-europe-1520337601.

Asmoredjo, K.C., A. Hovanesyan, S.M. To and C.M. Wong Loi Sing (2017), *Decentralized mortgage market: An open market for real-estate crowdsourcing*. Delft University of Technology. https:// repository.tudelft.nl/islandora/object/uuid:a20fc94f-a959-44ec-9c29-0cae8ad831ce?collection=education.

Bakker, S. (2017), Niet de technologieën maar het gedrag. Omslagverhaal De Ware disruptie. *Het Financieele Dagblad.* https://fd.nl/morgen/ 1197956/niet-de-technologie-maar-het-gedrag. [Not the technologies, but the behavior. Cover story De Ware disruption. *The Financial Times*.]

Bentum, J. van, E. Wiegerinck, E. Quispel, J. Veldhuizen, J.W. Santing, E. Nelson and W. Oosting (2017), *Slimme stenen.* Vastgoedmarkt. https://vastgoedbibliotheek.nl/#!/SingleDoc?find=TRF:blockchain&hitnr=10.

Bessems, P. and W. Bril (2017), *Blockchain organiseren.* Mijnmana-gentboek. https://www.managementboek.nl/boek/9789463426572/blockchain- organiseren-paul-Bessems. [*Organizing blockchain.* Mijnmana-gentboek.]

Bhushan, R. (2018), *Five Reasons Why Using Blockchain Technology Can Help Overthrow the Traditional Real Estate Limitations.* Rotterdam University of Applied Sciences. https://hogeschoolrotterdam.on.worldcat.org/search?queryString=blockchain%20real%20estate&databaseList=2375,2572,3441,3837,1875,3018,1697,2268,3313,2267,4028,3633,638,10036,3834,2264,3551,2263,2262,3450,2261,1271,2260,2281,1941,3448,2259,2237,203,2277,1708,3841,3988,3967&sortKey=BEST_MATCH&clusterResults=true&scope=wz:60078&page=1#.

Bikker, A. (2017), Blockchain pilot in commercial real estate. *ABN Amro.* https://www.abnamro.com/en/newsroom/press-releases/2016/Blockchain- pilot-in-commercial-real-estate.html.

Blein, S. (2018), *A real estate coin has two sides: a study on the effects of tokenisation of real estate on the business model of the investment manager.* Amsterdam School of Real Estate. https://vastgoedbibliotheek.nl/#!/SingleDoc?find=BI:blockchain&hitnr=2.

Blums, I., H. Weigaard (2017), *Financial reporting by a shared ledger.* Tilburg University. https://research.tilburguniversity.edu/en/publications/ financial-reporting-by- a-shared-ledger.

Boer, E. de (2018), *o-evolution of disruptive technologies for sustainable transformation : blockchain start-ups' interactions with incumbents in the energy sector.* University of Amsterdam. http://www.scriptiesonline.uba.uva.nl/cgi/b/bib/bib-idx?type=simple;lang=nl;c=uvascript;sid=8d80e100620b75f76d424842fee998c6;rgn1=entire%20record;q1=blockchain;Submit.x=0;Submit.y=0;sort=publicationyear;cc=uvascript;view=reslist;fmt=long;page=reslist;start=6;size=1.

Breidbach, C., B. Ellway, B.W. Keating, W. Byron, K. Kormusheva, C. Kowalkowski, C. Lim and P. Maglio, Paul (2018), *Operating without operations: how is technology changing the role of the firm?* Emarald.

https://www.emeraldinsight.com/doi/abs/10.1108/JOSM-05-2018-0127.

Buisman, A. (2018), *Een betere cfo door blockchain*. Vastgoedmarkt. https://www.vastgoedmarkt.nl/data-entechnologie/nieuws/2018/08/verslaggeving-verslaglegging-een-betere-cfo-door-blockchain-101135572.

Burazeri, A. (2018), *Blockchain is here to stay: an exploratory study upon blockchain technology in the Netherlands*. University of Amsterdam. http://www.scriptiesonline.uba.uva.nl/cgi/b/bib/bib-idx?type=simple;lang=nl;c=uvascript;sid=8d80e100620b75f76d424842fee998c6;rgn1=entire%20record;q1=blockchain;Submit.x=0;Submit.y=0;sort=publicationyear;cc=uvascript;view=reslist;fmt=long;page=reslist;start=7;size=1.

Ceba Vega, J. (2018), *Creation and conveyance of real property rights on Blockchain Technology: A conciliation between real property principles and Blockchain functions?* University of Amsterdam. http://www.scriptiesonline.uba.uva.nl/cgi/b/bib/bib-idx?type=simple;lang=nl;c=uvascript;sid=8d80e100620b75f76d424842fee998c6;rgn1=entire%20record;q1=blockchain;Submit.x=0;Submit.y=0;sort=publicationyear;cc=uvascript;view=reslist;fmt=long;page=reslist;start=8;size=1.

Cohen, L.R., S. Rinaudo, L. Samuelson and H. Katz (2017), *How Securitization Can Benefit from Blockchain Technology*. Journal of Structured Finance. http://jsf.iijournals.com/content/23/2/51.

Compton, S.H. and D. Schottenstein (2017), *Questions and answer about using blockchain technology in real estate practice*. The practical real estate lawyer. http://files.ali- cle.org/thumbs/datastorage/lacidoirep/articles/PREL1709_Compton_thumb.pdf.

Compton, S.H. and D. Schottenstein (2018), *Questions and answer about using blockchain technology in real estate practice*. Rotterdam University of Applied Sciences. https://hogeschoolrotterdam.on.worldcat.org/search?queryString=blockchain%20real%20estate&databaseList=2375,2572,3441,3837,1875,3018,1697,2268,3313,2267,4028,3633,638,10036,3834,2264,3551,2263,2262,3450,2261,1271,2260,228

1,1941,3448,2259,2237,203,2277,1708,3841,3988,3967&sortKey=BEST_MATCH&clusterResults=true&scope=wz:60078&page=1#.

Couwenhoven, R. (2018), *Blockchain and its effect on business models: a study focussed on the energy sector.* University of Amsterdam. http://www.scriptiesonline.uba.uva.nl/cgi/b/bib/bib-idx?type=simple;lang=nl;c=uvascript;sid=8d80e100620b75f76d424842fee998c6;rgn1=entire%20record;q1=blockchain;Submit.x=0;Submit.y=0;sort=publicationyear;cc=uvascript;view=reslist;fmt=long;page=reslist;start=10;size=1.

CPB (2018), *CPB risicorapportage financiële markten 2018.* Centraal Planbureau (CPB). https://files.vastgoedbibliotheek.nl/Server/getfile.aspx?file=docs/publicaties/site/CPB/CPB_Notitie_29_mei_2018_CPB_Risicorapportage.pdf. [*CPB risk report financial markets 2018*]

Crosman, P. (2018), *Better and Cheaper: Blockchain makes inroads in real estate lending*. Rotterdam University of Applied Sciences. https://hogeschoolrotterdam.on.worldcat.org/search?queryString=blockchain%20real%20estate&databaseList=2375,2572,3441,3837,1875,3018,1697,2268,3313,2267,4028,3633,638,10036,3834,2264,3551,2263,2262,3450,2261,1271,2260,2281,1941,3448,2259,2237,203,2277,1708,3841,3988,3967&sortKey=BEST_MATCH&clusterResults=true&scope=wz:60078&page=1#.

Crosman, P. (2018), *Could Blockchains Replace Banks In Real Estate Lending*? Rotterdam University of Applied Sciences. https://hogeschoolrotterdam.on.worldcat.org/search?queryString=blockchain%20real%20estate&databaseList=2375,2572,3441,3837,1875,3018,1697,2268,3313,2267,4028,3633,638,10036,3834,2264,3551,2263,2262,3450,2261,1271,2260,2281,1941,3448,2259,2237,203,2277,1708,3841,3988,3967&sortKey=BEST_MATCH&clusterResults=true&scope=wz:60078&page=1#.

Dandapani, K., (2017), *Electronic Finance - recent developments*. Florida International University. https://www.emeraldinsight.com/doi/abs/10.1108/MF-02-2017-0028.

Davis, A., (2018), *Bringing the blockchain to Lethbridge*. Rotterdam University of Applied Sciences. https://hogeschoolrotterdam.on.

worldcat.org/search?queryString=blockchain%20real%20estate&databaseList=2375,2572,3441,3837,1875,3018,1697,2268,3313,2267,4028,3633,638,10036,3834,2264,3551,2263,2262,3450,2261,1271,2260,2281,1941,3448,2259,2237,203,2277,1708,3841,3988,3967&sortKey=BEST_MATCH&clusterResults=true&scope=wz:60078&page=1#.

Deloitte (2018), *Blockchain Centre of Expertise*. Deloitte. https://www2.deloitte.com/nl/nl/pages/over-deloitte/articles/deloitte-opens-blockchain-center-of-expertise.html.

Deloitte (2018), *Real Estate Predictions 2018.* Deloitte. https://www2.deloitte.com/nl/nl/pages/real-estate/articles/blockchain-technology-for-real-estate-rome-wasnt-built-in-a-day.html.

Dutch Blockchain coalition - smart contracts workgroup (2018), *Smart contracts, als specifieke toepassing van blockchain-technologie*. Dutch Blockchain Coalition. https://search.saxionbibliotheek.nl/cgi-bin/koha/opac- detail.pl?biblionumber=22580. [*Smart contracts, as a specific application of blockchain technology*.]

Dutch Blockchain Coalition (2018), *Blockchain for Good. The vision and mission of the Dutch Blockchain Coalition.* Dutch Blockchain Coalition. https://visie.dutchblockchaincoalition.org/wp- content/uploads/2018/12/Visiedocument-brochure-Blockchain-For-Good- A4-ENGELS-WEB-031218.pdf.

Dutch Blockchain Coalition (2018), *Smart contracts als specifieke toepassing van de blockchaintechnologie.* Dutch Blockchain Coalition. https://dutchdigitaldelta.nl/uploads/pdf/Smart-contract-rapport-DBC.pdf. [*Smart contracts as a specific application of blockchain technology.*]

Dutra, A., A. Tumasjan and I.M. Welpe (2018), *Blockchain is changing how media and entertainment companies complete.* MIT Camebridge, Massachusetts. https://sloanreview.mit.edu/article/blockchain-is-changing-how-media-and- entertainment-companies-compete/.

Dijkstra, M. (2017), *Blockchain: Towards Disruption in the Real Estate Sector.* Univesity of Delft. https://www.google.nl/search?q=on+the+impact+of+Blockchain+technology+in+the+real+estate+management+process.&ie=&oe=.

Dutch Digital Delta (2017), *Knowledge and Innovation Agenda ICT 2016 – 2019*. Dutch Digital Delta. https://www.dutchdigitaldelta.nl/uploads/pdf/PDF-Kennis-en- Innovatieagenda-ICT-2016-2019_2015-10-06_254.pdf.

Dutch Digital Delta (2017), *Legacy Coalitie*. Dutch Digital Delta. https://www.dutchdigitaldelta.nl/uploads/pdf/ddd-Legacy-Flyer.pdf .

Edriouch, J., R. Bemelmans, M. Zoet and J. Beumers (2018), *Blockchain voor het hbo*. Zuyd Hogeschool. https://www.zuyd.nl/over-zuyd/nieuws/2018/07/verslag-zuyd-symposium- blockchain-in-het-hbo.

El Hri, A. (2018), *De blockchain als pandregister: Kan de registratie van pandrechten in de blockchain dezelfde waarborgen bieden als het kadaster voor hypotheekrechten?* University of Amsterdam. http://www.scriptiesonline.uba.uva.nl/cgi/b/bib/bib-idx?type=simple;lang=nl;c=uvascript;sid=8d80e100620b75f76d424842fee998c6;rgn1=entire%20record;q1=blockchain;Submit.x=0;Submit.y=0;sort=publicationyear;cc=uvascript;view=reslist;fmt=long;page=reslist;size=1;start=13. [*The blockchain as a pledge register: Can the registration of pledges in the blockchain offer the same guarantees as the land registry for mortgage rights?*]

Feng, Q. and J.G. Shanthikumar (2017), *How Research in Production and Operations Management May Evolve in the Era of Big Data*. Purdue University. https://onlinelibrary.wiley.com/doi/abs/10.1111/poms.12836.

Fischer, S. (2018), Blockchain finances commercial real estate loan. *Idaho Business Review*. https://tue.on.worldcat.org/search?databaseList=2375%2C2474%2C2572%2C2274%2C2175%2C3384%2C1931%2C1875%2C233%2C3018%2C3535%2C3413%2C2269%2C2401%2C1697%2C3313%2C2223%2C3652%2C4026%2C638%2C2507%2C3954%2C3879%2C2463%2C2221%2C2264%2C2462%2C3374%2C3195%2C3229%2C1842%2C2897%2C2237%2C2236%2C3544%2C2796%2C2795%2C2036%2C3909%2C2233%2C1847%2C3988&queryString=bloc kchain%2Bestate#/oclc/7755429846.

Grant, P. (2017), *Real-Estate Industry Explores Use of 'Blockchain' Technology*. Wall Street Journal. https://www.foxweek.com/news/real-estate-industry-explores-use- blockchain-technology.

Gout, B. (2017), *Block mortgage: Blockchain inspired businessmodel for mortgage funding marketplace*. Delft University of Technology. https://repository.tudelft.nl/islandora/object/uuid%3Abe64e8ed-6e28-489f- a84b-7661cae75e91.

Herian, R. (2018), *Legal recognition of Blockchain registries and Smart contracts*. Open University Law School. https://s3.amazonaws.com/academia.edu.documents/58014198/Legal_Recognition_of_Blockchain_Registries_and_Smart_Contracts_Final_Draft_ReportAppendix.pdf?AWSAccessKeyId=AKIAIWOWYYGZ2Y53UL3A&Expires=1546236789&Signature=VQkbjwrzOqk4vP3ceiRmBmk%2BBRg%3D&response-content-disposition=attachment%3B%20filename%3DLegal_Recognition_of_Blockc hain_Registri.pdf.

Henry, C. (2018), *Leadership and strategy in the news*. Emerald Publishing. https://www.emeraldinsight.com/doi/full/10.1108/SL-05-2018-139.

Hert, P. de (2018), *The future of privacy - Addressing singularities to identify bright- line rules that speak to us*. Tilburg University. https://research.tilburguniversity.edu/en/publications/the-future-of-privacy- addressing-singularities-to-identify-bright.

Hitesh, M. (2017), *Blockchain for commercial Real Estate*. SSRN Electronic Journal. https://sci-hub.tw/10.2139/ssrn.2922695.

Jongeneel, M. (2018), *De mogelijke bijdrage van blockchain aan een transparante vastgoedsector*. Fontys University of Applied Sciences. Not public.

Hoogeboom, B. (2018), *Blockchain kan een informatievuist vormen tegen ondermijning*. NRC. https://www.nrc.nl/nieuws/2018/10/19/blockchain-kan-een-informatievuist-vormen-tegen-ondermijning-a2628340.

JaeShup, O. and L. Song (2017), *A case study on business model innovations using Blockchain: focusing on financial institutions*. Emerald Publishing. https://www.emeraldinsight.com/doi/full/10.1108/APJIE-12-2017-038.

Janssen, R., P. Stam, J. Visser, D. de Vries and J. Wijnker, (2017), *Blockchaintechnologie in de gezondheidszorg*. Tilburg University. https://pure.uvt.nl/ws/portalfiles/portal/17518490/2017_08_09_Janssen_R.T. J.M.pdf. [*Blockchain technology in healthcare*]

JLL (2018), *How Blockchain is Reshaping the Real Estate Industry*. JLL. https://hogeschoolrotterdam.on.worldcat.org/search?queryString=blockchain%20real%20estate&databaseList=2375,2572,3441,3837,1875,3018,1697,2268,3313,2267,4028,3633,638,10036,3834,2264,3551,2263,2262,3450,2261,1271,2260,2281,1941,3448,2259,2237,203,2277,1708,3841,3988,3967&sortKey=BEST_MATCH&clusterResults=true&scope=wz:60078&page=1#.

Karpook, D. (2017), *Smart, connected and dangerous: Assessing the impact of digital business on real estate*. Corporate Real Estate Journal. https://planonsoftware.com/us/articles-and-whitepapers/article-smart-connected-and-dangerous-assessing-the-impact-of-digital-business-on-real- estate/.

Kleemans, J. and M. Jongeneel (2017), *Blockchain: transparantiemotor of gehypte techtoepassing? Een onderzoek naar de mogelijke bijdrage van blockchain aan een transparantere vastgoedsector*. University of Eindhoven. https://www.service-studievereniging.nl/magazine/artikel/blockchain- transparantiemotor-gehypte-techtoepassing/. [*Blockchain: transparency engine or hyped tech application? An investigation into the possible contribution of blockchain to a more transparent real estate sector*]

Kruijf, J. de and H. Weigaard (2017), *Ontologies for commitment-based smart contracts*. Tilburg University. https://research.tilburguniversity.edu/en/publications/ontologies-for-commitment-based-smart-contracts.

Kruijf, J. de and Weigaard, H. (2017), *Understanding the blockchain using enterprise ontology*. Tilburg University. https://research.tilburguniversity.edu/en/publications/understanding-the-blockchain-using-enterprise-ontology.

Lafarre, A. and C. van der Elst (2018), *Blockchain maakt vergaderen efficiënt*. Tilburg University. https://universonline.nl/2018/04/17/blockchain-maakt-vergaderen-efficient.

Lafarre, A. and C. van der Elst (2018), *Blockchain technology for corporate governance and shareholder activism.* Tilburg University. https://research.tilburguniversity.edu/en/publications/blockchain-technology- for-corporate-governance-and-shareholder-ac.

Lafarre, A. and C. van der Elst (2018), *Blockchain and smart contracting for the shareholder community*. Tilburg University. https://research. tilburguniversity.edu/en/publications/blockchain-and-smart-contracting-for-the-shareholder-community.

Lafarre, A. and C. van der Elst (2018), *Blockchain and the 21st century annual general meeting*. Tilburg University. https://research. tilburguniversity.edu/en/publications/blockchain-and-the-21st-century-annual-general-meeting.

Lafarre, A. and C. van der Elst (2018), *Blockchain Technology for Modernizing the Shareholder Dialogue*. Tilburg University.
https://www.tilburguniversity.edu/upload/1413437f-2ccb-4fe9-bc01-60aa0c7ec657_Blockchaintechnologyformodernizingshareholderdialo gueWP.pdf.

Lavrijssen, S., F. van der Velde, P. Köpsel San zand G. Heusschen (2018), *Onderzoek naar de mogelijke juridische integratie van de Elektriciteits-, Gas- en Warmtewet*. Tilburg University. https:// research.tilburguniversity.edu/en/publications/onderzoek-naar-de-mogelijke-juridische-integratie-van-de-elektric. [*Research into the possible legal integration of the Electricity, Gas and Heat Act*.]

Leeuwen, G. van (2018), *The day after tomorrow*. Amsterdam School of Real Estate. http://files.vastgoedbibliotheek.nl/Server/getfile. aspx?file=docs/MRE/18/Lee uwen_GJ.pdf.

Leeuwen, G. van (2018), *The day after tomorrow: vastgoedbanken vandaag, morgen en de dag na morgen*. Amsterdam School of Real Estate. https://vastgoedbibliotheek.nl/#!/SingleDoc?find=BI:block chain &hitnr=1.

Lier, B. van (2018), *Thinking about ecologies of autonomous cyber-physical systems and their ethics*. Rotterdam University of Applied Sciences. https://www.hogeschoolrotterdam.nl/onderzoek/eventitem/ openbare-les-ben- van-lier/112408/.

Lifthrasir, R. (2016), *Blockchain platforms: Speeding up the money & assets transfer process*. RICS. http://www.rics.org/nl/news/het-latest-.

Lipton, A. (2017), *Blockchains and distributed ledgers in retrospective and perspective*. MIT Cambridge, Massachusetts. https://www.emeraldinsight.com/doi/full/10.1108/JRF-02-2017-0035?utm_source=TrendMD&utm_medium=cpc&utm_campaign=Emerald_TrendMD_0&WT.mc_id=Emerald_TrendMD_0.

McClary, S. (2017), *Understanding blockchain for real estate*. Rotterdam University of Applied Sciences. https://hogeschoolrotterdam.on.worldcat.org/search?queryString=blockchain%20real%20estate&databaseList=2375,2572,3441,3837,1875,3018,1697,2268,3313,2267,4028,3633,638,10036,3834,2264,3551,2263,2262,3450,2261,1271,2260,2281,1941,3448,2259,2237,203,2277,1708,3841,3988,3967&sortKey=BEST_MATCH&clusterResults=true&scope=wz:60078&page=1#.

Mest, C.E. (2018), *Blockchain technology meets real estate investment at the St. Regis Aspen*. https://www.hotelmanagement.net/tech/blockchain-technology-meets-real- estate-investment-at-st-regis-aspen.

Meijaard, J. (2018), *Adoption of blockchain digital asset management systems: An empirical study*. http://www.scriptiesonline.uba.uva.nl/622830.

Moerel, L. and C. Prins (2016), *Privacy voor de homo digitali*. Tilburg University. https://pure.uvt.nl/ws/portalfiles/portal/11437684/Preadviezen_NJV_2016.pdf. [*Privacy for the gay digitali*]

Murtaza Haider, M. and S. Moranis (2018), *Blockchain, AI will reshape real estate*. Rotterdam University of Applied Sciences. https://hogeschoolrotterdam.on.worldcat.org/search?queryString=blockchain%20real%20estate&databaseList=2375,2572,3441,3837,1875,3018,1697,2268,3313,2267,4028,3633,638,10036,3834,2264,3551,2263,2262,3450,2261,1271,2260,2281,1941,3448,2259,2237,203,2277,1708,3841,3988,3967&sortKey=BEST_MATCH&clusterResults=true&scope=wz:60078&page=1#.

Navitas Capital (2018), *Exploring blockchain & transformative applications in real estate*. Navitas Capital. https://navitascap.com/wp-content/uploads/2018/08/Exploring-Blockchain-Transformative-Applications-in-Real-Estate-Whitepaper-1.pdf.

Nir, K. and J. Voas (2018), *Blockchain in Developing Countries*. IEEE. https://www.computer.org/csdl/mags/it/2018/02/mit2018020011-abs.html.

Noonan, L. (2018), *Riding a new wave of deals*. Financial Times.

Nordrum, A. (2017), *Govern by blockchain dubai wants one platform to rule them all, while Illinois will try anything.* IEEE Spectrum. https://www.semanticscholar.org/paper/Govern-by-blockchain-dubai-wants- one-platform-to-Nordrum/9829a48ad459dd1eb5f8e871d8c9d9098b376598.

Os, V.H.M. van (2017), *The emperor's new clothes: smart cities, smarter contracts & smartest decisions.* Tijdschrift voor bouwrecht. https://vastgoedbibliotheek.nl/#!/SingleDoc?find=TRF:blockchain&hitnr=13.

Pal, L.W.C. (2018), *Smart contracts : De juridische duiding van een smart contract naar Nederlands privaatrecht.* University of Amsterdam. http://www.scriptiesonline.uba.uva.nl/cgi/b/bib/bib-idx?type=simple;lang=nl;c=uvascript;sid=8d80e100620b75f76d424842fee998c6;rgn1=entire%20record;q1=blockchain;Submit.x=0;Submit.y=0;sort=publicationyear;cc=uvascript;view=reslist;fmt=long;page=reslist;size=1;start=22.

Palavesh, S. (2018), *Top 5 Industries that Need Blockchain Development*. Rotterdam University of Applied Sciences. https://hogeschoolrotterdam.on.worldcat.org/search?queryString=blockchain%20real%20estate&databaseList=2375,2572,3441,3837,1875,3018,1697,2268,3313,2267,4028,3633,638,10036,3834,2264,3551,2263,2262,3450,2261,1271,2260,2281,1941,3448,2259,2237,203,2277,1708,3841,3988,3967&sortKey=BEST_MATCH&clusterResults=true&scope=wz:60078&page=1#.

Peters, B. (2017), *Rental Equipment/Real Estate/Pot Company Is The Latest To Go Blockchain.* Investor's business Daily. https://www.investors.com/gdpr-agreement/?back_url=https%3A%2F%2Fwww.

investors.com%2Fnews%2Findia-globalization-capital-latest-blockchain-bump%2F.

Prins, C. (2018), *De Blockchain.* Tilburg University. https://pure.uvt.nl/ws/portalfiles/portal/13357217/NJB38_Vooraf.pdf. [*The Blockchain*]

Puthal, D., N. Malik, S.P. Mohanty, E. Kougianos and G. Das (2018), *Everything You Wanted to Know About the Blockchain: Its Promise, Components, Processes, and Problems.* University of Technology Sydney. https://ieeexplore.ieee.org/document/8386948.

Razaghi, M. and M. Finger (2018), *Smart Governance for Smart Cities.* École polytechnique fédérale de Lausanne (EPFL), Lausanne. https://ieeexplore.ieee.org/document/8326767.

Salmeling, M., and C. Fransson (2017), *The Land Registry in the Blockchain – testbed.* Landshypotek Bank. https://chromaway.com/papers/Blockchain_Landregistry_Report_2017.pdf.

Scheurwater, S. (2017), *The future of valuations; the relevance of real estate valuations for institutional investors and banks: views from a European expert group.* Royal Institute of Chartered Serveyors. https://files.vastgoedbibliotheek.nl/Server/getfile.aspx?file=docs/publicaties/site/RICS/Future_valuations_relevance_real%20estate_valuations_institutiona l_investors_banks.pdf.

Schols, F.W.J.M. and B.C.M. Waaijer (2018), *Blockchain as alternative for the notary public.* Tilburg University. https://research.tilburguniversity.edu/en/publications/blockchain-as- alternative-for-the-notary-public.

Seuren, F. F., (2018), *Introducing Blockchain to Commercial Real Estate: Exploring the applicability of blockchain technology in lowering transaction costs of the commercial real estate due diligence process.* Delft University of Technology. https://repository.tudelft.nl/islandora/object/uuid:e5266e5c-3c2c-45fe-a5df-5e9d1f5feec3?collection=education.

Shedroff, N. (2018), *Self-Managing Real Estate.* IEEE Computer Society. https://ieeexplore.ieee.org/stamp/stamp.jsp?tp=&arnumber=8267594.

Shedroff, N. (2018), *Self-Managing Real Estate*. Rotterdam University of Applied Sciences. https://hogeschoolrotterdam.on.worldcat.org/search?queryString=blockchain%20real%20estate&databaseList=2375,2572,3441,3837,1875,3018,1697,2268,3313,2267,4028,3633,638,10036,3834,2264,3551,2263,2262,3450,2261,1271,2260,2281,1941,3448,2259,2237,203,2277,1708,3841,3988,3967&sortKey=BEST_MATCH&clusterResults=true&scope=wz:60078&page=1#.

Skinner, C. (2016), *Valueweb: how Fintech firms are using mobile and blockchain technologies to create the Internet of Value*. Saxion University of Applied Sciences. http://opcprod.utsp.utwente.nl/DB=20/LNG=NE/PPN?PPN=401130630.

Suzuki, B., T. Taylor and G. Marchant (2018), *Blockchain: How It Will Change Your Legal Practice*. Rotterdam University of Applied Sciences. https://hogeschoolrotterdam.on.worldcat.org/search?queryString=blockchain%20real%20estate&databaseList=2375,2572,3441,3837,1875,3018,1697,2268,3313,2267,4028,3633,638,10036,3834,2264,3551,2263,2262,3450,2261,1271,2260,2281,1941,3448,2259,2237,203,2277,1708,3841,3988,3967&sortKey=BEST_MATCH&clusterResults=true&sco pe=wz:60078&page=1#.

Tan, W.K. (2018), *Dubai Land Department to conduct all transactions through blockchain*. Rotterdam University of Applied Sciences. https://hogeschoolrotterdam.on.worldcat.org/search?queryString=blockchain%20real%20estate&databaseList=2375,2572,3441,3837,1875,3018,1697,2268,3313,2267,4028,3633,638,10036,3834,2264,3551,2263,2262,3450,2261,1271,2260,2281,1941,3448,2259,2237,203,2277,1708,3841,3988,3967&sortKey=BEST_MATCH&clusterResults=true&scope=wz:60078&page=1#.

Tjong Tjin Tai, E. (2015), *De redelijke derde en de blockchain*. Tilburg University. https://research.tilburguniversity.edu/en/publications/the-reasonable-third- party-and-the-blockchain. [*The reasonable third and the blockchain.*]

Tjong Tjin Tai, E. (2017), *Formalization of contract law for smart contracts*. Tilburg University. https://research.tilburguniversity.edu/en/activities/formalization-of-contract- law-for-smart-contracts.

Tjong Tjin Tai, E. (2017), *Juridische aspecten van blockchain en smart contracts*. Tilburg University. https://research.tilburguniversity.edu/en/publications/legal-issues-of- blockchain-and-smart-contracts. [*Legal aspects of blockchain and smart contracts.*]

Tjong Tjin Tai, E. (2017), *Legal issues of blockchain and smart contracts*. Tilburg University. https://research.tilburguniversity.edu/en/publications/legal-issues-of- blockchain-and-smart-contracts.

Tjong Tjin Tai, E. (2018), *De blockchain als alternatief voor de notariële praktijk*. Tilburg University. https://www.tilburguniversity.edu/nl/webwijs/show/t.f.e.tjongtjintai_nl.htm. [*The blockchain as an alternative to the notarial practice*.]

Tjong Tjin Tai, E. (2018), *Smart contracts en het recht*. Tilburg University. https://research.tilburguniversity.edu/en/publications/smart-contracts-and- the-law. [*Smart contracts and the law*]

Tjong Tjin Tai, E. (2018), *The reasonable third party and the blockchain*. Tilburg University. https://research.tilburguniversity.edu/en/publications/the-reasonable-third- party-and-the-blockchain.

Tushar, W., C. Yuen, H. Mohsenian-Rad, T. Saha, P. Tapan, H. Poor, W. Vincent and K.L. Kristin L. (2018), *Transforming Energy Networks via Peer-to-Peer Energy Trading: The Potential of Game-Theoretic Approaches*. University of Queensland, Brisbane. https://ieeexplore.ieee.org/document/8398582.

University of Groningen (2018), *Blockchain, public trust, law and governance*. University of Groningen. https://www.rug.nl/rechten/congressen/archief/2018/blockchain-public-law-public-trust/blockchain-conference-programme.pdf.

Unknown (2016), *Blockchain platform targets property financing opportunities in China*. Rotterdam University of Applied Sciences. https://hogeschoolrotterdam.on.worldcat.org/search?queryString=blockchain%20real%20estate&databaseList=2375,2572,3441,3837,1875,3018,1697,2268,3313,2267,4028,3633,638,10036,3834,2264,3551,2263,2262,3450,2261,1271,2260,2281,1941,3448,2259,2237,203,2277,1708,3841,3988,3967&sortKey=BEST_MATCH&clusterResults=true&scope=wz:60078&page =1#.

Unkown (2018), *Latest blockchain real estate platform offers cashback and rewards.* Rotterdam University of Applied Sciences. https://hogeschoolrotterdam.on.worldcat.org/search?queryString=blockchain%20real%20estate&databaseList=2375,2572,3441,3837,1875,3018,1697,2268,3313,2267,4028,3633,638,10036,3834,2264,3551,2263,2262,3450,2261,1271,2260,2281,1941,3448,2259,2237,203,2277,1708,3841,3988,3967&sortKey=BEST_MATCH&clusterResults=true&scope=wz:60078&page =1#.

Unkown (2018), *Leveraging blockchain technology to democratize the real estate industry.* Rotterdam University of Applied Sciences. https://hogeschoolrotterdam.on.worldcat.org/search?queryString=blockchain%20real%20estate&databaseList=2375,2572,3441,3837,1875,3018,1697,2268,3313,2267,4028,3633,638,10036,3834,2264,3551,2263,2262,3450,2261,1271,2260,2281,1941,3448,2259,2237,203,2277,1708,3841,3988,3967&sortKey=BEST_MATCH&clusterResults=true&scope=wz:60078&page=1#.

Veldhuizen, J. and J.W. Santing (2017), *Meer transparantie en vertrouwen door blockchain.* Vastgoedmarkt. https://vastgoedbibliotheek.nl/#!/SingleDoc?find=TRF:blockchain&hitnr=10.

Vermeend, S. and P. Smit (2017), *Blockchain de technology die de wereld radicaal veranderd.* Einstein Books. https://www.managementboek.nl/boek/9789492460141/blockchain-de-technologie-die-de-wereld-radicaal-verandert-simone-vermeend. [*Blockchain the technology that is radically changing the world*]

Vermeulen, E.P.M. (2018), *How Blockchain will Disrupt Corporate Organizations*. Harvard Law School Forum. https://www.tilburguniversity.edu/students/news/show/news-vermeulen-blockchanin-harvard/.

Vermeulen, E.P.M. and M. Fenwick (2018), *Technology and Corporate Governance: Blockchain, Crypto, and Artificial Intelligence.* Tilburg University.https://www.tilburguniversity.edu/research/law/news/news-vermeulen-on- technology-and-corporate-governance/.

Veuger, J. (2017), *Attention to disruption and blockchain creates a viable real estate economy.* Journal of USA-China Public Administration.

https://davidpublisher.org/index.php/Home/Article/index?id=33918.html.

Veuger, J. (2017), *A viabele real estate economy with disruption and blockchain.* Hanze University of Applied Sciences. https://www.corporaterem.nl/wp-content/uploads/Blockchain-complete.pdf.

Veuger, J. (2017), *Blockchain: kantelpunt in de vastgoedsector.* Vastgoedmarkt. https://research.hanze.nl/ws/portalfiles/portal/16542880/Jan_Veuger_Blockc hain_5245_.pdf.

Veuger, J. (2017), *Blockchain: vertrouwen in een wendbare vastgoedeconomie.* VastgoedJournaal. [*Blockchain: trust in an agile real estate economy.*]

Veuger, J. (2017), *Een wendbare vastgoedeconomie met disruptie en Blockchain, Real Estate in control.* Reasult. https://youtu.be/a91s_DP_ymw. [*An agile real estate economy with disruption and Blockchain, Real Estate in control.*]

Veuger, J. (2017), *Noordelijk Vastgoedcongres 2017: disruptie, blockchain en vastgoed.* Hanze University of Applied Sciences. https://youtu.be/dg_PW_pyJik. [*Northern Real Estate Congress 2017: disruption, blockchain and real estate.*]

Veuger, J. (2017), The true meaning of the blockchain technology for real estate still needs to be investigated. *International Journal of Engineering and Sciences (IJES).*

Veuger, J. (2017), *Trust in a viable real estate economy with disruption and blockchain.* Journal Facilities. https://www.emeraldinsight.com/doi/full/10.1108/F-11-2017-0106.

Veuger, J. (2018), *A real game changer in real estate: blockchain.* American Real Estate Society (ARES). https://www.etnpconferences.net/ares/ares2018/PaperSubmissions/Submissions2018/S-2018-233.pdf.

Veuger, J. et al. (2018), *Barometer public real estate: special issue 2018.* Spryg. https://www.corporaterem.nl/barometers/.

Veuger, J. (editor) (2019), *Blockchain Technology and Applications* (Editor 8 chapters). Nova Science Publishers New York.

Veuger, J. (2019), Blockchain Technology and Applications: Influence of blockchain applications and digitalization on real estate. In: *Blockchain Technology and Applications*. Nova Science Publishers New York.

Veuger, J. and J. Bronckers (2019), Blockchain Technology and Applications: Blockchain technology looking for a problem in real estate. In: *Blockchain Technology and Applications*. Nova Science Publishers New York.

Veuger, J. and W. Hulsebos (2019), Blockchain Technology and Applications: Start up GetaBrick in real estate. In: *Blockchain Technology and Applications*. Nova Science Publishers New York.

Veuger, J. (2019), *Digitalization Real Estate on American Real Estate Society 2018*. Saxion University of Applied Sciences. https://www.corporaterem.nl/wp-content/uploads/Publicaties-Jan-Veuger.pdf#zoom=100.

Vrielink, H.K. and L.S. ten Have (2018), *De impact van Blockchain-technologie op businessmodellen.* Saxion University of Applied Sciences. https://postit.saxion.nl/document/details?pid=EA24C9FA-37FD-4898- 89ECCC32A0BE8752. [*The impact of Blockchain technology on business models.*]

Vos, J. (2016), *Blockchain based land registry: panacea, illusion or something in between*? European Land Registry Association. Registry.pdf.

Water, G. van den (2017), *Blockchain ballot*. Tilburg University. https://www.tilburguniversity.edu/upload/57359745-a33a-4fe5-bf76-f645336d4887_Masterthesis%20Gijs%20van%20de%20Water.pdf.

Water, G. van den (2017), *Blockchain ballot. Electoral Enhancement or Danger to Democracy*? https://www.tilburguniversity.edu/students/news/show/news-can-blockchain-contribute-to-combating-electoral-fraud.htm.

Weihs, B. (2018), *Blockchain enabled asset management in the case of XDecks: cooperation enhanced by decentralization in the building industry*. Delft University of Technology. http://files.vastgoedbibliotheek.nl/Server/getfile.aspx?file=docs/scripties/Delft/Weihs_B.pdf.

Wilkinson, S., D. Halvitigala and H. Antoniades (2017), *Educators, professional bodies and the future of the valuation profession.* Emarald. https://www.emeraldinsight.com/doi/abs/10.1108/PM-04-2017-0027.

Windesheim en Hogeschool Rotterdam (2018), *RAAK project: kansen en bedreigingen blockchain MKB.* Windesheim en Hogeschool van Rotterdam. https://www.windesheim.nl/over-windesheim/nieuws/2018/juli/onderzoekers-blockchain-biedt-kansen-voor- het-mkb/.

World Banking (2018), *International and National Economies.* World Bank. https://onlinelibrary.wiley.com/doi/abs/10.1111/woba.5467.

Wynder, E. (2018), *Real estate execs dismiss bitcoin frenzy.* Rotterdam University of Applied Sciences. https://hogeschoolrotterdam.on.worldcat.org/search?queryString=blockchain%20real%20estate&databaseList=2375,2572,3441,3837,1875,3018,1697,2268,3313,2267,4028,3633,638,10036,3834,2264,3551,2263,2262,3450,2261,1271,2260,2281,1941,3448,2259,2237,203,2277,1708,3841,3988,3967&sortKey=BEST_MATCH&clusterResults=true&scope=wz:60078&page=1#.

Zaal, R. (2017), *TU-Delft heeft Blockchain-hypotheek werkend.* Delft University of Technology. http://agconnect.nl/artikel/tu-delft-heeft-Blockchain-hypotheek-werkend.

Zlotowitz, I. (2018), *Way of the Future: Will blockchain disrupt established CRE processes?* Rotterdam University of Applied Sciences.https://hogeschoolrotterdam.on.worldcat.org/search?queryString=blockchain%20real%20estate&databaseList=2375,2572,3441,3837,1875,3018,1697,2268,3313,2267,4028,3633,638,10036,3834,2264,3551,2263,2262,3450,2261,1271,2260,2281,1941,3448,2259,2237,203,2277,1708,3841,3988,3967&sortKey=BEST_MATCH&clusterResults=true&scope=wz:60078&page=1#.

In: The Future of Real Estate
Editor: Jan Veuger
ISBN: 978-1-53619-414-2

Chapter 2

PRINCIPLE OF SUBSTITUTION IN THE FACE OF COVID-19 PANDEMIC: AN APPLICATION TO TENANTS' CHOICE IN COMMERCIAL REAL ESTATE MARKETS

Ephraim Kabunda Munshifwa[1,*], PhD, Niraj Jain[1], MPhil, Anthony Mushinge[1], PhD and Roy Alexander Chileshe[2], PhD

[1]Department of Real Estate Studies,
Copperbelt University, Kitwe, Zambia
[2]Department of Urban and Regional Planning,
Copperbelt University, Kitwe, Zambia

[*] Corresponding Author's E-mail: ephraim.munshifwa@cbu.ac.zm.

ABSTRACT

The principle of substitution is an important concept in economics and valuation of real estate. The principle postulates that the upper limit of the market value will be set by the cost of acquiring a similar substitute property. This means that no investor will be willing to pay more for an investment property than the amount it would cost to build or buy a similar one. However, most studies on the application of this principle are focused on assessment of value and less on tenants' choice. The recent COVID-19 pandemic, which has resulted in a barrage of scholarly articles on its impact to various sectors of the economy, provides an opportunity for the investigation of the principle of substitution from the tenant's perspective. While most studies have focused on the investors' side, as it relates to vacancies and loss of business, little attention is being paid to the behavioural changes amongst tenants as clients of these services. As explained within the concept of the principle of substitution, tenants are trading-down (especially in the residential market) or being forced to work from home, in essence abandoning commercial space. Thus the question that emerges is: what is the future of real estate in a post COVID-19 environment? The paper undertakes a detailed analytical review of emerging literature on measures to combat COVID-19 (such as social distancing, working from home, etc) in relation to levels of rentals and vacancies in residential and commercial real estate rental markets. The paper then goes further to investigate these dynamics within the Zambian context.

Keywords: substitution, COVID-19, commercial real estate, tenant's choices, rent, Zambia

INTRODUCTION

Recent media reports[1,2,3,4]show demands by tenants to renegotiate occupation terms, especially rent payable, due to the impact of the Coronavirus Disease (COVID-19) pandemic. In cases of unsuccessful re-

---

[1] Hammond, Edge-Cliffe-Johnson and Morris, "WeWork offers Rent Discounts to Covid hit."
[2]Stibbe, "Provisional Rental Discount in times of COVID-19."
[3] Brown, "Apartments for Rent."
[4] Queensland Government, "Negotiating commercial rent relief during Covid-10."

negiatations, a number of tenants are failing to keep up with their monthly obligations, hence opting out or substituting commercial for residential space. This is being seen in increased vacancies in commercial real estate. This chapter asserts that those opting out often settle for cheaper substitutes or smaller spaces[5,6], and during this COVID-19 pandemic, this includes working from home. The principle of substitution in economics, which postulates that no investor will pay more for an investment in property than the cost to build or buy a similar one, then finds application during this period. However, most of its application is to the valuation of property and less on the tenant's choice. When perceived from the perspective that tenants have to pay rent, which is the price for the use of space, then the principle becomes equally applicable to tenants' choices.

The objective of this study is to show how the principle of substitution can be used to provide insight into tenants' behaviour, as consumers of commercial real estate, during the COVID-19 pandemic period. The application of this principle at market level is underpinned by classical and neo-classical debates on the relationship between price, rent and cost. The theoretical discussion later in this chapters aims at discussing these links. However before that, the next section reviews literature to understand key determinants of tenants' choice in commercial real estate.

TENANTS' CHOICE IN COMMERCIAL REAL ESTATE

A review of literature in this section highlights the key determinants of rent as they relate to tenants' choice in modern real estate markets. Generally speaking, there is a long term relationship between price, rent and macroeconomic variables such as employment, interest rates, exchange rate and general economic growth[7]. Dobson and Gooddard[8] argued that

[5]Khisa, "Kampala tenants opt for small office space."
[6]Thakker, "Are Corporate tenants reworking office space strategy to beat pandemic woes?"
[7]Zawir et al., "The Determinants of Rental Rates and Selling Prices of Office Spaces in Jakarta," 165-178.
[8]Dobson and Goddard, "The determinants of commercial property prices and rents," 301-321.

commercial price and rent are sensitive to employment and residential property values (and rents). Thus a fall in employment levels within the catchment area of the sub-real estate market will result in a fall in prices and rent. Furthermore, there is a relationship between commercial and residential markets in that failure to pay rent for retail and office space will force potential occupants into other markets, in many instances the residential market is seen as a closer substitute.

Celka[9] outlined a number of factors that influence tenant selection of office space, namely: location, lease terms and conditions (include rent), accessibility, building characteristics, building features, fit-out and other ad-on factors (e.g., vicinity of fitness centre, office area lighting, etc. Crosby et al.[10] also found that lease terms, structure and lengths have a bearing on tenant choice. Five terms were especially found to be important, namely: lease length, break clauses, assignment and sub-letting, repairs and insurance and rent review type[11]. Udoekanem et al.[12] also found that real GDP and vacancy rates accounted for 83% of variations in rentals.

Even before the COVID-19 pandemic, firms have been attempting to transform themselves to maintain competitiveness. For instance, noting the changes in the business environment, Lizieri[13] argued that there is an assumption that the property production system would equally respond to this change, and yet the institutional structure prevents this from happening. This follows a number of studies investigating the need to construct buildings which can accommodate the flexibility of a changing business environment[14,15,16]. The COVID-19 pandemic is therefore just another aspect exerting pressure on the business environment. A more

---

9Celka, "Determinants of office space choice," 108-114.
10Crosby, Gibson and Oughton, "Lease structures, Terms and Lengths."
11Crosby, Gibson and Oughton, "Lease structures, Terms and Lengths."
12Udoekanem, Bassey and Nuhu "Determinants of commercial property rental growth in Minna, Nigeria," 60-75.
13Lizieri, "Occupier requirements in commercial real estate markets," 1151-1169.
14Horgen et al., "Excellence by design."
15Vischer, "Workspace strategies."
16Meel and Vos. "Funky offices," 322-334.

recent study by Zhang[17] examined the effect of e-commence on the demand for commercial real estate in China. Findings from this study revealed that there was a relationship between the growth of e-commence and slowing growth rates of commercial property sales between 2009 and 2013. In essence, even before the advent of COVID-19, the trajectories in the e-commence growth and commercial real estate were in opposite direction; the "stay home" policy during the pandemic could be said to have accelerated these trajectories. Zhang et al.[18] further found that different forms of commercial properties were affected differently.

Literature revealed a number of factors as being important considerations in tenants' choice, namely: location, accessibility, lease terms and conditions (including rent), building characteristics, building features, fit-out and other ad-on factors (e.g., vicinity of fitness centre, office area lighting, break clauses, assignment and sub-letting, repairs and insuance and rent review type. Recent media reports though show increased demands for rent discounts by tenants and policy provisions on re-negotiating rentals in the UK, Netherlands, US, Australia and across the globe[19,20,21,22]. Clearly, rent and lease terms have been shown to be key considerations for tenants in choosing or staying in a commercial space during this pandemic. The next section then explores the theoretical underpinning of rent in economics in order to appreciate its relevance in this chapter.

---

[17]Zhang, Zhu, and Ye, "The effects of e-commerce on the demand for commercial real estate," 106-120.

[18]Zhang, Zhu, and Ye, "The effects of e-commerce on the demand for commercial real estate," 106-120.

[19] Hammond, Edge-Cliffe-Johnson and Morris, "WeWork offers rent discounts to Covid hit."

[20]Stibbe, "Provisional rental discount in times of COVID-19."

[21] Brown, "Apartments for Rent."

[22] Queensland Government, "Negotiating commercial rent relief during Covid-10."

THEORY OF RENT

Classical economics defines rent as an income derived from the ownership of land. Over time this has come to be applied to the temporary use of any property (or asset) such as real estate, vehicles, plant and equipment. A number of classical, neo-classical and contemporary economists have debated the theory of rent, starting with Adam Smith, von Thunen, Alfred Marshall, David Ricardo and William Alonso and others. It is therefore important for this chapter to put in perspective the contribution of theoretic thinkers on the subject of rent.

Adam Smith (1723–1790) on Rent

Adam Smith viewed rent both as a monopoly price and surplus[23]. It was viewed as a monopoly price in that people who owned land, which is a limited resource, could extract something from consumers not because they used their labour or capital but by simply owning a finite resource[24]. As a surplus, rent was defined as the difference between the price of a product and the cost of producing it. During Smith's time the main product of discussion was the growing of corn from the land. Thus the thinking was that the rent payable to the landlord should be the surplus of the income from the sale of corn and the cost of producing that corn. Hence the difference (surplus) between this price and cost was the rent.

Thomas Robert Malthus (1766-1834) on Rent

Like Adam Smith, Thomas Malthus also saw rent as a surplus on agricultural land. Malthus defined costs to include outgoings belonging to its cultivation, such as profits on capital employed and wages[25]. Malthus

[23]Smith, "An Inquiry Into the Nature and Causes of the Wealth of Nations."
[24]Smith, "An Inquiry Into the Nature and Causes of the Wealth of Nations."
[25]Malthus, "An inquiry into the nature and progress of rent."

then presented what were seen as the key determinants of rent, namely: employment of capital, population increase, technological advancement and increased demand without corresponding fall in the cost of production[26]. Each of these factors could be discussed further as they relate to the increase in the amount and size of land cultivated (supply side) and increase in the amount of product sold or purchased (demand side). In other words, an increase in the quantity of corn produced, with no corresponding increase on the cost side, would result in an increased surplus.

Johann Heinrich von Thunen (1783-1850) on Rent

Von Thunen's approach was to study rent from a location perspective. Using an imaginary scenario of an "isolated state," von Thunen argued that the amount a tenant will be willing to pay for the land (bid rent) will be determined by the distance to the market for his/her agricultural products and the cost incurred to get them to such markets[27.] This meant that an increase in transport costs would affect the net income from the sale of the product resulting in less available for the payment on the use of the land. In other words, rent is a surplus after the deduction of costs, key amongst these is the transport cost. This basic understanding was later applied by William Alonso and others in what came to be known as the bid-rent theory.

David Ricardo (1772-1823) on Rent

Although Thomas Malthus developed the same ideas on rent from the study of Adam Smith, more credit was given to Ricardo on what came to

---

[26] Malthus, "An inquiry into the nature and progress of rent."
[27]vonThünen, "The isolated state."

be known as the differential cost theory or the Ricardian theory[28]. Ricardo defined rent as the "portion of the produce of the earth which is paid to the landlord for the use of the original and indestructible powers of the soils"[29]. For Ricardo, population growth was also a key determinant of the size and quality of land cultivated; arguing that population growth forces the cultivation of inferior land, in the process creating rent (surplus) for the superior land[30]. In this rent equation, capital and labour were important variables on the cost side; since Ricardo also defined rent as the difference between the produce, on one hand, and capital and labour employed, on the other.

Alfred Marshall (1842-1924) on Rent

For Alfred Marshall, price depended on the marginal productivity of a factor of production. Marshall qualified the rent as surplus concept to Producer Surplus, which was defined as the excess of the gross receipts less prime costs[31]. Marshall further pointed out that the surplus, which a piece of land yields, will depend on the market of the products produced on that land. Thus the implication is that the price of a product will be set in comparision with the price of substitute products on the market, in a way justifying the "marginal" concept in economics. Thus Marshall argued that Ricardian rent theory had a firm foundation.

Richard Muth (1927-2018) on Rent

The Thunen model was also used by others, such as Richard Muth[32], to argue that the decline in population density with distance from the CBD

---

[28]Lackman, "The Classical Base of Modem Rent Theory," 287-300.
[29] Ricardo, "Principles of political economy and taxation."
[30] Ricardo, "Principles of political economy and taxation."
[31]Marshall, "Principles of economics: unabridged eighth edition."
[32]Muth, "Cities and housing."

was mainly as a result of the decline in the value of housing produced per unit of land. Muth[33] investigated how the equilibrium use and rents of land change with changing market conditions; similarly Edwin Mills used von Thunen's model as a basis for the development of an aggregative model of resource allocation[34]. The relationship between transport costs, distance to the markets and rent is thus central to Muth's theory.

William Alonso (1933-1999) on Rent

Literature in urban economic theory also show that by the 1960s the assumptions of the von Thunen's theory and models adopted from such thinking were already being questioned by thinkers such as William Alonso[35]. This led to the development of a theory on residential land and the static bid-rent model by Alonso who postulated a decline in land rent and density as distance increases away from the centrally located work places[36].

Synthesis of Theoretical Literature

Although not based on the growing of corn in a purely agricultural economy, modern real estate economics relies heavily on these theoretical thinkers of the past. For instance, in commercial real estate, whether office or retail occupation, the link between receipts (income) from the use of the space will have a direct bearing on the rent (surplus) the tenant will be willing to pay to the landlord. In other words, productivity of the space is a key element impacting on the amount the tenant will be willing to pay as rent.

---

[33]Muth, "Economic change and rural-urban land conversions."
[34] Mills, "An aggregative model of resource allocation in a metropolitan area," 197-210.
[35]Alonso, "A theory of the urban land market," 149-157.
[36]Alonso, "Location and land use."

While this section discusses the bare-bones of the thinking on rent by Adam Smith, Thomas Malthus, David Ricardo and others, it nonetheless captures its essence to enable the application of theory on rent to a modern real estate rental market. For instance, it can be concluded from the preceding discussion that the differential theory of rent was based on the basic idea that rent is a surplus (difference) of price of a product and its cost of production. In other words, rent was seen as price-determined[37].

It is clear from the discussion above that the setting on which the above theories were based was more simplistic than the current realities; nevertheless they underpin current understanding in most theoretical frameworks on land and real estate. It is also evident from the literature that the basis of modern understanding of rent is from the classical thinking that "rent is a surplus"; that is, the difference between the cost and price of a product after subtracting profits and wages.

Applied to the modern commercial real estate market, rent is therefore the net income from the productivity of a property, hence the capitalisation of net income to assess market value in commercial valuations. The implication of this understanding is that tenants in commercial real estate will vacate or substitute commercial space when their difference between income and costs of their occupation starts to narrow, as this will affect their ability to pay rent to the landlord. Rent then becomes price-determined. When applied to modern real estate rental markets, rent of retail space will be determined by the prices of products sold in that space. When applied to valuation of real estate, rent is price-determining in that it is the net rent (net income as a surplus of receipts and costs) which is capitalised to arrive at capital value. In this way price, rent and cost are related.

It can therefore be argued that the principle of substitution in real estate economics permeates through the arguments of Adam Smith, Malthus, von Thunen, Alfred Marshall, Ricardo and other early thinkers, particularly when viewed at the market level. Marshall could therefore

---

[37]Lackman, "The Classical Base of Modem Rent Theory."

argue that this principle applies to almost every field of economics[38]; for this chapter, it is applied to tenants' choice in the occupation of commercial real estate space.

In the modern application of von Thunen's agricultural model, William Alonso argued that the value of real estate will be determined in relation to its proximity to the central business district (CBD). Thus different uses of land, retail, office or residential, will compete for the most accessible land with the more profitable use bidding higher for land closer to the CBD. Unlike in agricultural economies where growing of corn was the most profitable use, in modern economies real estate is the more productive use, hence agricultural land having the lowest value.

COVID-19 Measures and Commercial Real Estate in Zambia

Zambia had recorded 19,234 cases and 381 COVID-related deaths by 25th December 2020[39]. Compared to Europe and America, these numbers are relatively low, however the impact of the pandemic on the economy has been severe. For instance, Gross Domestic Product (GDP) is expected to drop by 2.6% by the end of the year with the worst impacted sectors being education, transport and catering and accommodation[40]. A survey of 706 large, medium, small and micro enterprises conducted in May 2020 by the Zambian government through the Ministry of Commerce, Trade and Industry, with the support of the United Nations Development Programme (UNDP), revealed that 71% of firms were partially closed during 2020, 14% were totally closed with only 15% reporting normal operations[41]. A number of enterprises reported various challenges during the year which included loss of customers (77%), had disruption in the supply chain (38%)

---

[38] Marshall, "Principles of economics: unabridged eighth edition."

[39] World Health Organisation, "Health Emergency Dashboard."

[40] Government of the Republic of Zambia, "Business Survey Report: The impact of COVID-19."

[41] Government of the Republic of Zambia, "Business Survey Report: The impact of COVID-19."

and experienced late payments (32%). As a response to these challenges many firms had to layoff workers or reduce salaries (37%), shift to flexible hours (34%) or shut down production lines and outlets (23%). The overall effect has been shrinkage in economic activities and redundancies.

In response to the pandemic, Zambia has put in place a number of measures. For the purpose of this chapter, these measures can be categories in five areas: health policies, social policies, monetary policies, fiscal policies and real estate policies.

- Health policy relates to measures such as testing, contact tracing, vaccination and hospitalisation. By September 2020, Zambia had established seven testing centres for its 10 provinces.
- Social policy relates to measures such as hand washing, sanitising, social distancing, masking up and movement restriction. In March, 2020, the Ministry of Health issued a statement on the passing of Statutory Instrument No. 22 of 2020 which provided additional regulations to facilitate management and control of COVID-19[42].
- Monetary policy includes reduction in interest and policy rates to reduce the cost of borrowing. In August 2020, the Bank of Zambia lower the Monetary Policy Rate by 125 basis points to 8% in order to provide stability to the financial sector and safeguard people's lives and livelihoods in the wake of COVID-19 pandemic[43].
- Fiscal policy relates to measures to cut expenditure from other sectors in order to fund health expenses. In May 2020, Ministry of Finance instituted additional fiscal measures to mitigate the impact of COVID-19, these included: easing liquidility, tax relief, building new and sustainable value chain and engaging multilateral organisations[44].

---

[42]Minsitry of Health, "Press Briefing on COVID-19 and additional Preventive and Control Measure."

[43] Bank of Zambia, "Monetary Policy Committee Statement: August 2020."

[44] EY Zambia, "Zambia issues additional fiscal measures to mitigate the impact of COVID-19."

- Real state policy relates to rent moratoriums on eviction. Although not effected, the Zambia government in April 2020 considered asking landlords to forgo rentals due to the impact of Covid-19 on tenants[45].

The effect of these measures on the real estate market has been varied. Thus the gravity of the effect of COVID-19 on commercial real estate has been reported differently in different markets. It is however indisputable that the restriction of movement meant closure of office and retail spaces with workers encouraged to continue working from homes. This has seen the plummeting of demand for office and retail spaces and consequently an increase in vacancies in commercial properties[46,47]. The work-from-home measure, forced firms to substitute commercial with residential space.

The rest of this section presents a synopsis of the effect of COVID-19 on the Zambian real estate market, using examples from the city of Lusaka. As discussed in the literature reviewed, there is a link between retail sales volumes and rent, defined as a surplus from occupation of commercial space. The higher the retail sales, the higher the net income and the amount a tenant would be willing to pay as rent. Zambian reports, though, show a decline in sale volumes in 2020, attributed to the effects of COVID-19; this is clearly evident in the closure of a number of retail stores due to dwindling profits. Furthermore, the local currency (Kwacha) has depreciated by 42% within 2020[48] further affecting profitability. As a result of these pressures EDCON Limited, owners of clothing stores Edgars and Jet, shut down their operations in Zambia citing loss making due to COVID-19 impacts and weakening of the local currency, in the process laying off 270 workers. Food retailers, Spar and Food Lovers, also announced closure of their Zambian stores in March and August, 2020, respectively (see Table 1 below). Other retailers, such as Mr Price (clothing) and Pick n Pay (Foods) although still operational, have either

[45]Malunga, "We're considering asking landlords to forego rentals amids COVID-19: Siliya."
[46] Knight Frank, "Africa Retail Report."
[47] Wilson, "COVID-19 Impacts on Real Estate in Zambia."
[48] Wilson, "COVID-19 Impacts on Real Estate in Zambia."

scaled down or having challenges[49]. This has resulted in hundreds of workers losing their jobs. The closed retailers had multiple stores in major malls around the country, which included Mukuba Mall in Kitwe, Kafubu Mall in Ndola, Arcades and East Park Malls in Lusaka and others across the country.

Table 1. Closure of retail shops

	Retailer	Product	Date of Closure	Potential Job losses	Country of origin
1	Spar	Food	March, 2020		South Africa
2	Edgar	Clothing	April, 2020	270	South Africa
3	Jet Store	Clothing	April, 2020		South Africa
4	Food Lovers	Food	August, 2020	100+	South Africa
5	Carnival Furnishers	Furniture	November, 2020	200+	South Africa

Source: Various media sources.

The effect of this fall in sales volumes can be analysed in terms of increase in vacancies, decrease in rentals and property values and increase in unemployment. The Lusaka real estate rental market has seen a fall in average rentals for Grade A and B office space from US$25 in 2015, US$20 in 2019 stabilising at US$18 in 2020[50,51]; a fall of 39%. With the COVID-19 pandemic, this situation has worsened with recent statistics showing further fall in rentals and increase in vacancies in office space and shopping malls. Furthermore, in the third quarter of 2020, Lusaka saw a fall in retail sales by 5.2% and over the same period occupancy rates fell to 80%[52]. As noted above, fall in sales is leading to closure and increase in vacancies. As seen earlier, rent is a surplus from sales (receipts) of the the product being sold in that space. It thus goes without saying that a fall in sales (receipts) of a product, with no reduction in the cost of operation

[49] Pick n Pay, "Integrated Annual Report."
[50] Knight Frank, "Africa Retail Report."
[51] United Africa Real Estate, "Lusaka Real Estate Market Report."
[52] Knight Frank, "Africa Retail Report."

(such as wages), will inevitability affect the amount available to pay as rent (surplus).

Redundancies have had an indirect effect on occupancy rates and rentals in the market through its contribution to unemployment. As unemployment increases, purchasing power of potential consumers falls. As seen under theoretical discussions, employment levels will have an effect on rent and prices. Although Zambia's economic conditions were weakening even before the COVID-19 pandemic, these worsened with closure of borders, work-from-home measures and reduced economic activities which impacted the real estate market. Thus landlords have been forced to undertake measures such as lease concessions and rent discounts.

Weakening sales can also partly be attributed to consumers substituting "luxury" goods with essentials such as food and shelter, thus spending less on furniture and clothing. This has contributed to low sales for clothing retailers, such as Edgars and Jet, and furniture retailers, such as Creation Furnishers and Carnival Furnishers, who have closed a number of their retail stores in various parts of Zambia.

Retail space, especially large space, has been more adversely affected than smaller spaces and office use. The reason is that Zambia has predominantly small to medium businesses which opt for smaller low grade commercial spaces; which explains why the majority of large space occupiers in most shopping malls are South African firms.

THE FUTURE OF REAL ESTATE

The work-from-home measure has shown that it is possible for most employees to work from their homes, hence residential space becomes an important substitute for commercial space. Working from home has then pointed to a number of challenges which include inadequancy of current designs to accommodate work activities, limitation of Information and Communication Technology (ICT) facilities, and work-life balancing. In many cases, homes are not designed as work environments resulting in frequent disruptions. Thus there is need to think through designs of future residential properties to accommodate both residence and working spaces. Integration of ICT facilities in the design of residential space also reinforces the concept of "Smart Cities," which is a tall-order for most developing countries.

For the developed economies, as online purchasing increases, the need for retail space will keep decreasing. For the developing countries with serious deficiencies in ICT infrastructure, the need for physical retail space may persist for a long time, but mainly for food outlets and less for luxury products. Nonetheless, the immediate lesson from the COVID-19 pandemic is that in the long term residential space has the potential to substitute for most functions performed by commercial space.

With specific reference to property services, the COVID-19 pandemic has also reinforced the rise and importance of Property Technology (Proptech) firms. For instance, reports show that investment in Proptech companies had increased from US$200 million in 2011 to US$2.5 billion in 2016[53]. Although current statistics show an adverse effect to investments in Proptech during the COVID-19 pandemic period, long term projection are for a realigned real estate and Proptech relationship[54,55].

CONCLUSION

The entry point for the chapter was a review of literature on key determinants of commercial real estate. This was followed by a review of the theory on rent underpinning its application in economics, before the discussion of COVID-19 measures and their impacts on the commercial real estate sector. The chapter revealed that the negative relationship between growth in e-commence and commercial real estate started before the COVID-19 pandemic as businesses strived to adapt to the changing environment. The advent of COVID-19 pandemic has merely exacerbated

[53] ING Economics Department, "Technology in the real estate sector."
[54] Blondeau, "Why COVID-19 has Spurred Innovation in Proptech."
[55] Donati, "What's next for real estate and Proptech after COVID-19."

an already changing landscape. The rise of online shopping and Proptech had already changed the *modis operandi* of real estate. This implies that the long term trend is for space users to substitute commercial space with residential. Literature though showed that the rate of substitution will dependent on the commercial real estate sub-market.

REFERENCES

Alonso, William. "A theory of the urban land market."*Papers in regional science* 6, no. 1 (1960): 149-157.

Alonso, William. "Location and land use. Toward a general theory of land rent."*Location and land use. Toward a general theory of land rent.* (1964).

Bank of Zambia. *Monetary Policy Committee Statement*: August 2020. https://www.boz.zm/monetary_policy_committee_statement_august_2020.pdf.

Blondeau, Gregory. Why COVID-19 has Spurred Innovation in Proptech. *Computer Business Review*. August 17, 2020. https://www.cbronline.com/opinion/innovation-in-proptech.

Brown, Dalvin. Apartments for Rent: Americans don't want yearlong leases amid pandemics, neither do landlord. *USA Today*. August 17, 2020.

Celka, Krzysztof. "Determinants of office space choice."*Journal of International Studies* 4, no. 1 (2011): 108-114.

Crosby, Neil, Virginia Gibson, and Melanie Oughton. "Lease structures, Terms and Lengths: Does the UK lease meet current business requirements." *Reading, University of Reading/RICS* (2001).

Dobson, Stephen M., and J. A. Goddard. "The determinants of commercial property prices and rents." *Bulletin of Economic Research* 44, no. 4 (1992): 301-321.

Donati, Angelica K. What's next for real estate and Proptech after COVID-19. *Forbes*. May 27, 2020. https://www.forbes.com/sites/

angelicakrystledonati/2020/05/27/whats-next-for-real-estate-and-proptech-after-covid-19/?sh=1a35c1f07694.

EY Zambia. Zambia issues additional fiscal measures to mitigate the impact of COVID-19. *Global Tax Alert*. April 24, 2020. https://www.ey.com/en_gl/tax-alerts/zambia-issues-additional-fiscal-measures-to-mitigate-the-impact-of-covid-19.

Government of the Republic of Zambia (GRZ). *Business Survey Report: The impact of COVID-19 on Zambian Enterprises. GRZ/UNDP*. 2020. https://www.zm.undp.org/content/zambia/en/home/presscenter/pressreleases/2020/business-survey-reveals-adverse-effects-of-covid-19-on-businesse.html.

ING Economics Department. *Technology in the real estate sector: Proptech reduces risks and increases value*. June 2018. https://think.ing.com/uploads/reports/ING_EBZ_PropTech-Technlogy_in_the_real_estate_sector-June_2018_tcm162-148619.pdf

Hammond, George, Edge-Cliffe-Johnson, Andrew and Morris, Stephen. WeWork offers Rent Discounts to Covid hit. *Financial Times*. October 4, 2020. https://www.ft.com/content/742d321a-6c40-42cd-b78d-59110aac4650.

Horgen, Turid, Michael L. Joroff, William L. Porter, and Donald A. Schon. *Excellence by design: Transforming workplace and work practice*. John Wiley & Sons, 1999.

Khisa, Issac. Kampala tenants opt for small office space. *The Independent*. February 4, 2020. https://www.independent.co.ug/kampala-tenants-opt-for-small-office-space/.

Knight Frank. *Africa Retail Report*. December, 2020. https://www.knightfrank.com/research/africa-retail-report-december-2020-7645.aspx.

Lackman, Conway L. "The Classical Base of Modem Rent Theory." *American Journal of Economics and Sociology* 35, no. 3 (1976): 287-300.

Lizieri, Colin Martyn. "Occupier requirements in commercial real estate markets." *Urban Studies* 40, no. 5-6 (2003): 1151-1169.

Malthus, Thomas Robert. *An inquiry into the nature and progress of rent, and the principles by which it is regulated.* For J. Murray, and J. Johnson and Company, 1815.

Marshall, Alfred. *Principles of economics: unabridged eighth edition.* Cosimo, Inc., 2009.

Malunga Julia. We're considering asking landlords to forego rentals amidst COVID-19: Siliya. *News Diggers.* April 7, 2020. https://diggers.news/local/2020/04/07/were-considering-asking-landlords-to-forego-rentals-amid-covid-19-siliya/.

Meel, Juriaan van, and Paul Vos. "Funky offices: Reflections on office design in the? new economy?." *Journal of Corporate Real Estate* 3, no. 4 (2001): 322-334.

Mills, Edwin S. "An aggregative model of resource allocation in a metropolitan area." *The American Economic Review* 57, no. 2 (1967): 197-210.

Ministry of Health. *Press Briefing on COVID-19 and additional Preventive and Control Measure.* March 17, 2020. https://www.moh.gov.zm/?wpfb_dl=145.

Muth, Richard F. *Cities and housing: The spatial pattern of urban residential land use.* University of Chicago Press, (1969).

Muth, Richard F. "Economic change and rural-urban land conversions." *Econometrica: Journal of The Econometric Society* (1961): 1-23.

Pick n Pay. *Integrated Annual Report.* 2020. https://www.picknpay investor.co.za/downloads/annual-report/2020/pick-n-pay-iar.pdf.

Queensland Government. *Negotiating commercial rent relief during Covid-10.*https://www.business.qld.gov.au/running-business/support-assistance/qsbc/negotiating-rent-relief.

Ricardo, David. *Principles of political economy and taxation.* G. Bell and sons, 1891.

Simon, Zainal Zawir, Noer Azam Achsani, Adler H. Manurung, and Roy Sembel. "The Determinants of Rental Rates and Selling Prices of Office Spaces in Jakarta: A Macro-econometric Model Using VECM Approach." *International Journal of Economics and Finance* 7, no. 3 (2015): 165-178.

Smith, Adam. (1791). *An Inquiry Into the Nature and Causes of the Wealth of Nations: By Adam Smith,* (Vol. 4). JJ Tourneisen; and JL Legrand.

Stibbe. *Provisional Rental Discount in times of COVID-19.* August 14, 2020. https://www.stibbe.com/en/news/2020/august/provisional-rental-discounts-in-times-of-covid-19.

Thakker, Bhavin. *Are Corporate tenants reworking office space strategy to beat pandemic woes*? https://www.moneycontrol.com/news/business/real-estate/are-corporate-tenants-reworking-office-space-strategy-to-beat-pandemic-woes-5850751.html.

Udoekanem, Namnso Bassey, and James Idemudia Nuhu. "Determinants of commercial property rental growth in Minna, Nigeria." *LAÜ Sosyal Bilimler Dergisi* 5, no. 1 (2014): 60-75.

United Africa Real Estate (UARE) *Lusaka Real Estate Market Report*. August 17, 2018. https://www.slideshare.net/CatrinJones8/uare-lusaka-real-estate-report-2018-111736953.

Vischer, Jacqueline C. *Workspace strategies: Environment as a tool for work*. Springer Science & Business Media, 2012.

von Thünen, J. H. *The isolated state.* Wartenberg, CM trans. Translation of: *Der isolierte Staat (1826).*"(1966).

Wilson, Elaine. *COVID-19 Impacts on Real Estate in Zambia.* https://www.cushmanwakefield.com/en/insights/covid-19/covid-19-impacts-zambia-real-estate#:~:text=The%20retail%20market%20has%20been,case%20of%20a%20nationwide%20lockdown.

World Health Organisation. Health Emergency Dashboard https://covid19.who.int/region/afro/country/zm.

Zhang, Danlei, Pengyu Zhu, and Yanmei Ye. "The effects of E-commerce on the demand for commercial real estate." *Cities* 51 (2016): 106-120.

In: The Future of Real Estate
Editor: Jan Veuger
ISBN: 978-1-53619-414-2

Chapter 3

SELECTED ASPECTS OF THE SLOVENIAN LEGISLATION ON LEASE OF AGRICULTURAL LAND AND FORESTS

Marijana Kunc*[1], *MSc*, *Boštjan Aver*[1], *PhD* and *Alenka Temeljotov Salaj*[2,*], *PhD
[1]European Faculty of Law, New Univeristy,
Nova Gorica, Slovenia
[2]Department of Civil and Environmental Engineering,
Norwegian University of Science and Technology,
Trondheim, Norway

ABSTRACT

The article presents the legal provisions on the lease of agricultural land and forests in Slovenia, as well as some of the issues arising from the current Agricultural Land Act (ZKZ) and Forest Act (ZG). These two

* Corresponding Author's E-mail: alenka.temeljotov-salaj@ntnu.no.

laws feature several specific limitations in leasing out farmland, some of which have been kept from the socialist times of former Yugoslavia. Under the ZKZ, a landowner who wishes to lease out agricultural or forest land must first publish their intent and wait for applicants. Each agricultural lease agreement must be approved by the relevant administrative unit and entered in the land register. Moreover, the law grants pre-emption rights to certain persons (existing tenant, tenants or owners of neighbouring plots, etc.). The long and complicated procedure, as well as the inability to freely choose the tenant result in a large majority of landowners leasing out their agricultural land without the mandatory procedure, although court practice considers such agreements null and void. This often leaves tenants without the legal protection intended for them by law (e.g., minimum lease duration). Nevertheless, even tenants with contracts that have not been approved have the possibility of registering actual use of agricultural land, which is a requirement for direct payments to farmers under the EU's common agricultural policy. Because the Farmland and Forest Fund of the Republic of Slovenia, which manages publicly owned farmland and forests, is virtually the only one to fully comply with the provisions of the ZKZ, the authors propose removing some of the limitations. While the obligation of publishing a lease offer may be appropriate for publicly owned land, it is a disproportionate intervention in the property rights of private landowners. Moreover, the pre-emption rights have proved problematic, since they allow existing tenants on state- and municipality-owned agricultural land to extend their leases indefinitely, and they also limit the right of private landowners to freely choose their tenants.

Keywords: agricultural land, forest, lease, legislation, Slovenia

INTRODUCTION

Article 71 of the Constitution of the Republic of Slovenia tasks the legislature to ensure special protection of agricultural land by law. The protection of farmland was first regulated with the Agricultural Land Act of 1973 (ZKZ-73), which included several institutions aimed at reducing fragmentation of agricultural land and preventing farmland from ending up in the hands of non-farmers (e.g., farmer status; pre-emption rights of neighbours, existing tenants and agricultural organisations to buy land; cap on farmland ownership; land reallocation and consolidation). After

Slovenia declared independence from Yugoslavia, the Constitutional Court annulled in 1992 the provisions of the ZKZ-73 on maximum farm size (Constitutional Court Decision U-I-122/91), and in 1995 repealed the ZKZ-73 in its entirety (Constitutional Court Decision U-I-184/94), based on the assessment that the different conception of property in the new legal order meant several parts of the law were in conflict with the Constitution. A new Agricultural Land Act (ZKZ) was adopted in 1996, however, it did not bring much change, since most of the previous provisions were preserved.

Agricultural land lease is regulated in the relevant provisions of the ZKZ pertaining to trading in farmland, which remained similar to those from 1973.

In order to conclude a lease contract for an agricultural or forest plot, an offer must first be published on the notice board of the relevant administrative unit and the national e-administration website. Any natural or legal person can accept the offer, but the ZKZ gives pre-emption rights to certain persons (existing tenant, tenants or owners of neighbouring plots, etc.) based on the presumption that they will manage the land or forest better.

The administrative unit with jurisdiction over the relevant plot approves the legal transaction with an official notice. The lease contract for the agricultural land or forest is concluded in writing and is entered in the land register and land cadastre.

This complicated tenancy regulation—particularly the obligation to publish an offer before being able to lease out agricultural land—means that landowners rarely follow the procedure stipulated in the ZKZ. A large majority of landowners lease out their agricultural land without prior publication and approval by the administrative unit because they wish to choose their tenant themselves.

However, case law considers such contracts null and void because they are not signed in accordance with the mandatory procedure, so the question arises in (the rare cases of) litigation as to which property law should be used here.

In this article, we take a look at the Slovenian legislation pertaining to the lease of agricultural land and forests, as well as some of the issues arising from the current Agricultural Land Act (ZKZ) and Forest Act (ZG).

Slovenian Regulations on Lease of Agricultural Land and Forests

In Slovenian legislation, the conclusion of tenancy or lease agreements is regulated in the Obligations Code (OZ), but in the case of agricultural land and forest leases the provisions of the ZKZ and ZG are used as a *lex specialis*. According to the ZKZ, the object of lease is the relevant agricultural land, along with the associated facilities, equipment and permanent crops (ZKZ Article 26). Agricultural land refers to plots defined as agricultural areas in the planning documents of local communities, and may be classified as agricultural areas under permanent protection or other agricultural areas (ZKZ, Article 2). Unless elsewhere otherwise specified, the relevant provisions of the ZKZ are also used for forests (ZKZ Article 1). Farmland lease is regulated in the relevant provisions of Articles 19 – 24 (with the exception of the first, second and third paragraph of Article 23), which set down the transaction rules for agricultural land, forests and farms (ZKZ Article 27). A landowner who intends to rent out a piece of agricultural land, must submit a lease offer with the administrative unit responsible for the area where is located. The administrative unit then publishes the offer on its notice board and the national e-administration website. Anyone interested in leasing the offered land may send a written acceptance of the offer to the administrative unit by registered mail or submit it there in person within 30 days. If no one accepts the offer by this deadline, the owner must repeat the process in order to lease out the land.

The law sets the following order of priority for pre-emption rights in agricultural land lease:

- tenant,
- tenant or owner-farmer on an adjacent plot to the one being leased out,
- other farmer, agricultural organisation or sole proprietor who needs the land or farm for their agricultural or forestry activity (ZKZ Article 27).

With forests, pre-emption rights are granted to owners of adjacent land plots. If they do not exercise them, the rights are passed on to the owner of the next nearest forest land plot. In certain cases (protected forests and forests of special interest), pre emption rights are reserved for the state or municipality on whose territory the forest lies (ZG Article 47).

The natural or legal person concluding the lease with the farmland or forest owner must submit the legal transaction to the administrative unit for approval within 30 days after the original deadline for accepting the offer. The administrative unit may approve or deny the transaction. Only upon approval of the administrative unit can the tenancy be recorded in the land register and land cadastre.

Under the ZKZ, a lease agreement is signed for a fixed minimum term of 10, 15 or 25 years (depending on the type of land use), and is renewed automatically for another tenure of equal duration unless one of the parties gives a six-months' written notice of termination before its expiration (ZKZ Article 31). The owner and tenant may also agree on a hereditary lease (ZKZ Article 26).

The provisions of the ZKZ apply to all owners of agricultural land. Nevertheless, the Farmland and Forest Fund of the Republic of Slovenia, which manages the land owned by the state and municipalities, is more or less the only one to fully comply with the provisions of the ZKZ. Private landowners normally wish for their land to be managed by someone they choose themselves, so they mostly enter into agricultural land lease agreements without the prescribed procedure. However, such legal transactions cannot be entered in the land register and land cadastre, since such records require the approval of the relevant administrative unit.

In the past, the question of records of actual users of agricultural land arose, in particular in relation to the implementation of the common agricultural policy (CAP) and distribution of direct payments to farmers (i.e., subsidies). When the Ministry of Agriculture, Forestry and Food first set up the Register of Agricultural Holdings and records of actual use in 2003, the Agency for Agricultural Markets and Rural Development made a prior conclusion of lease agreements a condition for registration of reference parcels or land use units (known as GERKs)—a requirement for CAP payments. Since approved lease agreements were almost non-existent in practice, the procedure was eased and registration of land use units only required the actual user of an agricultural land parcel to deposit a signed statement on record at the relevant administrative unit. This is how GERKs are still registered today. For tax purposes, the 2017 changes to the Tax Procedure Act (ZDavP-2J) introduced the possibility of registering actual farmland use with the Financial Administration. An actual user of agricultural land or forest land whose right to use that particular plot is not recorded in the land register or land cadastre can declare actual use of the plot with the Financial Administration. The submitted declaration must be accompanied by proof of actual use (e.g., statement on the use of the plot signed by both the user and the registered landowner). If the Financial Administration establishes that a plot of land is not used by its owner, it may also determine ex officio the actual user and assign them the cadastral income for this plot (ZDavP Article 316.c). The cadastral income is a form of flat-rate Property Tax in Slovenia. More details about cadastral income can be found in Aver, Kunc and Temeljotov Salaj (2017, 63 - 88).

It is quite common that a GERK is assigned to the landowner although the land is actually cultivated by someone else. As a result, Slovenia still has a relatively high number of small agricultural holdings that are not in fact active farms since their land is cultivated by others. This practice is also not entirely in line with EU regulations on direct payments in agriculture. The European Court of Justice (ECJ) has ruled on several occasions that direct payments per hectare are eligible if the area is used by the farmer for his own agricultural activities in his name and on his own behalf (e.g., ECJ ruling in Case C-61/09).

Case law has clearly shown that lease agreements concluded without prior approval of the relevant administrative unit are null and void (VSC Ruling Cp 1326/2006). Miha Juhart (2004) also believes that we can assume a sanction of nullity from the general rules, based on the rule that a lease of agricultural land must be entered in the land register. If an agreement is found to be null and void, the court examines whether it meets the conditions of validity as a different type of contract (OZ Article 89). In one of the cases, the court ruled that the agreement between the two parties was a loan for use contract without specification of the duration and purpose of the precarium (VSK Ruling Cp 593/2009). Precarium is an agreement whereby one allows another the use of an agricultural land gratuitously. When the use of a land is onerous, is such an agreement null and void. It is common that the duration and purpose of the precarium are not specified, so the lender may demand the return of their property at any given time (OZ Article 583). Unless otherwise agreed, the lessor may therefore terminate the informal lease contract or precarium at any time, which can have unfavourable consequences for the tenant farmer. Before use, agricultural land must often be prepared for cultivation of different crops (setting up a plantation, access roads and water management, fertilisation, different kinds of amelioration of agricultural land, etc.), which means costs that may turn to profit only after several years of using the leased land. Farmers rarely choose to perform extensive maintenance works on informally leased land because there is no guarantee that the tenancy will continue for a longer period of time. And if the farmer is registered as the actual user of the land parcel, the termination of the lease or precarium also means a decrease in subsidies, and in some cases even an obligation to return subsidies already received. If the owner decides to sell the farmland, the farmer with only an unofficial lease agreement has no pre-emption rights over other prospective buyers, since according to case law, tenancy constitutes a basis for pre-emption only when proved with a written lease agreement concluded in accordance with the provisions of the ZKZ (UPRS Ruling U 1130/2004). In this respect, ECJ case law shows that pre-emption rights of certain categories of buyers (e.g., tenant farmers) are justified in some cases for the general aims of agricultural policy (see

European Commission 2017). Tenants' pre-emption rights in sale of agricultural land stipulated in the ZKZ are therefore not in contradiction of the *acquis communautaire*, but the predominance of informal leases in Slovenia means they rarely apply in practice.

To protect tenants, the ZKZ sets the minimum lease duration for different types of agricultural land. The tenure must not be shorter than:

- 25 years for vineyards, orchards and hop fields,
- 15 years for plantations of fast-growing trees,
- 10 years for other purposes.

However, since informal leases prevail in Slovenia, this legal protection of tenant farmers is hollow in practice (despite the mandatory minimum tenure set down in the ZKZ).

In comparison, German law does not feature any mandatory minimum duration for leases, while the Austrian Agricultural Lease Act (Landpachtgesetz) only provides guidelines on lease duration (*Richtpachtzeiten*) for different land uses, which is shorter than prescribed by the ZKZ:

- 15 years for lease of agricultural holdings used mostly for profit-oriented horticulture, viticulture or fruit production,
- 10 years for lease of agricultural holdings for other sectors and individual land plots used mostly for profit-oriented horticulture, viticulture or fruit production, and
- 5 years for all other purposes (Landpachtgesetz Article 5).

The Swiss Federal Agricultural Lease Act (LPG) defines the minimum lease duration separately for first lease (LPG Article 7) and lease renewal or extension (LPG Article 8). The first lease of an agricultural holding must be for at least nine years, while the minimum duration for individual land plots is six years. Shorter lease agreements are only valid if approved by the relevant authority, and an application for the exemption must be submitted within three months after the lease starts (Puhr 2011).

Kunc, Aver and Temeljotov Salaj (2018, 199) stated that, according to provisions in ZKZ, the lease agreement for agricultural land has to be concluded in writing and entered in the land register and in the land cadastre. In literature, the ZKZ is criticised for the mandatory recording of leases in the land register and land cadastre (Juhart 2004, 644). The relevant legislation in Germany, Austria and Switzerland, for instance, does not require special form or procedure for agricultural lease agreements. Lease agreements may even be concluded orally, although written form is preferable as proof. However in Germany if the land lease agreement for a period longer than two years is not concluded in writing, it is valid for an indefinite period (BGB, Article 585a). Because of its protective function is, according to the general understanding, the requirement mandatory (Schumacher 2016, 87). In Austria, entering leases in the land register is optional. The parties may agree to record the lease in the land register, which affects real property rights also in relation to third persons (ABGB Article 1095). In all three countries, lease agreements must be announced to the tax authorities, as agricultural land leases affect the calculations of taxes and social security contributions.

Compared to the EU average, agricultural land rents in Slovenia are relatively low (cf. Annex of European Commission 2017). In this respect, we should point out that the Slovenian Statistics Office currently only collects data on rents from the Farmland and Forest Fund (Puc 2020), since data on rents on privately owned land are not accessible. But according to unofficial information, rents paid to the Fund are much lower than rents on privately owned land (Šuler 2013, 11; Šubic 2016).

Conclusion

In Slovenia, there are certain specific limitations in concluding agricultural land lease agreements. The right of landowners to choose the tenant is limited by the pre-emption rights granted in the ZKZ. Owners of agricultural land and forests are also limited by the provisions on minimum lease duration and entering leases in the land register and cadastre. All these limitations, but particularly the mandatory publication of an offer to lease agricultural land, means that landowners rarely adhere to the prescribed procedure.

Given that the provisions of the ZKZ on agricultural and forest lease are hardly followed in practice, we believe the legislator should consider removing some of the limitations. In our opinion, the obligation of publishing the intent to lease out agricultural land or forest land should be kept for publicly owned surfaces, while the mandatory publishing of offers is inappropriate for privately owned land and represents a disproportionate intervention in the property rights of landowners.

The pre-emption rights to land lease should likewise be abolished, since they allow existing tenants on state- and municipality-owned agricultural land to extend their leases indefinitely. Moreover, they limit the right of private landowners to freely choose their tenants. In the future, it would also be necessary to reconsider the mandatory entry of lease agreements in real property records.

Acknowledgments

The presented study is a part of the project Legal statutory definition of farmer and farm in Slovenia, including with economic, environmental and social measurements, funded by ARRS (V5-1607).

References

Aver, Boštjan, Kunc, Marijana and Temeljotov Salaj, Alenka. 2017. "Opredelitev kmetije za potrebe izvajanja davčne politike". *Dignitas: Revija za Človekove Pravice,* 75/76: 63 - 88. [A definition of the farm for the tax policy implementation needs. *The Slovenian Journal of Human Rights,* 75/76:63 - 88]. (Aver, Kunc and Temeljotov Salaj 2017, 63 - 88).

Juhart, Miha. 2004. "Zakupna (najemna) pogodba". In *Obligacijski Zakonik s Komentarjem 3. Knjiga: Posebni Del),* edited by Juhart Miha and Plavšak, Nina. 633 - 722 [Leese agreement. In *Obligations Code with Comments 3. Book: Special Part.* 79/80: 633 - 72]. Ljubljana: GV Založba (Juhart 2004, 644).

Kunc Marijana, Aver, Boštjan, Starman, Marko and Temeljotov Salaj, Alenka. 2018. "Zakup kmetijskih zemljišč v Sloveniji". *Dignitas: Revija za Človekove Pravice,* 79/80: 189 - 208 [Agricultural tenancies in Slovenia. *The Slovenian Journal of Human Rights,* 79/80: 189 - 208] (Kunc, Aver and Temeljotov Salaj 2020, 199).

Puc, Helena. 2020. "Metodološko pojasnilo, Cene njiv in trajnega travinja in zakupnine kmetijskih zemljišč". Statistics Office of the Republic of Slovenia. Accessed May 20, 2020. ["Methodological explanation, Prices of fields and permanent grassland and leases of agricultural land." Statistics Office of the Republic of Slovenia]. http://www.stat.si/StatWeb/File/DocSysFile/8609/15-759-MP.pdf (Puc, 2020).

Puhr, Nataša. 2011. "Posebnosti zakupa kmetijskih zemljišč". Master's thesis, University of Maribor, Faculty of Agriculture and Life Sciences, 152) [Peculiarities of agricultural land lease. Master's thesis]. Ljubljana: GV Založba (Puhr, 2011, 76).

Schumacher, Dirk. 2016. "Gesetz über die Anzeige und Beanstandung von Landpachtverträgen (Landpachtverkehrgesetz – LPachtVG)". In *Agrarrecht.*, edited by Düsing Mechtild and Martinez, José. strani 1-287. München: Verlag C. H. Beck OHG. [Law on the notification and objection of land lease contracts (Land Lease Traffic Act – LpachtVG. In *Agricultural law*] (Schumacher 2016, 87).

Šubic, Petra. 2016. "Kako od sklada kmetijskih zemljišč in gozdov najamete kmetijsko zemljišče". *Finance*, Accessed May 17, 2018 [How to rent agricultural land from the Agricultural Land and Forest Fund. *Finance*]. https://agrobiznis.finance.si/8848212_(Šubic, 2018).

Šuler, Nadija. 2013. "Zakup kmetijskih zemljišč kot neizrabljen proračunski vir". *Pravna praksa,* 32(24/25):11 - 12. [Leasing of agricultural land as an unused budgetary resource. *Legal practice,* 24/25: 11/12] (Šuler, 2013, 11).

Acts

Agriculture Act – ZKme-1 (*Official Gazette of the Republic of Slovenia* [*Uradni list RS*], No. 45/08, 57/12, 90/12, 26/14, 32/15, 27/17 and 22/18).

Agricultural Land Act – ZKZ-73 (*Official Gazette of the Socialist Republic of Slovenia* [Uradni list SRS], No. 26/73, 24/75, 23/77, 1/79-popr., 11/81, 1/86, 7/86 – popr., 17/86, 29/86 – popr., 32/89, 83/89, 42/89, 5/90, 9/90, 14/90 – popr., and *Official Gazette of the Republic of Slovenia* [Uradni list RS], No. 5/91, 8/91, 10/91, 17/91 – ZUDE, 46/92 – Odl. US, 13/93, 66/93, 71/93, 29/95 – ZPDF, 58/95 – Odl. US and 70/95 - ZDKG).

Agricultural Land Act – ZKZ (*Official Gazette of the Republic of Slovenia* [Uradni list RS], No. 59/96, 31/98 – odl. US, 1/99 – ZNIDC, 54/00 – ZKme, 68/00 – odl. US, 27/02 – odl. US, 58/02 – ZMR-1, 67/02, 110/02 – ZUreP-1, 110/02 – ZGO-1, 36/03, 55/03 – UPB1, 43/11, NPB12, 71/11 – UPB2, 58/12, 27/16, 27/17 – ZKme-1D and 79/17).

Allgemeines bürgerliches Gesetzbuch (ABGB, JGS, Nr. 946/1811, last changes BGBl. I Nr. 16/2020 (NR: GP XXVII IA 397/A AB 112 S. 19. BR: AB 10288 S. 904.).

Bundesgesetz über die landwirtschaftliche Pacht (LPG) of 4 October 1985, last changes Verordnung über die abschliessende Inkraftsetzung der Änderung vom 22. März 2013 des Landwirtschaftsgesetzes. [Federal Law on Agricultural Lease (LPG) of 4 October 1985, last changes Ordinance on the final implementation of the amendment of 22 March 2013 to the Agriculture Act.]

Bundesgesetz vom 26. November 1969, mit dem Bestimmungen über landwirtschaftliche Pachtverträge getroffen werden (Landpachtgesetz) StF: BGBl. Nr. 451/1969 (NR: GP XI RV 1216 AB 1434, p. 157. BR: p. 284.), last changes BGBl. I Nr. 58/2018 (NR: GP XXVI RV 195 AB

221 S. 34. BR: AB 10018 S. 882). [Federal Act of November 26, 1969, with which provisions on agricultural leases are made (Land Lease Act) StF: Federal Law Gazette No. 451/1969 (NR: GP XI RV 1216 AB 1434, p. 157.BR: p. 284.), last changes in Federal Law Gazette I No. 58/2018 (NR: GP XXVI RV 195 AB 221 p. 34. BR: AB 10018 p. 882).]

Forest Act – ZG (*Official Gazette of the Republic of Slovenia* [Uradni list RS], No. 30/93, 56/99, 67/02, 110/02, 115/06, 110/07, 106/10, 63/13, 101/13, 17/14, 22/14, 24/15, 9/16 and 77/16).

Obligations Code – OZ (*Official Gazette of the Republic of Slovenia* [Uradni list RS], No. 97/07, 64/16 and 20/18).

Tax Procedure Act – ZDavP-2 (*Official Gazette of the Republic of Slovenia* [Uradni list RS], No. 13/11 – UPB, 32/12, 94/12, 101/13 – ZDavNepr, 111/13, 22/14 – odl. US, 25/14 – ZFU, 40/14 – ZIN-B, 90/14, 91/15, 63/16, 69/17, 13/18 – ZJF-H, 36/19 and 66/19).

Case-Law

Administrative Court of the Republic of Slovenia (Upravno sodišče Republike Slovenije – UPRS). Ruling U 1130/2004 of 20 December 2005.

Celje Higher Court (Višje sodišče v Celju – VSC). Ruling Cp 1326/2006 of 24 May 2007.

Constitutional Court of the Republic of Slovenia (Ustavno sodišče – US RS). Decision U-I-122/91 of 10 September 1992. Available at: http://www.us-rs.si/documents/0f/76/u-i-122-912.pdf [14 October 2020].

Constitutional Court of the Republic of Slovenia (Ustavno sodišče – US RS). Decision U-I-184/94 of 14 September 1995. Available at: http://www.us-rs.si/documents/54/bb/u-i-184-942.pdf [14 October 2020].

Koper Higher Court (Višje sodišče v Kopru – VSK). Ruling Cp 593/2009 of 15 December 2009.

European Commission. 2017. *Commission Interpretative Communication on the Acquisition of Farmland and European Union Law* (C/2017/6168). Official Journal of the European Union, C 350/5.

European Court of Justice. 2010. *Judgment of the Court* (First Chamber) of 14 October 2010 (reference for a preliminary ruling from the Oberverwaltungsgericht Rheinland-Pfalz (Germany)) — Landkreis Bad Dürkheim v Aufsichts- und Dienstleistungsdirektion (Case C-61/09). ECLI:EU:C:2010:606.

In: The Future of Real Estate
Editor: Jan Veuger
ISBN: 978-1-53619-414-2

Chapter 4

LAND VALUE CAPTURE'S POTENTIAL IN NORWEGIAN PROJECTS

Alexander Bergsland Finsnes*[1] *and Alenka Temeljotov Salaj*[2,*], *PhD

[1]Vedal AS, Oslo, Norway

[2]Department of Civil and Environmental Engineering, Norwegian University of Science and Technology, Trondheim, Norway

ABSTRACT

The paper discusses the potential for implementing Land Value Capture (LVC) strategies in Norway. In order to evaluate such a potential, case studies have been oriented both to look at a re-zoning's effect on real estate value and to understand how private infrastructure contributions are gathered in Norway today. Methodology used is a literature review for establishing knowledge regarding LVC instruments, an analytical study regarding relevant Norwegian legislation for private infrastructure contributions, and a case study. The results show that several

* Corresponding Author's E-mail: alenka.temeljotov-salaj@ntnu.no.

professionals, mainly real estate developers and academics, have been consulted regarding the matter throughout the work, as well as basic estimations and calculations have been carried out in the study. The land value of the properties assessed in the case study, which are a subject for re-zoning and a new local plan, turned out to be highly dependent of the utilization degree. The implications show a possibility to develop a new system for gathering private infrastructure contributions in Norway, based on replacing both development agreements and the infrastructure work up duty with a re-zoning fee, that captures plan made values, where the revenues shall be spent on nearby, necessary infrastructure measures.

Keywords: development agreement, LVC, private infrastructure contribution, re- zoning fee, Norway

INTRODUCTION

Most of the infrastructure projects today are financed solely by public authorities, or by public authorities and private investors as a cooperation. The execution of infrastructure projects often gives positive bi-effects to neighboring stakeholders, more specifically increased land value to adjacent properties. If the project owner, usually a public authority, could benefit from this value increment after the project was done, parts of the project funding could then be captured, and more projects could be carried out. A principle involving this idea is called Land Value Capture (LVC). The concept behind LVC is that a project owner of an infrastructure project wants to be rewarded for its investments that increases the land value of an adjacent property it does not own itself. That can typically be exemplified by a public authority building a sub-way station nearby a property owned by an unaffiliated private company. The value of the property is then expected to increase, and the public authority would want a share of the increased land value.

LVC has been implemented in jurisdictions for several hundred years, and the principles behind it were mentioned already in the works by the economist Adam Smith. Special Assessments (SA), which is one of the methods classified as LVC, was used as early as 1691 in New York City for funding the construction of a drainage system and street pavements (Zhao and Larson, 2011). In more modern history, specifically in 1976, LVC was included in the founding document for UN- Habitat, the Vancouver Action Plan (Walters, 2013). At the document's time of publishing, several methods of LVC had been used frequently during periods over the last 100 years, especially in U.S.A. (Zhao and Larson, 2011). There are several strategies and instruments that may be referred to as LVC, a lot because of the wide definitions. As a result, several countries are using LVC strategies, without actually categorizing them as such. The strategies can interfere with each other, as well as some countries use strategies very similar to the more theoretical LVC strategies. Different countries have different applicable laws, meaning LVC strategies will in most cases need adaption to each and every country. Another aspect is that most countries write their laws in languages different to English, meaning an expression like LVC would usually not be used in a country where English is not the official language. The judgment whether a country uses LVC strategies or not, may therefore in some cases be considered subjective. An important reason that LVC has become especially interesting and relevant today, is the green change, meaning that revenues from motor fuel taxes are falling. This results to more environmental friendly and public ways of transport (Zhao et al., 2012a). The definition of LVC seems fairly wide so far, but there exist several concrete policies involving the concept of value capture (Salaj et al. 2018). All stakeholders for the public private partnerships rely on the users' perceived value (Temeljotov Salaj, 2005) and their expectations for supplyers' offers (Grum and Kobal Grum, 2020).

The paper aim is to establish an overview of how public authorities gather private funding for public infrastructure and see the potential for implementing LVC strategies, especially with the focus on the status of LVC in Norway.

THEORETICAL BACKGROUND

LVC involves four main steps (Walters, 2013): 1) an increment of land value as a result of infrastructure improvements must occur; 2) an estimation of the changed land value due to the improvements and a value that a tax or fee can be based on; 3) the tax or fee to be implemented and kept for a sufficient amount of time in order to cover the budgeted costs of the project; and 4) the efforts in collection to be sufficient enough to realize the increased value. Another important aspect is that the amount captured due to increased land value cannot exceed the benefits received from the infrastructure project (Zhao et al., 2012a). Many scientists have their own definitions and assumptions that have been in place for a value capture process to be successful. A partnership consisting of the UN Habitat together with Hendricks and Tonkin (2010) resulted in the following assumptions that has to be in order to implement a well-functioning LVC:

- Existence of a well-functioning political system including a leader with support from the inhabitants, a de-centralized authority and a good and functional system for property tax.
- The effectiveness of LVC during the implementation phase through effective land use management.
- Adequate training for a functional LVC system for: policy makers, administrators and land developers.
- The land valuation has to be precise, efficient and in its time.
- All tools for LVC should be considered when a jurisdiction chooses to use the concept.

One of the LVC strategies is called Tax Increment Financing (TIF) (Zhao et al., 2010), used in transportation finance is based on that development and execution of projects improving the infrastructure will in most cases contribute to rising property values in their adjacent areas. The rising property values then lead to increased property taxes, and the purpose of TIF is to direct this increment towards the financing of the infrastructure project. In order to do so, the difference between the previous and the new property tax must be calculated and earmarked back to the project. It is therefore necessary to use temporary funding such as bonds and loans while waiting for TIF to deliver revenue. The method is often misunderstood as an extra tax burden, but no taxes are changed in the strategy, as the only actual action is earmarking the increased tax revenue. There are two different strategies for earmarking the increased taxes: Project- and district based. TIF can in other words be used for financing a single project, or several projects in a designated district. The district-based method can be hard to execute, as there are often a lot of stakeholders, opinions and goals within a district. Large single projects can often involve just as large amounts of money as a whole district, but the goals and funding of a single project are usually more set and agreed upon than for a collection of projects within a district.

Special Assessments (SA) involves introducing an extra fee for funding infrastructure projects in contradiction to Tax Incremental Financing. The concept is however also similar to TIF, as it involves defining a so called "Special Assessment District" (SAD) where all inhabitants are levied a fee for certain public projects that all residents' properties are expected to benefit from (Zhao and Larson, 2011). Some general principles lay the grounds for Special Assessments: (1) The property owners are levied a fee for financing specific public improvements. (2) The SAD has to be defined, and all properties covered by the district must benefit from the improvements. (3) The fee that is to be levied must correspond with the amount of benefits the property owner receives. That implies that the within the SAD, the properties' distance to the improved infrastructure may be taken into consideration and thereby differentiate the fees levied. (4) If a district has reached their limits of property tax collected, revenues from Special Assessments may exceed these, as they are not related.

There are several definitions of Joint Development (JD), but Landis and Hall (1991) puts it this way:

> Joint development is any formal agreement or arrangement between a public transit agency and a private individual or organization that involves either private sector paying to the public sector or private sector sharing capital costs with the public sector, in mutual recognition of the enhanced real-estate development potential created by using a public transit facility.

Joint development projects could be looked upon as public-private partnerships, but they also include other types of projects; for instance when public authorities participate directly in developing real estate for profitability purposes, when governments sell or lease property rights for making revenues or when private companies only contribute with revenue for adjusting the density standards or usage rights (Zhao et al., 2012b).

There are also others as a Land Value Tax, Transportation Utility Fees, a Development Impact Fee, Air rights. In practice developers try to use the most promising model that suits their needs, based on the possibilities for the investment and market analysis (Salaj et al., 2018).

Norwegian Legislation

The term LVC is not commonly known in Norway today, but some of the principles and instruments are in use. There are also laws and regulations that have relevance to the principles related to it. When considering how LVC can be implemented in a jurisdiction, it is important to look at the already existing legislation to map the jurisdiction's adaptability.

The group of decisions that are taken by the *Land consolidation court* is called *land consolidation*. These decisions concern land and properties that are difficult to use in an adequate way, due to various circumstances. The problems may regard undivided joint properties, rights of use or inappropriate property borders. If the land owners are unable to resolve their issues themselves, their cases are subject for the Land consolidation court (Falkanger, 2017). Laws similar to the law of land consolidation have been present in Norway since "Magnus Lagabøtes landslov" from 1274 (Gisle, 2016). The amount of urban areas was very limited at the time, meaning the laws regarding land consolidation have primarily been written in regards of rural land. Today, the amount of urban areas has increased greatly, which has led to the need of land consolidation not only for rural land, but also urban. The purpose of the Land consolidation court is to resolve issues between land owners by changing property borders and re-arranging properties so they become more suitable for their use (Gisle, 2016). Private and public landowners, as well as persons with rights of use of land, are entitled to try their case in the Land consolidation court, if they are not able to solve their issues themselves. In case of an appeal against the court's decision, the cases will be tried in the Norwegian High Court.

The term "urban land consolidation" is considered imprecise as there exists no separate urban land consolidation, but it is used to specify land consolidation occurring in urban areas. As mentioned, land consolidation has its origin in regulating farm land and other rural land, but the law of land consolidation is also used for urban areas and a specification can therefore be found necessary (Reusch, 2017a). However, urban land consolidation is a tool used to split a value increment between multiple properties and property right holders within a zoned development- or transformation area. It is often used to work out zoning- or local plans, but it can only be used if the current local plans allowit.

Urban land consolidation may for instance involve to:

- Develop more suitable property borders prior to land planning
- Coordinate and gather properties and right owners based of available resources prior to the zoning plan work and development starts
- Distribute development value- and cost potential when executing an approved zoning plan
- Establish cooperatives for facility management of completed real estate development

A peculiar part in the Law of land consolidation states the land consolidation court's right of judging a joint action. The law of land consolidation §2e states that when in need of common measures, for instance establish a road or put up a fence, in order to make land more usable or capable of development, the court may judge a joint action. It means that all land owners affected are obliged to participate in the financing of the measures, given that the benefits are proportionate to the investment amount for all affected land owners (Myrvold, 2012). This sub-section of the law may also be utilized in cases concerning urban land consolidation.

Plans for area development are given by three authority levels in Norway; government, regional and municipal. The two first mentioned levels are usually superior and are not considered relevant when studying infrastructure contributions. The plans given by the municipalities are on the other hand of relevance. On top of the municipal plan hierarchy, is the land-use part of the municipal master plan, which states the future intended use of a block or a city district. An example could be office-, residential- or mixed-use of an area. The second level is local plans. These plans contain more details and concern more limited areas, but multiple lots. They may for instance include height limitations, percentage limitations of residences or offices, as well as indications of what type of buildings the municipality would approve at certain lots. The last plan level is the zoning plan, which is the most detailed plan in the Norwegian plan hierarchy. This plan gives exact limitations for an erection on a lot and may for instance involve GIA, heights and aesthetics. An important part of a zoning plan when discussing development agreements, is the development conditions. They are described in Section 2.2.6 (Maehlum, 2018).

As mentioned, development conditions are found in zoning plans, but may also be found in the land-use part of the municipal master plan. The conditions are sequential, as they are numbered where the one condition has to be fulfilled before the other. It is also stated what conditions needs to be fulfilled before erection on a lot may begin. Thus, they are deciding relatively at what time erection of a building may start. The other function of development conditions, is that they deal with infrastructure, green areas and other facilities, meaning they assure that all of these living-necessities are in place before erection (Byggordboka, 2018).

A type of agreements between developers and municipalities that are in charge of building matters are called development agreements and are established by law in The Norwegian Planning and Building act, §17. The agreement is based on provisions in municipal regulative plans, meaning the land-use part of the municipal master plans and zoning plans. The contents of the agreements may concern relations in the mentioned plans, as well as limitations of the amount of buildings, smallest and largest GIA and other appropriate regulations. The agreement may also give the municipality first options on a decided number of units, in case of residential development. A highly discussed part of these agreements is that they may set the real estate developer to completely or partly finance measures necessary for completion of the decisions made in the prevailing plans.

It is important to emphasize that the measures must be necessary, and they must be proportionate with the developments' size and cost. They must also be proportionate to the liability the real estate development causes the municipality (Norges Lover, 2009). §17-7 states that the municipalities are not allowed to make exemptions from the law, but approval from the Norwegian Ministry of Local Government and Modernization may be requested. Some other limitations of the development agreements are: They can only be approved by the municipal council, meaning they are not subject for implementation in single building matters. There are also requirements regarding public transparency of the processes (Norges Lover, 2009).

Development agreements can be looked upon as a kind of Joint Development, that we find in the LVC literature. Development agreements have historically been professionally misconducted in Norway, meaning that real estate developers have been required to finance municipal developments that have not been economically proportional or relevant to the development carried out. According to the real estate broker consulted for the case study in Section 4, a developer have for instance been asked to build a school in one part of a city, in order to obtain permission for establishing housing units in another part of the city. Development agreements concerning social infrastructure like schools, preschools and old people's homes were therefore forbidden in Norway in 2006, while agreements regarding relevant technical- and green infrastructure remained legal (Reusch, 2017b). This was ruled in the secondary law "Forskrift om forbud mot vilkår om sosial infrastruktur i utbyggingsavtaler." FOR-2006-04-20-453.

According to the Planning and building Act §18-3, first paragraph; the person that wants to make, change or expand authorized public road or public pipelines for water or sewage, may require their expenses refunded by other property owners who benefit from the works. The law applies for both private and public persons and the road does not have to be in a zoning plan. There does however exist an exception for private road exits and roads that are not publicly approved. Already developed properties are not obliged to refund the expenses, but if the property ever is re-developed, the duty of refund is triggered. The local municipalities are responsible for approving the refunds as well as the future accounts of them (Nicolaisen and Brinker, 2017).

§105 in the Norwegian constitution states that if the state demands a person to give up movable or immovable property for public use, he or she should be fully compensated by the Exchequer. As this is the stated in the constitution, it rules over other laws that have been released since, that for instance indirectly have claimed specific land exaction cases to have reduced right to compensation other countries' practice (Falkanger and Reusch, 2018).

Even though the constitution states that the right of expropriation is for the state, the right is also frequently used by counties and municipalities, as well as private persons, naturally with limitations. Immovable property is usually the subject for expropriation, but it is also used for movables, rights of use and even labor. In general, the expropriation has to be authorized by "the King," a ministry or another public authority, even though in practice, the authorization has been subject for professional judgment in several cases.

As the person expropriated has the right of a full compensation, the question of valuation in expropriation cases has qualified for the Supreme court in several occasions. The valuation process is to be executed in regards of interests protected by law, meaning that affection value and similar is to be excluded from the judgment. There are three main principles for valuations, where the highest value should be considered applicable; (1) The market price, (2) The utilization value for the owner, especially applicable for factories and other production sites and (3) The replacement value (Falkanger and Reusch, 2018).

The Planning and Building Act's §18 explains *opparbeidelsesplikt*, freely translated to infrastructure work up duty. It assures that sufficient infrustructure road, water and sewage infrastructure is achieved at all times, as new real estate development occurs. Triggering factors for the duty could for instance be splitting of buildings, new buildings, substantial expansion of existing buildings or changed used of existing buildings. It means that if for instance a building is expanded in such a degree that a sewage pipe with larger capacity is needed, the responsible actor for the building's expansion is obligated to upgrade the appurtenant sewage infrastructure (Trondheim Kommune, 2019).

Case Study: A Re-Zoning's Effect on Real Estate Market Value

Several of the LVC-strategies relate to decisions made by public authorities, where public plan work is of high importance. Some of the strategies capture plan-made values, a value that for instance is created by a changed zoning plan or local plan. It is therefore considered interesting to look further into how plan-made values are created and what factors influence them. This is a step to gather arguments and knowledge to answer RQ2 and RQ3. There is also a clear connection between development agreements and re-zoning, as development agreements in Oslo only are entered after a re-zoning is performed. If the re-zoning does not create any value, the development agreement will often not be sustainable for the developer. This case study does in other words investigate how real estate market prices are affected by a re-zoning.

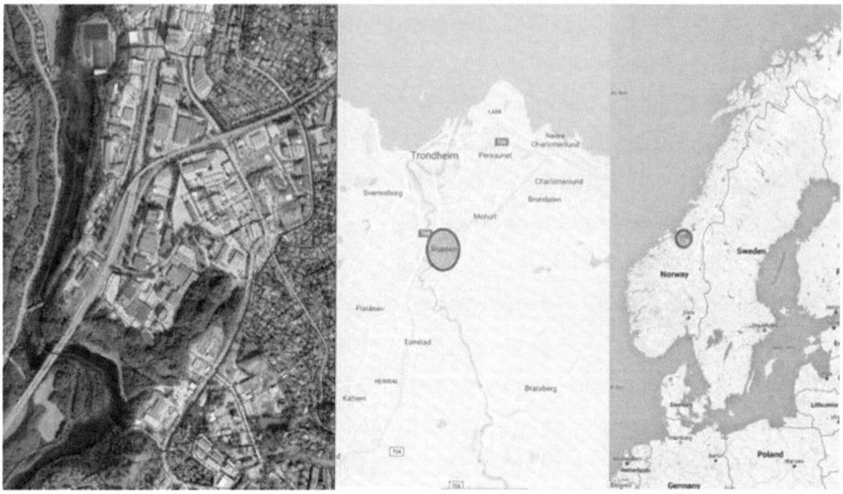

Figure 1. Sluppen, Norway. Maps retrieved from Google Maps.

The area subject for study is Sluppen, located at the southern borders of Trondheim city in Norway, shown on a map in Figure 1. The red line in all three maps draws the border of the area. The area is chosen because it is known that the area is facing a large transformation, meaning that the local municipalities are currently planning a re-zoning of the area and several investors have been working to facilitate a development of the area the last years. Sluppen, together with its neighboring areas, Valøya and Tempe have been considered to be in need of development. Today, the areas contain properties used for bus parking, car garages, unattended storehouses, offices and abandoned buildings. These properties are highly area consuming and have a low degree of area utilization. All three areas are lacking a superior structure for recreation, green areas, social meeting points and accessibility for pedestrians and cyclists. Due to the situation described, a local plan covering all three areas together was made in 2014 by Trondheim Municipality, with the mandate of transforming the area into an extension of Trondheim city. During these works, it was decided that the areas should contain private housing, student housing, commercial properties including commerce, offices and public services, as well as recreational services (Tondheim Kommune, 2014). The development of the neighboring areas, Tempe and Valøya, has already resulted in a large, new office building and the construction of a larger block of flats. Sluppen is however still awaiting new zoning plans, which is the reason why it is chosen as the subject for this case study. An air photo of the Sluppen-area can be seen in Figure 2, which situated below the red line in the picture.

Figure 2. Sluppen, Norway. Photo by Trondheim Municipality.

Progress

Trondheim Municipality carried out a new municipal plan in 2012, where the land-use part stated that Sluppen should be developed as a central part of the city with large green and wet areas. So far, a Local Plan Program feasibility study of the area was performed by "Forum Sluppen" and was published in December 2017. Forum Sluppen is a cooperation between Trondheim Municipality, Trøndelag County, The Norwegian Public Roads Administration and a large real estate investor, R. Kjeldsberg

AS (Forum Sluppen, 2017). The study presents four main concepts for how Sluppen can be developed from now until 2050 and it serves as inspiration for the zoning plan program that was sent out for public inquiry during the summer of 2018. In the end of October, 2018, the motion for the local plan program was carried out, meaning that the objective of the zoning works and process, as well as the level of external stake holder influence was affirmed (Bygningsrådet, 2018).

The planned progress is to establish a selection of principles for the transport communications of the area by February 2019. This is important because two of the major roads in Trondheim are intersecting Sluppen and it is also planned to improve the public transport systems greatly in the area. The proposal for the local plan will be sent for inquiry in June 2019, possibly containing two different alternatives. After the public hearing, the local plan is likely to be affirmed during November and December 2019 (Byplankontoret, 2018). It is critical that the local plan is finished by 01.01.2020, as this is the deadline for submitting suggestions for contents to the National Plan of Transportation (NTP), which works as the basis for Norway's national distribution of transportation financing.

As mentioned, the local plan program for Sluppen was affirmed by the building council of Trondheim Municipality in October 2018. As this case study is focusing on how a re-zoning impacts real estate values within the zoning area, it is relevant to consider what improvements the new zoning plan is likely to entail. So far, the zoning plan program states the following focus areas (Byplankontoret, 2018):

- New main road system
- "Omkjøringsveien" (E6) will be laid in a tunnel
- Sluppen will be established as an expansion of Trondheim city centre with appurtenant district functions
- New public transport hub
- Metro-bus
- Higher degree of area utilization (such as high risers)
- Prepare for future construction of residential areas
- Prepare for future construction of a light rail system

In order to perform a study of the changing real estate values at Sluppen, it is necessary to make an overview of the relevant properties within the area. The work resulted in map with an appurtenant legend, showing who the owners of the properties are, as well as the last recorded transaction for each property. The map is to be found in Figure 3.

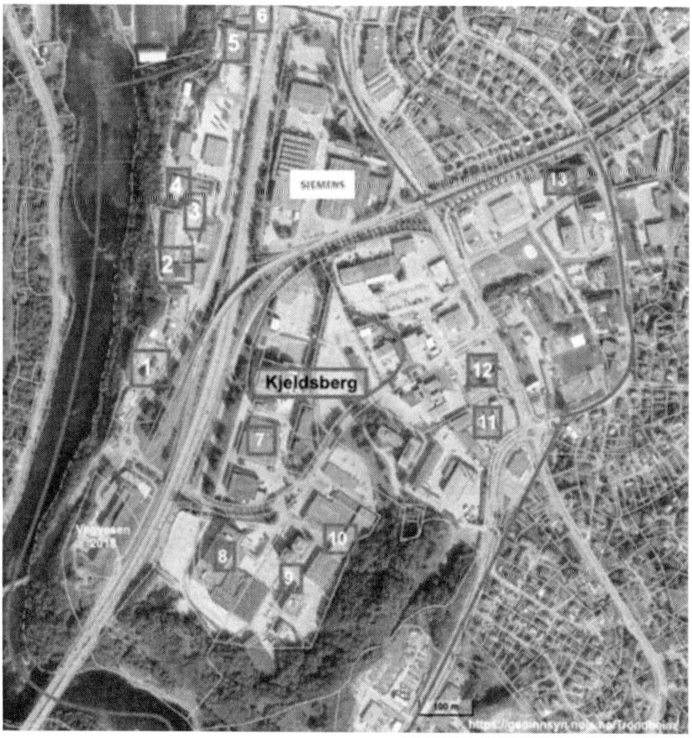

Figure 3. Property overview, Sluppen. Map by Trondheim Municipality.

All the relevant details that are found for the properties marked in Figure 3 are listed in Table 1. In addition to the table, the Siemens property in the upper half of the map may be noted. The number (#) in the table refers to the numbers marking the properties in Figure 3. The address field presents the street address as well as the lot's national grid number (ngn) and property number (pn), written (ngn/pn). ''Owner'' represents who the owner of the property is today and ''Transaction info'' provides details of the latest transaction of the property, if found. The ''Previous owner'' column describes who the property was acquired from and the "Area" describes the size of the lot, as well as price per square meter if available.

The reason why some of the fields are marked as "Not available (N/A)" is that they are either not found, or the address exists of several smaller lots combined into a larger one. If a large area is split into too many lots, the analysis of the property will be considered too complicated if no inside information regarding the relations between them is known.

Table 1. Property details, Sluppen

	Address (ngn/pn)	Owner	Transaction info	Previous owner	Area (m^2) Price (NOK/m^2)
1	Tempevegen 41 og 43	B.N. Eiendom	N/A	Lastebilcentralen	N/A
2	Tempevegen 35 (73/89)	Angel Næringsbygg v/Koteng	22 MNOK, 10.10.2000	Hegvold	10,391 2,117
3	Tempevegen 33 (73/82)	Angel Næringsbygg v/ Koteng	4.5 MNOK, 10.10.2000	Hegvold	2,527 1,780
4	Tempevegen 31 (73/112)	Helland A Transport AS	5 MNOK, 10.10.2002	Kreftforeningen	3,162 1,589
5	Tempevegen 23 (73/16)	Tempeveien 23 AS	23.8 MNOK, 24.06.2014	Stokke	4,966 4,792
6	Tempevegen 21 (65/20)	Laguna Fabrikker AS	5 MNOK, 05.09.2016	Nidarbø AS	4,244 1,179
7	Kjeldsberg area	R. Kjeldsberg AS Veidekke owns 50% of Lysgården		N/A	N/A
8	Sluppenvegen 14 (73/115)	Sluppenvegen 14 AS v/ Heglund	N/A, 07.04.2014	Posten Norge AS	17,950
9	Sluppenvegen 12	KLP	N/A	N/A	N/A
10	Sluppenvegen 8 og 10	R. Kjeldsberg AS	N/A	N/A	N/A
11	Bratsbergveg en 25 (73/83)	Frodal	N/A	N/A	4,618
12	Sluppenvegen 2 (73/87)	G H Gården AS v/ Heglund	18.5 MNOK, 30.04.2012	Heglund	4,586 4,034
13	Klæbuveien 194 (73/101)	Klæbuveien 194 AS v/ Koteng	N/A, 27.06.2008	Gjensidige Nor	9,303

Moving on to the actual case, a selection of properties have been selected for further research of their market values. Four lots have been chosen, each with unique characteristics, as a measure for understanding how different types of real estate are affected by re-zoning processes. An overview of the chosen lots may be seen in Figure 4.4. The lots are marked with their national grid number (ngn) and property number (pn) in the syntax (ngn/pn). The background map is retrieved from the feasibility study of Sluppen, and makes an example of how ''Omkjøringsveien" (E6) can be laid in a tunnel, making space for a new main road system at Sluppen.

Property A: Lysgården, Sluppenvegen 19 (73/255)

This property was made over from Kjeldsberg to Sluppenvegen 19 AS at 26.05.2015. Sluppenvegen 19 AS is owned 50/50 by R. Kjeldsberg AS and Veidekke Eiendom, where the last mentioned is a contractor who is going to use the property as their headquarters in this region. They are also the contractor for the building process that is currently going on. The property lies within a separate zoning plan that was developed for this lot, along with four other lots that are located on a line further south of it. The other properties are also owned by R. Kjeldsberg AS and they have all been part of a common development in the area.

Before this development started, the property was empty and could have been characterized as a lot that would typically have a potential for industry development. According to the real estate broker consulted, these lots often contain warehouses or production facilities, have a utilization degree of 50 - 70% and have a rental income of 1,500 - 2,500 NOK/m^2. The area of the lot is 3,433 m^2, while the gross internal area (GIA) is planned to be 12,000 m^2 pursuant to the project plans. According to proff.no, Sluppenvegen 19 AS' value of property and real estate was set to 14.12 MNOK prior to construction start in 2016, meaning the lot's value was probably assessed to this amount prior to the new zoning plan. Divided by the size of the lot, it results in a price per m^2 of 4,113 NOK, which is fairly similar to what can be seen from the latest transactions in Table 1.

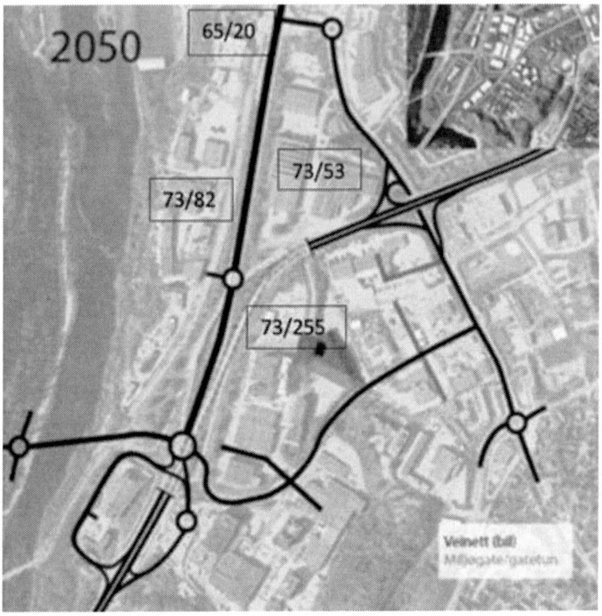

Figure 4. Overview of the lots subject for study. Map by Trondheim Municipality.

Figure 5. Location of Lysgården in an animation from Trondheim Municipality's feasibility study for Sluppen.

A land value of 14.12 MNOK is therefore considered to be prevailing before the re-zoning of the property in 2011. The lot's location is shown in a sketch-up from Trondheim Municipality's feasibility study in Figure 5. This exact property is interesting to analyze, because it was re-zoned as early as 2011 and can therefore make an actual example of how the land value changes with a re-zoning.

The new zoning plan allows what is being built today, meaning a GIA of 12,000 m^2, while the expected net rental income per m^2 is set to 1,750 NOK. The building costs are expected to be 23,000 NOK/m^2 and the uncertainty of this cost is set to 5%. The developers desired return of investment is set fairly high, at 15% and the financial costs are set to 9%. All these figures are provided by the real estate broker consulted and should be considered as round numbers, but are not far from the actual figures, as they have facilitated the broking of the property. Equation 4.1 shows that the residual land value is estimated to be 54 MNOK. This is according to the broker not far from the actual value that was settled for the transaction. The value equals a price per m^2 of 15,730 NOK.

$$\begin{aligned}
\text{Expected revenue} \quad & 12,000m^2 \times 1,750MNOK/m^2 = 21MNOK \\
\text{Property value} \quad & \frac{21MNOK}{5\%} = 420MNOK \\
\text{Building costs (BC)} \quad & 23,000NOK/m^2 \times 12,000m^2 = 278MNOK \\
\text{Uncertainty BC} \quad & 278MNOK \times 5\% = 14MNOK \\
\text{Financial costs} \quad & 292MNOK \times 9\% = 26MNOK \\
\text{Return of investment} \quad & 318MNOK \times 15\% = 48MNOK \\
\text{Residual land value} \quad & 420MNOK - 366MNOK = 54MNOK
\end{aligned}$$

Table 2. Summary figures, Property A

Post	Value
Property value before re-zoning	14.12 MNOK
Land value after re-zoning	54 MNOK
Value increment	382%
Utilization degree before re-zoning	60%
Utilization degree after re-zoning	350%
Utilization degree increment	290%
Ratio value/utilization increment	1.32

When considering 14.12 MNOK as the property's land value before the re-zoning and 54 MNOK as the property's value after re-zoning, it represents a value increment of 382%. As mentioned, the typical utilization degree before re-zoning could have been between 50 - 70%, which is fairly high compared to neighbouring properties with the same characteristics. For simplification purposes, this degree is set to 60%. According to the current zoning plan, the utilization degree is now exploited fully, meaning that it is currently approximately 12, 000m2/3, 433m2 = 350% (Byplankontoret, 2011). This implies an increment of the utilization degree of 350% − 60% = 290%. The ratio between the land value and utilization degree increment is thus 1.32. A summary of the assessment's key figures (Table 2).

Property B: Tempevegen 21 (65/20)

The property was sold for 5 MNOK by Nidarbø AS to Laguna Fabrikker AS at the 05.09.2016. The area of the lot is 4,244 m^2, resulting in a price per m^2 of 1,179 NOK. As it can be seen in Figure 4.6, the lot holds an old factory building that seems to be abandoned today. According to Trondheim Municipality's register, the property is currently used for transport and storage services. In addition to the old factory building, the lot also contains a residential house at the backside of the factory (Figure 6).

Figure 6. Tempevegen 21 today. Photo by Google Streetview.

The property is interesting to indicate how a re-zoning process affects the real estate value of a property that will have a completely different potential before and after re-zoning. As the property is abandoned today and may be used to develop new housing or offices in a potentially attractive area after the re-zoning, there is a large probability for a value increment. The property is also of interest because of the latest transaction, that holds an unusually low property cost. It is therefore assumed that a private deal was agreed upon in addition to the public available transaction data.

This property has not been zoned since 1973 and is therefore a subject that will need re-zoning in order to be developed. The yield method is used to assess today's value. By measuring the buildings' dimensions in Trondheim's map service, the factory building's GIA is set to 1.235 m^2 and the residential house at the back of the lot is set to 758 m^2. This results in a utilization degree of 47%.

$$\text{Expected revenue (1)} \quad 1{,}235m^2 \times 500NOK/m^2 = 617{,}500NOK$$

$$\text{Expected revenue (2)} \quad 758m^2 \times 2{,}000NOK/m^2 = 1{,}516{,}000NOK$$

$$\text{Expected costs} \quad 2{,}133{,}500NOK \times 15\% = 320{,}025NOK$$

$$\text{Property value} \quad \frac{2{,}133{,}500NOK - 320{,}025NOK}{7.5\%} = 24.18MNOK$$

Even though the factory building is abandoned today, it is estimated to have a potential of yielding 500 NOK/m^2 (Revenue 1) and the residential house at the back is estimated to have a revenue of 2,000 NOK/m^2 (Revenue 2), as it is inhabited today. The maintenance and operations cost are set to 15% of the revenue, as the buildings are old and the required yield is of the same reason set to 7.5%. Based on these assumptions, Equation 4.2 assesses a present property value of 24.18 MNOK. This value is not representative of today's situation, as the factory is not rented out today, but shows the present potential value.

This property is assumed to be zoned for similar purposes as Property A and a utilization degree of 350% is also for this lot considered realistic, which results in a GIA of $4,244m^2 \times 350\% = 14,854m^2$. For simplification purposes, this value assessment will be based on a commercial use of the property. The other parameters for calculating the future land value of the property will be similar to Property A.

$$\text{Expected revenue} \quad 14,854m^2 \times 1,750MNOK/m^2 = 26MNOK$$

$$\text{Property value} \quad \frac{26MNOK}{5\%} = 520MNOK$$

$$\text{Building costs (BC)} \quad 23,000NOK/m^2 \times 14,854m^2 = 341MNOK$$

$$\text{Uncertainty BC} \quad 341MNOK \times 5\% = 17MNOK$$

$$\text{Financial costs} \quad 358MNOK \times 9\% = 32MNOK$$

$$\text{Return of investment} \quad 380MNOK \times 15\% = 57MNOK$$

$$\text{Residual land value} \quad 520MNOK - 447MNOK = 73MNOK$$

The residual land value is according to Equation 4.3 73 MNOK and implies a land value per m^2 of 17,200 NOK. The increment of the utilization degree is 350% − 47% = 303%, while the land value is increased by 302%. The ratio between the land value and utilization degree increment is thus 1.00. A summary of the assessment's key figures are found in Table 3.

Table 3. Summary figures, Property B

Post	Value
Property value before re-zoning	24.18 MNOK
Land value after re-zoning	73 MNOK
Value increment	302%
Utilization degree before re-zoning	47%
Utilization degree after re-zoning	350%
Utilization degree increment	303%
Ratio value/utilization increment	1.00

Property C: Tempevegen 33 (73/82)

The property was sold for 4.5 MNOK on 10.10.2000. The lot area is 2,527 m^2 and a price per m^2 of 1,780 NOK. The lot contains an office building that can be seen in Figure 4.7 with a measured footprint of 530 m^2. Multiplied with 2.5 floors, as the building is expected to entail a mix of offices and storage facilities, the GIA measures 1,325 m^2 and is rented out today. The property is interesting because approximately only half of the lot's area is utilized, meaning there is a large potential for increasing the degree of utilization. This estate can be considered typical for the area, containing an old office building and is thus interesting because it may be a measure of how the general real estate value will change after the re-zoning.

Figure 7. Tempevegen 33 today. Photo from www.koteng.no.

Today's utilization degree of the lot is 1, 325m2/2, 527m2 = 52%. According to the consulted real estate broker, an expected present rental income is set to 750 NOK/m2, as the building is fairly old and probably entails both offices and storage facilities. Because of the age, the maintenance and operations costs are set to 15% and the desired yield to 7.5%. The present property value is thus assessed to 11.26 MNOK in Equation 4.

$$\text{Expected revenue} \quad 1,325m^2 \times 750\,NOK/m^2 = 993,750\,NOK$$

$$\text{Expected costs} \quad 993,750\,NOK \times 15\% = 149,062\,NOK$$

$$\text{Property value} \quad \frac{993,750\,NOK - 149,062\,NOK}{7.5\%} = 11.26\,MNOK$$

This property is assumed to be zoned for similar purposes as Property A and B and a utilization degree of 350% is considered realistic, which results in a GIA of 2, 527m2 × 350% = 8, 845m2. For simplification, this value assessment will also be based on a commercial use of the property. The other parameters for calculating the future land value of this property will be similar to Property A and B.

$$\begin{aligned}
\text{Expected revenue} &\quad 8,845m^2 \times 1,750\,MNOK/m^2 = 15.5\,MNOK \\
\text{Property value} &\quad \frac{15.5\,MNOK}{5\%} = 310\,MNOK \\
\text{Building costs (BC)} &\quad 23,000\,NOK/m^2 \times 8,845m^2 = 203\,MNOK \\
\text{Uncertainty BC} &\quad 203\,MNOK \times 5\% = 10\,MNOK \\
\text{Financial costs} &\quad 213\,MNOK \times 9\% = 19\,MNOK \\
\text{Return of investment} &\quad 232\,MNOK \times 15\% = 35\,MNOK \\
\text{Residual land value} &\quad 310\,MNOK - 267\,MNOK = 43\,MNOK
\end{aligned}$$

The residual land value assessed in Equation 5 is 43 MNOK, implying a land value per m2 of 17,016 NOK. The increment of the utilization degree is 350% − 52% = 298%, while the land value is increased by 382%. The ratio between the land value and utilization degree increment is thus 1.28. A summary of the assessment's key figures is found in Table 4.

Table 4. Summary figures, Property C

Post	Value
Property value before re-zoning	11.26 MNOK
Land value after re-zoning	43 MNOK
Value increment	382%
Utilization degree before re-zoning	52%
Utilization degree after re-zoning	350%
Utilization degree increment	298%
Ratio value/utilization increment	1.28

Property D: Siemens, Bratsbergvegen 5 (73/53)

There have not been recorded any recent transactions for this property, as it has been owned by Siemens for as long as the real estate data at 1881.no goes back. The area of the property is measured to 60,856 m2, making it the largest privately owned lot in the area. The lot is today used for offices, production, R&D and parking and it has a unique value for Siemens, but has also a potential for value increment. A satellite photo of the lot with its borders is shown in Figure 8.

Figure 8. The Siemens lot today. Satelite view by Trondheim Municipality.

Property D is interesting because of its size and its location within Sluppen, as it is Sluppen's closest lot to the city centre. Its use today is also interesting, as it is unsure how its assets may be utilized optimally after a re-zoning.The value of this property is assumed to mainly be based on its inventories, as Siemens have invested large sums in the production and R&D facilities at the site. Due to a lack of knowledge regarding the facilities' area and revenues, the value assessment of this property is considered too complicated seen in the perspective of this thesis' scope. The property is however included in the Case study, as it represents a unique real estate category that should be taken into consideration when assessing a re-zoning's impact on real estate value.

Discussion and Conclusion

Re-Zoning's Impact on RE Value

In the theoretical approach multiple strategies or principles can be used for capturing land and real estate in situations where the value is changed as a result of a public authority's decision and actions. A significant factor of a zoning plan's effect on real estate prices is the allowed degree of utilization, which the case study from Sluppen supports. Seen in the perspective of LVC, one could argument for that a land owner should pay compensation to the municipalities when the utilization degree is increased, as the land value will increase. The Norwegian legislation acts as a barrier to this public revenue opportunity, as §17 in the Planning and Building Act limits the amount a public authority can receive as compensation for a changed zoning plan. As mentioned, the law was intended to protect real estate developers from the municipality's misuse of power, by demanding disproportionate measures from the developers for their plans to be accepted. This problem is discussed by Hauge and Holth (2018), in an article regarding a high riser at Fornebu in Bærum, that a developer wants to erect. There are currently no buildings of the planned height in the area, meaning that if the high riser will be accepted by the municipalities, it implies a great change of the lot's zoning plan. The municipality's alternatives for receiving benefits by doing this change are very limited and the fairest decision would probably be to disallow the proposal of the high riser. The authors of the article however address a change in the laws, as the way the legislation is today, it does not allow large benefits to be compensated for a re-zoning. In order to investigate this assumption further, a highly relevant question is: "If the utilization degree is increased with 100%, will the land value increase proportionally?"

The case study that has been performed does only treat three unique land value assessments, meaning it is inaccurate to draw patterns based on the findings. On the other hand, the three assessments give fairly similar ratios between the properties' value and utilization increment, which are juxtaposed in Table 5. This ratio is in fact very close to 1, meaning that the value increment of the three properties is almost proportionate with the utilization degree increment.

Table 5. Summary of figures, all properties

Post	Property A	Property B	Property C
Property value before re-zoning	14 MNOK	24 MNOK	11 MNOK
Land value after re-zoning	54 MNOK	73 MNOK	43 MNOK
Value increment	382%	302%	382%
Utilization degree before re-zoning	60%	47%	52%
Utilization degree after re-zoning	350%	350%	350%
Utilization degree increment	290%	303%	298%
Ratio value/utilization increment	1.32	1.00	1.28

An aspect to be pointed out, is that the three properties have quite different characteristics and are selected for assessment of that very reason. Property A did not contain any buildings prior to the ongoing development, meaning there was no existing property value to be assessed, except for the land value. Property B and C both contain existing buildings today, that are considered revenue generating. Property B entails a residential building in addition to the commercial area, which usually results in a higher yield than commercial buildings and is considered to affect the ratio of the value/utilization increment. Property C does on the other hand contain a commercial building consisting of offices and storage facilities, generating revenues comparable with the expected future, rental revenues. One matter that should be taken into consideration when assessing the proportionality between land value and utilization degree, is that it cannot be constant. According to the real estate broker consulted in the case study, the average renter of a commercial property demands 350 m^2 in small cities like

Trondheim, but in Oslo the average demand is 2,000 m^2. This substantiates the claim that above a given utilization degree, the value increment will fall, as the market cannot deliver enough renters to fill the buildings capacity. As an example, if a skyscraper was allowed in a zoning plan situated in Trondheim, the land value would probably not increase proportionally with the utilization degree increment.

Implementation of LVC in Norway

The Norwegian political system could be categorized as socialistic, meaning benefits should be shared among all inhabitants, while the financing of the Norwegian public services is mainly based on user-implementation of LVC in Norway related fees and tax revenues. This should lay the grounds for a possible political implementation of LVC in Norway, as it does not demand a radical change in the people's mindset regarding public financing. As in most other countries, taxation is an important topic, meaning more fair and balanced taxation based on LVC could be welcome. When it comes to Hendricks and Tonkin's criteria for successful implementation of LVC, the groundwork is already in place. It is common knowledge that the Norwegian political system is well functioning, the leader has solid support from the people, the authorities are de-centralized as well as the property tax system functions well. However, the Norwegian property tax is heavily discussed, and removal of the property tax has become a popular topic for politicians. The land use management in the country functions well, at least within each separate county. The practices of land use management within the different counties is however often quite different. Another aspect is that the way LVC strategies have been implemented in other countries, may not be applicable for Norwegian circumstances, given the population and size of the country's cities. However, an interesting point of view is to see how LVC strategies correlates with relevant existing, Norwegian legislation. Several strategies have been provided, along with an extract of relevant Norwegian legislation. Most of the strategies could be considered plausible for implementation in Norway, as they are all based on principles of sharing benefits among people, which is exactly what the rationale of the Norwegian land consolidation court is, in a smaller scale.

The Norwegian land consolidation court is working to share benefits equally between the affected landowners, when one of them is improving adjacent facilities. From this perspective, the Norwegian land consolidation and all principles related to it, may be interpreted as a weak or vague LVC system, as it shares benefits equally, but only between persons that actually own affected land. The LVC policies are taking the case one step further as they are sharing the benefits received by land and real estate owners with the public. It is therefore interesting to see what potential LVC-strategies have for implementation in Norway, seen in comparison with the Norwegian legislation that has been presented.

- Tax Increment Financing is a solution that potentially could be implemented in Norway. A challenge could be the lack of areas that can be classified as central business districts, which are the areas where TIF has proved its greatest potential. Oslo have a couple of qualified areas, such as Aker Brygge, Tjuvholmen, Barcode and Bjørvika, but the other cities lack these. The Norwegian economy can on the other hand be considered strong with a large purchasing power, opening for the possibility of implementing TIF in more regular high-priced districts. As with every other financing strategy, people have to be informed and prepared to adapt to it, so that implementation can be politically plausible. A positive feature of the strategy is that is does not involve the introduction of a new tax or fee, it simply redirects the tax revenues. The implementation is also expected to demand for legislative changes, which are considered to be rather large by Zhao. It would in other words require a law to allow for differentiation of a single property tax, in terms of who receives what parts of the tax revenues. Another issue could possibly be if the property tax will be abolished, due to populist politics. In such a case, TIF would have little chance of being implemented, as it would implicate re-implementation of a property tax. A weak spot related to TIF, is that it could be discussed that the tax revenue increment could have occurred without the tax increment financed project, due to market variations and other external factors. The tax increments would in such a case have been spent for other causes. When seen in comparison with the Norwegian legislation, there are not a lot of aspects related to land consolidation that could substantiate the implementation of TIF in Norway.

- Special Assessments would be possible to implement in Norway, but would most probably demand a lot of work regarding people's attitude regarding the matter, as even property tax is a hot and disliked topic these days. The strategy involves introduction of a fee additional to the existing taxes and fees, which usually is quite unpopular. However, if people or companies would see the potential benefits received large enough, a special assessment could be possible to implement. It is not known that such system exists in the country today, and the relevant legislation would therefore need adaption. The Norwegian tradition is more based on voluntary work in order to improve an area in need of transformation and as SA implies forcing inhabitants to contribute to an improvement financially, it could be hard to obtain acceptance for the measure from the people. The Norwegian legislation presented in this thesis is not considered to be relevant for the plausibility of implementing SA.
- Joint Development already exists in certain forms in Norway, but there is still a potential for expanding the amount of joint development. The use of joint development for financing infrastructure is not common in the country, even though public private partnerships (PPPs) have increased in use over the last years. These partnerships does however mostly involve private companies to operate and maintain roads after they have built them themselves and thereby share a part of the building costs, as they greatly affect the future maintenance cost. There are also several examples of counties and municipalities taking shares in real estate

development projects and thereby benefiting from the yield. The public authority's role in such a partnership is often as a land owner, as large parts of the Norwegian vacant land is owned by the public. The potential for increased used of join development in Norway is considered large, for instance through receiving continuous revenues for adjusting usage rights or density standards, or by selling or leasing property rights.

As stated for each strategy, several of these have a potential for implementation in Norway and some are already utilized to a limited extent. Special Assessments might have the least potential, as it does not seem to comply with any existing tax or fee collection. The other strategies will probably be feasible to implement in Norway and could thereby improve the fairness of public value capture based on land and real estate. As stated for several of the LVC strategies, some of them have common features with the Norwegian development agreements. This could support the need of developing these agreements further in legislative terms, which is also substantiated by the article of Hauge and Holth (2018). LVC strategies with connections to development agreements may with that be considered as more plausible for implementation, as they are based on an already existing principle in the Norwegian legislation. It is hard to say whether one of the described strategies, a combination of them or the development of a new, accommodated strategy would be optimal. This question will however be discussed further in the following sections.

Two models are suggested to be interesting in Norway: A development fee, similar to Great Britain's Community Infrastructure Levy and a re-zoning fee, similar to what we find in Switzerland and used to find in Denmark. An advantage with both models is that they both avoid today's issues regarding VAT and adjustment agreements, as they are both based on fees and no self-performed measures. The two models are fairly similar, and the main difference is what part of the development area they appoint to be levied. A summary and comparison of the two models may be found in Table 6.

Both models are intended to fund the same infrastructure measures, but the basis for calculating the contribution is different. It could therefore be discussed for both models whether there should be a limitation of what share the contributions may take in funding a measure. A suggestion could be that infrastructure contributions should stand for maximum 50% of a measures funding, so that the municipality also has to raise funds to carry out a measure.

By doing so, the municipality has to commit to the measure with monetary values, meaning it is less of a chance that the municipality will misuse their power for gathering contributions. The question whether a contribution measure is necessary or not will probably in such a case be less relevant, as the municipality is less likely to require an un-necessary measure if they are obligated to contribute financially themselves.

Table 6. Summary of the suggested development fee and re-zoning fee

Feature	Development fee	Re-zoning fee
What is levied?	Total developed area, including existing renovated area. Excluding existing area that is not renovated.	Only additional area according to the new zoning-plan.
Pros	Levies all real estate development.	Levies plan made values that are unavailable to everyone except for the land owner. Increased renovation of older buildings. Less demolishing.
Cons	May decrease the real estate development and renovation. Could lead to older building masses. More demolishing and re-building.	Less area to be levied for the municipalities.
Common features	Upper limit fee per m^2 is set by a council. The council may also treat complaints. May replace both development agreements and infrastructure work up duty. Voluntary implementation in the municipalities.	

The development fee is intended to be a fee calculated per GIA, covering 100% of a projects GIA. That would imply also non-added GIA in a renovation case. An example could be renovation and expansion of an existing office building with a GIA of 5,000 m^2, and an expansion of 2,000

m^2, resulting in a new total GIA of 7,000 m^2. Only 4,000 of the original 5,000 m^2 is supposed to be renovated, meaning a total 6,000 m^2 would be developed in this case. The development fee would therefore be based on 6,000 m^2 and not the total GIA of 7,000 m^2. Some negative features of such a model is that it would levy renovation of existing buildings, possibly leading to less renovation and older building masses. The most extreme case could be that the fee would lead to an increased trend of complete demolition and re-building of buildings. It would in other words highly increase the renovation cost. It is hard to find any argumentation for that it is fair to levy renovation, as it does not necessarily lead to increased load on existing infrastructure. A model similar to OM's current practice for development agreements could be charging a fee for all 7,000 m^2, but it remains hard to find any legitimate argumentation for such a practice. The figures for the examples are clearly set out in Table 7.

Table 7. Overview of suggested practice example

Example figures for Suggested practice	
Existing GIA	5,000 m^2
Renovation	4,000 m^2
Expansion	2,000 m^2
New total GIA	7,000 m^2
Basis for development fee	6,000 m^2
Basis for re-zoning fee	2,000 m^2

The maximum rate of the development fee would be decided by a council, as for the re-zoning fee, which is described in the following section. The revenues from the fee would have to be used for nearby, necessary infrastructure measures, that are to be decided by the responsible municipal agency. The agency would have to present a cost estimate for these measures, calculated by a third-party, where the total amount of these costs would be the finite maximum total cost of the development fee. That means that if the maximum rate per GIA multiplied by the GIA would exceed the total cost of the necessary infrastructure measures, no more than the cost of the infrastructure measures could be charged. Like the re-zoning fee, the same council that sets the rate per GIA, would also be able to handle any potential complaints from developers of municipal agencies. The only difference between the development fee and the re-zoning fee is really what area the fee is calculated from. More detailed information regarding the two fees follows in the next section.

A re-zoning fee would on the other hand only levy the additional GIA, meaning 2,000 m^2 in the previous example, set out in Table 7. The intention of such a fee would be to tax plan made values, for instance through increased utilization degree. This value is as mentioned only available to the owner of the re-zoned lot, meaning it could be considered fair to require the developer to pay a fee for the received benefit, that may be considered exclusive. The owner should however only be levied a fee if it takes advantage of the increased utilization degree, by expanding the building as in the mentioned example. The fee is in other words only triggered if the allowed expansion is developed. The revenues made from the re-zoning fee should be ear-marked nearby, necessary infrastructure measures.

Due to all the issues with today's development agreements, it is suggested to replace the development agreements with a re-zoning fee. This fee is optional for the municipalities to use, in case it may be considered to decrease real estate development in less-populated areas. When used, it is however intended to replace both development agreements and infrastructure work up duty. It is important to stress that the infrastructure work up duty will still be prevailing for the cases where the re-zoning fee is not applied. The fee is intended to cover expenses the municipalities may have for establishing near-by, necessary infrastructure; a little similar to the intention of today's development agreements. It is based on inspiration from two LVC-instruments; Negotiated Exactions and Development Impact Fees, as well as similar strategies implemented in Great Britain, Switzerland and Denmark.

The fee is based on levying plan made values, such as increased utilization degree of a lot. That means if a lot's utilization degree is re-zoned from 5,000 m^2 to 7,000 m^2, the fee shall be levied for 2,000 m^2 when the increased utilization degree is utilized. A council should be appointed in order to set a maximum rate to be charged per m^2 for a whole municipality or a certain area within the municipality, in order to differentiate the infrastructure development costs. Thereafter, the responsible municipal agency must document what measures the fee is intended to cover and a cost estimate of these measures must be made by a third-party. If the total cost of these exceed the maximum rate multiplied by the amount of m^2 to be levied, the latter rate will be determining. If the total cost of the measures is less than the maximum rate; it is the total cost of the measures that is determining. The re-zoning fee may in other words not be higher than the rate set by the council, nor the cost estimate for the necessary measures. The council should consist of at least one representative from the municipality, a real estate developer trade association, a neutral third party and a government official. The same council may also treat any potential complaints regarding costs or definitions of necessities.

REFERENCES

Falkanger, T. 2017. *Jordskifte.* Retrieved 2018.11.19. URL https://snl.no/jordskifte. [*Land change.*]

Falkanger, T., Reusch, M. 2018. *Utbyggingsavtale*. Retrieved 29.11.2018. URL https://snl.no/ekspropriasjon.

Finsnes, A. B. 2019. *Land Value Capture's potential in Norway. Master thesis in Civil and Environmental Engineering.* Norwegian University of Science and Technology, Trondheim. p.91.

Forum Sluppen, 2017. *Mulighetsstudie Sluppen. Trondheim Kommune.* [*Feasibility study Sluppen. Trondheim municipality.*]

Gisle, J. 2016. *Jordskifterett.* Retrieved 18.11.20. URL: https://snl.no/jordskifterett.

Grum, B., Kobal Grum, D. 2020. Concepts of social sustainability based on social infrastructure and quality of life. *Facilities,* 38(11/12): 783-800.

Hauge, K. B., Holth, F. 2018. Problematisk om fornebu-skyskraper. Published in *Dagens Næringsliv*, 15.11.2018.

Hendricks, M., Tonkin, A. 2010. *LVC taxation (lvc/t) scoping study—final report*. Cape Town, South Africa: Development Action Group.

Landbrukskvartalet, 2019. Retrieved 19.03.2019. URL https://www.landbrukskvartalet.no/.

Landis, J., R. C., Hall, P. 1991. Transit joint development in the USA: Inventory and policy assessment. *Environment and Planning*, 9(4):431.

Maehlum, L. 2018. Arealplan. Retrieved 16.04.2019. URL https://snl.no/arealplan.

Mathur, S., Smith, A. 2013. *LVC to fund public transportation infrastructure: Examination.*

Nicolaisen, C., Brinker, M. 2017. *Eindomsutvikling: Når har man krav på refusjon for oppabeidelse av teknisk infrastruktur?* Retrieved 2018.11.20. URL: eindomsutvikling-refusjon-teknisk-infrastruktur.html. [*Real estate development: When are you entitled to a refund for the development of technical infrastructure?*]

Norges Lover, 2009. *Lov om planlegging og byggesaksbehandling (plan- og bygningsloven).* Retrieved 16.04.2019. URL https://lovdata.no/dokument/NL/lov/2008-06-27-71/KAPITTEL_3-3#. [*Act on Planning and Building Case Processing (Planning and Building Act).*]

Reusch, M. 2017a. *Urbant jordskifte*. Retrieved 2018.11.20. URL https://snl.no/urbant_jordskifte. [*Urban land change*]

Reusch, M. 2017b. *Utbyggingsavtale.* Retrieved 2018.11.20. URL https://snl.no/utbyggingsavtale. [*Development agreement.*]

Salaj, A., Roumboutsos, A., Verlič, P., Grum, B. 2018. LVC strategies in PPP – what can FM learn from it? *Facilities* 36 (1/2): 24-36.

Temeljotov Salaj, A. (2005). The synergetic effect of the observer on the built environment. *Urbani izziv* 16 (2): 163-167.

Temeljotov Salaj, A. et al. (2010). Knowledge, skills and competence in spatial planning. *Urbani izziv* 21 (1): 136-143.

Trondheim Kommune, B. 2014. *Tempe, valøya og sluppen, områderegulering.* Retrieved 2018.11.27. URL https://www.trondheim.kommune.no/aktuelt/kunngjoring-arealplan/arkiv-planer-kunngjort/Tempe-Valoya-Sluppen-omraderegulering/. [*Tempe, valøya and sluppen, area regulation.*]

Walters, L.C. 2013. LVC in policy and practice. *Journal of Property Tax Assessment & Administration* 10 (2): 5.

Zhao, Z., Das, K., Larson, K. 2010. Tax increment financing as a value capture strategy in funding transportation. *Transportation Research Record* 2187 (2187): 1–7.

Zhao, Z., Iacono, M., Lari, A., Levinson, D. 2012a. Value capture for transportation finance. *Procedia - Social and Behavioral Sciences* 48 (C): 435–448.

Zhao, Z. J., Das, K. V., Larson, K. 2012b. Joint development as a value capture strategy in transportation finance. *Journal of Transport and Land Use* 5 (1): 5–17.

Zhao, Z. J., Larson, K. 2011. Special assessments as a value capture strategy for public transit finance. *Public Works Management and Policy* 16 (4): 320–340.

In: The Future of Real Estate
Editor: Jan Veuger
ISBN: 978-1-53619-414-2

Chapter 5

ENVIRONMENTAL STRESS AND CONTEMPORARY UNDERSTANDING OF HUMAN-BUILT ENVIRONMENT RELATIONS: STUDY CASE ON ZERO-WASTE CITY LJUBLJANA

Bojan Grum[1,*], PhD and Darja Kobal Grum[2], PhD

[1]European Faculty of Law, Ljubljana, Slovenia
[2]Department of Psychology, University in Ljubljana, Slovenia

ABSTRACT

In the paper, we systematically review the impact that research on environmental stress, i.e., poor housing and neighbourhood quality, has had on the current understanding of the relationship between humans and the environment. It is shown that poor quality housing, high noise levels, lack of natural light in the house, poorer physical quality of

* Corresponding Author's E-mail: bgrum@siol.net.

neighbourhoods, living in low-income neighbourhoods, etc. are associated with increased physiological and psychological stress. We believe that built environmental relationships are closely related to attitudes towards waste in the neighbourhood. We focus on transforming our society so that all unnecessary waste is disposed of and everything that is produced can be reused, repaired, composted, or returned to the system. In a growing number of regions, local groups of individuals, businesses and municipalities are taking significant steps to eliminate waste in our society. We highlight the case study: Zero Waste City Ljubljana, which is the first European capital to be on the way to Zero Waste. We confirmed the hypotheses that there is a strong sustainable interaction between the psychological processes underlying human behaviour and the built environment and that among sustainable construction environmental factors waste management expresses these interactions at night. We believe that the positive effects of research can only be achieved with sustainable interactions between the psychological processes underlying human behaviour and the built environment.

Keywords: sustainable solutions, zero waste, human behaviour, built environment, Ljubljana, Slovenia

INTRODUCTION

In the paper, we systematically review the impact that research of environmental stress, namely, poor housing and poor neighbourhood quality had on contemporary understanding of human-built environment relations. Poor housing conditions can lead to pessimism, passivity, chronic stress, and general discontent (Cohen et al. 2005). Due to the economic crisis, which is part of the economic cycle and a phenomenon when economic activities increase or decrease, it is increasingly necessary to coordinate the interests of potential buyers' expectations for buying decisions. However, problems in the real estate market are not to be exclusively attributed to the global financial and economic crisis. In the case of the housing bubble, Shiller et al. (2010) note that the strong increase in real estate prices was especially caused by psychological expectations and financial instruments that allow speculation with real estate. It is shown that substandard quality of the house, high noise, lack of natural light in the house, poorer physical quality urban neighbourhoods, living in a low-income neighbourhood etc. are linked to elevated physiological and psychological stress. If a purchase takes place and satisfies the buyer's needs, then it has fulfilled the buyer's expectations, and individuals' buying decisions result in their satisfaction, which becomes part of their experience.

In this context, expectations can be understood as buyers' wishes or needs, or as their perception of what the supplier should offer (Lewis & Spyrakopoulos, 2001). Through purchases, buyers look for products with features that best meet their needs, and there is a human values system behind this, that influences an individual's preferences towards certain products. People tend to decide to buy products that show their role and position in society. Although they belong to the same sub-cultural group, social class, or profession, they may vary by lifestyle (Heijs et al. 2011). Research on sustainable interactions between psychological processes underlying human behaviour and built environment in housing is based on similar contexts.

In the case study, Zero waste City Ljubljana, we focus on re-designing our society so that all superfluous waste is eliminated and everything that is produced can be re-used, repaired, composted or recycled back into the system. In a growing number of regions, local groups of individuals, businesses and city officials are taking significant steps towards eliminating waste in our society. Zero Waste means strengthening the top three priority tasks in waste management - waste prevention/reduction, product reuse and recycling of materials. Ljubljana is the first European capital to move towards Zero Waste. We believe that the results could be reached only with sustainable interactions between psychological processes underlying human behaviour and the built environment. We believe that the results could help the local governments to contribute to reducing climate change, protect the health, create green jobs, and promote local sustainability and of course help increase the interests of potential buyers' expectations for buying decisions. Zero Waste is a critical stepping-stone to other necessary steps in the efforts to protect the health, improve equity and reach sustainability. Zero Waste can be linked to sustainable agriculture, architecture, energy, industrial, economic, and community development (Zero Waste International Alliance, 2015). We followed the hypotheses that there is a strong sustainable interaction between psychological processes underlying human behaviour and built environment and that among the sustainable built environment factors the waste management expressed these interactions at night. In the paper we systematically review the impact that research of environmental stress, namely, poor housing and poor neighbourhood quality had on contemporary understanding of human-built environment relations. Poor housing conditions can lead to pessimism, passivity, chronic stress, and general discontent (Cohen et al. 2005).

A built environment is closely connected with the living environment factors, where we observed proximity to public green areas, substandard quality of the houses, waste management, sustainable agriculture, architecture, built environment and proximity to health centres (Grum & Kobal Grum, 2015). We believe that built environment relations are closely connected with the attitude to waste in the neighbourhood.

Since market conditions have changed over time, the buyers' behaviour has become more complex, so, they now differ in psychological and social needs and preferences. Research shows that people vary in their decision to buy a home in numerous factors (Grum & Kobal Grum, 2015). Grum and Kobal Grum (2015) in their study focus on the following ones: financial, physical, living environment and socioeconomic factors. The goal of their study was to verify the hypothetical model of psychological factors in the decision to buy real estate. It clarifies in the integrated and relational way the role of psychological characteristics of real estate buyers in their expectations regarding the decision to buy which was established previously. Based on the analysis carried out, the authors (Grum & Kobal Grum, 2015) assume about setting up a hypothetical model of psychological factors in the decision to buy real estate, which in an integrated and relational way clarifies the role of psychological characteristics of real estate buyers in their expectations regarding the decision to buy. As shown, the living environment factors are those to which the psychological factors are most connected.

The results point out four main psychological factors in the decision to buy real estate, which are: basic psychological needs, self-esteem, subjective emotional well-being, and personal growth. The model assumes that these same four psychological factors are those, which from a set of partial individual and social psychological factors integrate and connect psychological characteristics that connect potential buyers of real estate. All four factors significantly correlate with the living environment factors: basic psychological needs ($r = .324$), self-esteem ($r = .242$), subjective emotional well-being ($r = .224$) and personal growth ($r = .256$). It also shows that psychological factors are entirely independent of the financial and physical factors of real estate. It seems, therefore, that when buying real estate the price, age, size, etc. are not as important as good infrastructure, quick access to everyday vital facilities, and other positive qualities of the living environment including proximity to public green areas, substandard quality of the houses, waste management, sustainable agriculture, architecture, built environment and proximity to health centres. Fulfilled basic psychological needs, stable self-esteem, subjective emotional well-being, and sense of personal growth are associated with this decision.

We can talk about sustainable interactions between psychological processes underlying human behaviour and the built environment. We focus on re-designing our society so that all superfluous waste is eliminated and everything that is produced can be re-used, repaired, composted, or recycled back into the system. The living environment is strongly connected with pollution (noise, air, and water pollution, waste...) In a growing number of regions, local groups of individuals, businesses and city officials are taking significant steps towards eliminating waste in our society (Temeljotov Salaj, 2005; Temeljotov Salaj et al. 2020). We highlight the case study: Zero waste City, Ljubljana. Zero Waste means strengthening the top three priority tasks in waste management - waste prevention/reduction, product reuse and material are recycling. Ljubljana is the first European capital to move towards Zero Waste. We believe that the positive effects of research could be reached only with sustainable interactions between psychological processes underlying human behaviour and the built environment. This could be achieved by addressing the three pillars of sustainability (Zero Waste International Alliance, 2015):

a) Environment: extending the usability of consumer goods through waste prevention and reuse and repair; improving waste sorting and recycling via technical innovations.
b) Society: engaging communities and businesses in resource-efficient behaviours through social innovation; developing a multi-stakeholder approach for increased collaboration and finding solutions how this collaboration will ensure a faster transition towards resource efficiency.
c) Economic: boosting green jobs in the waste sector.

In ten years, the number of recovered materials in Ljubljana increased from 16 kg per person in 2004 to 145 kg in 2014. By 2014, the average resident produced just 283 kg of waste, 61% of which was recycled or composted (Zero-waste Europe, 2015). This means that the amount of waste being sent to landfill decreased by 59% in ten years, and total waste generation decreased by 15%. This reduction is even more remarkable when considering that Ljubljana already generated relatively low amount of waste for European standards, being its generation of 2014 a 41% less than the EU average (481 kg per person) (Zero Waste Europe, 2015). At the same time, the average monthly waste management costs for households decreased, reaching 7.96 € in 2014. The costs for households in Ljubljana are among the lowest in Slovenia. The average yearly cost across the country is 150 €, compared to less than 100 € in Ljubljana.

The influence of the development level of the living environment factors on health inequalities is widely known, but there is still poor understanding of the precise relationship between area-based conditions and neighbourhood environmental quality. Fobil et al. (2010) showed wide variation in levels of association between the socioeconomic variables and environmental conditions, with strong evidence of a real difference in environmental quality across the five socioeconomic classes with respect to total waste generation, waste collection rate, sewer disposal rate, non-sewer disposal, the proportion of households using public toilets. Socioeconomic conditions related to the living environment are therefore important drivers of change in environmental quality. And, urban environmental interventions aimed at prevention and control of infectious disease, if effective, could benefit from simultaneous implementation with other social interventions.

METHODS

Participants

1.270 participants volunteered. There were 545 men and 725 women. Participants' age range was from 18 to 55 years, with an average of 21.15 years (SD = 4.6). As to education, most participants have secondary education (57.3%), which is followed by graduate degree education (38.1%). As to the number of children in a joint household, the most participants are without children (45.6%). The most participants live in the city centre (43.3%) or on the city outskirts (34.1%). The sample includes participants who were selected according to cultural identity, gender, age, employment, marital or family status and economic social status.

Measures

We used two types of measures, the first one for measuring participants' expectations, and the second one for measuring their psychological characteristics. The main questionnaire for measuring real estate expectations was the questionnaire set up within the context of broader research (blank – self-identifying citation). Of the three main types of questions (Keats 2000), open-ended, multiple-choice, and rank ordering, the latter two types of questions were used. Using a five-point Likert scale, the participants assessed the importance of their personal and external expectations regarding the acquisition of real estate rights. The statistical analysis includes the factor analysis and the reliability analysis of the questionnaire (Cronbach's alpha).

General Need Satisfaction Scale (GNSS, Gagne 2003) was used to measure the level of satisfaction of three basic psychological needs in life. It is a 21-item measure consisting of three subscales: autonomy, competence, and relatedness. Participants were asked to read each statement and rate on a 7-point scale how characteristic these statements are of them. Gagne (2003) reports the following reliability coefficients: .69 for autonomy, .86 for relatedness and .71 for competence. In the present study, reliability for autonomy was .69, .79 for relatedness and .61 for competence.

Personal Growth Attitude Scale (Ryckman et al. 1996) consists of 15 items. Participants were asked to read each statement and rate on a 5-point scale how often they behave according to various statements. Ryckman et al. (1996) reported reliability of .90. In the present study, internal reliability was .87.

Status motivation scale (Ryckman et al. 1990) consists of 26 items. Participants were asked to read each statement and rate on a 5-point scale how often they behave according to various statements. Authors reported reliability of .91. In the present study, internal reliability was .77.

Positive and Negative Affect Scale (PANAS; Watson et al. 1988) measures two dimensions: positive and negative effects. Positive affect refers to a state of good mood, enthusiasm, and action, whereas negative affect refers to a state of depression, anxiety, distress, and nervousness. Each subscale consists of 10 items. Participants were asked to read each statement and rate on a 5-point scale how often they experience various emotions in general. The authors reported reliability coefficients between .47 and .68 for positive affect and from .39 to .71 for negative effect. In the present study, internal reliability was .79 for positive affect and .85 for negative effect.

Self-esteem questionnaire (SLCS-R; Tafarodi & Swann 2001) measures two dimensions of the general self-esteem: self-liking and self-competence. The self-competence subscale measures the part of self-esteem originating in an individual's feelings of ability and efficacy, while the self-liking subscale measures the part of self-esteem depending on the society. Each subscale consists of eight items. Participants were asked to read each statement and rate on a 5-point scale how characteristic these statements are of them. The scale's reliability is .90 for the self-liking subscale and .82 for the self-competence subscale (Tafarodi & Swann 2001), in our research .87 was for self-liking and .77 for self-competence.

Contingent Self-esteem Scale (Paradise & Kernis 2002) measures to what degree an individual's self-esteem depends on achieving standards, goals, and positive feedback. The scale consists of 15 items. Participants were asked to read each statement and rate on a 5-point scale how characteristic these statements are of them. Thc scale's test-retest reliability is .77 (Kernis & Goldman, 2006). In the present study, internal reliability was .78.

Data Analysis

Data were treated using IBM SPSS Statistics for Windows, version 24.0. The internal consistencies of all scales were estimated, as well as the mean scores for each scale and the correlations between them. Subsequently, an explanatory factor analysis (EFA) of the variables was conducted.

Research Findings and Discussion

A questionnaire, which measures potential real estate buyers' personal expectations, covers 30 variables. Eight factors explain over 71 percent of the variance. Factors extracted by the factor analysis are partly covered by factors, which have been extracted from the questionnaire. Under the first factor are highly saturated items which, according to the questionnaire, fall within the scope of physical factors. Under the second factor are highly saturated items that, according to the questionnaire fall within the scope of living environment factors. Under the third factor are highly saturated items that, according to the questionnaire, fall within the scope of socioeconomic factors. The factor analysis classifies the variables - maintenance costs and a sense of economic status - under physical factors, but the correlation in socioeconomic factors is similarly high, which is why we classify it with the set of latter factors. Under the fourth factor are highly saturated items that, according to the questionnaire, fall within the scope of socioeconomic factors. Under the fifth factor is highly saturated the item that according to the questionnaire falls within socioeconomic factors (maintenance costs). It is also highly reflected under physical factors as maintenance costs are linked to the physical condition of the real estate. Under the sixth factor are highly saturated items that, according to the questionnaire, fall within the scope of physical factors. Under the seventh factor is a highly saturated item, which falls within the scope of general factors. Under the eighth factor are highly saturated items that fall within financial factors. The Kaiser-Meyer-Olkin measure of sampling adequacy is .861. Bartlett's test (BT = 2654.756), which is statistically significant, also shows that extracted factors can be interpreted. The results are shown in Table 1.

By merging variables into four main factors: physical factors, living environment factors, socioeconomic factors, and financial factors, we find that physical factors explain 79% of the variance, living environment factors 13%, socioeconomic factors 6%, while financial factors explain a total of only 1% variance.

Factor analysis thus confirms the hypothesis according to which the principles related to the real estate itself were divided into four real estate factors. These are (1) financial factors (interest rates, household income, credit availability, GDP), (2) physical factors related to physical characteristics of real estate (location, size of the apartment, presence of the balcony, natural lighting, peacefulness, age of the building and neighbourhood, parking options, the infrastructure of the apartment), (3) living environment factors (proximity to vital facilities, accessibility, substandard quality of buildings, waste management, agriculture, architecture, built environment) and (4) socioeconomic factors (maintenance costs, neighbourly relations, sense of security, sense of social connection, sense of suitable economic status).

Table 1. Rotated factor matrix of score results of the factor scale

Variables	Factors							
	1	2	3	4	5	6	7	8
Location of the apartment	**0.814**	0.245	0.169	-0.019	0.067	-0.126	0.006	-0.005
Size of the apartment	**0.868**	0.123	0.096	0.024	0.045	-0.050	-0.031	0.090
Balcony / terrace	**0.845**	0.074	0.082	0.063	0.017	0.175	0.031	0.101
Brightness – natural lighting	**0.738**	0.208	0.207	0.048	0.131	0.221	-0.045	0.062
Open view	**0.737**	0.148	0.240	0.047	0.295	0.127	-0.108	-0.040
Peaceful, not noisy apartment	**0.584**	0.233	0.434	0.001	0.162	0.218	-0.106	-0.030
Age of the building	**0.700**	0.195	0.121	-0.097	-0.100	0.222	0.241	-0.068
Age of the neighbourhood	**0.528**	0.255	0.183	-0.083	-0.036	0.343	0.310	0.144
Parking options	**0.614**	0.222	0.310	0.035	0.142	0.249	-0.158	-0.062
Internet access	**0.271**	0.378	0.003	0.103	0.059	0.751	0.075	-0.013
Central heating	**0.380**	0.245	0.232	0.110	-0.038	0.737	0.069	0.042
Proximity to public green area	0.215	**0.846**	0.090	0.035	-0.055	0.168	-0.030	0.078
Substandard quality of the house	0.371	**0.696**	0.206	0.158	-0.022	0.138	0.090	-0.075
Waste management	0.209	**0.857**	0.187	0.020	0.100	0.048	-0.003	0.009
Sustainable agriculture	0.298	**0.779**	0.154	0.013	-0.011	-0.006	0.126	0.013
Sustainable architecture	0.172	**0.838**	0.099	0.016	0.019	0.126	0.118	-0.012
Proximity to health centres	0.115	**0.844**	0.188	-0.069	0.143	0.151	-0.024	-0.067
Sustainable built environment	0.027	**0.792**	0.124	-0.074	0.023	0.096	-0.021	0.206
Maintenance costs	0.439	0.300	**0.363**	0.011	0.369	0.302	-0.148	0.008
Relationships with neighbours	0.282	0.261	**0.738**	0.026	0.095	0.117	0.130	0.004
Sense of security	0.367	0.243	**0.725**	0.157	0.006	0.177	-0.011	0.000
Social affiliation	0.256	0.327	**0.725**	-0.065	0.010	-0.096	0.152	0.098
A sense of economic status	0.590	0.309	**0.499**	0.027	0.014	0.104	0.178	-0.021
Other factors	0.050	0.031	-0.031	-0.038	0.406	0.014	**0.771**	0.145
When to buy property	-0.456	-0.195	0.196	-0.057	-0.157	0.065	0.212	**-0.311**
Social security	-0.072	0.149	0.104	**0.666**	0.237	0.215	-0.062	0.172
Suitable economic status	0.239	0.043	-0.103	**0.556**	0.176	-0.248	0.062	-0.396
Sense of independence	-0.090	-0.079	0.043	**0.781**	-0.155	0.041	0.004	-0.165
Sense of complacency	0.074	-0.029	-0.005	**0.833**	-0.206	0.025	-0.053	0.071
Main financial resources	-0.161	-0.060	0.010	0.136	-0.021	0.031	-0.003	**-0.742**

Table 2. Correlations between expectations of potential real estate buyers and their motivational and emotional characteristics

	Financial	Physical	Living environment	Socioeconomic	Social status	Independence	Self-contentment	Autonomy	Competence	Relatedness	Status motivation	Self-liking
Financial	1	.255**	0.112	0.142	-0.055	0.07	0.108	0.034	0.051	0.074	-0.083	-0.05
Physical	.255**	1	.280**	0.064	-0.052	0.038	0.068	0.036	0.131	0.127	0.08	-0.135
Living environment	0.112	.280**	1	.399**	-0.054	-0.074	0.006	.230**	.264**	.324**	-0.139	0.125
Socioeconomic	0.142	0.064	.399**	1	-0.059	-0.024	-0.009	0.132	0.165	0.146	0.035	0.13
Social status	-0.055	-0.052	-0.054	-0.059	1	.405**	.380**	-0.105	-0.023	-0.095	.228**	-0.039
Independence	0.07	0.038	-0.074	-0.024	.405**	1	.617**	-0.101	-0.057	-0.012	.227**	-0.083
Self-contentment	0.108	0.068	0.006	-0.009	.380**	.617**	1	-.202*	-0.079	-0.105	.205*	-0.053
Autonomy	0.034	0.036	.230**	0.132	-0.105	-0.101	-.202*	1	.564**	.572**	-.296**	.536**
Competence	0.051	0.131	.264**	0.165	-0.023	-0.057	-0.079	.564**	1	.490**	-.298**	.563**
Relatedness	0.074	0.127	.324**	0.146	-0.095	-0.012	-0.105	.572**	.490**	1	-.339**	.408**
Status motivation	-0.083	0.08	-0.139	0.035	.228**	.227**	.205*	-.296**	-.298**	-.339**	1	-.350**
Self-liking	-0.05	-0.135	0.125	0.13	-0.039	-0.083	-0.053	.536**	.563**	.408**	-.350**	1

Table 2 shows the correlation between expectations to purchase real estate and psychological factors. Among these correlations, which are according to participants decisive to purchase real estate, are: financial, physical, socioeconomic, living environment factors and basic motivational and emotional factors, subjective well-being and self-esteem.

The results show that neither physical nor financial factors, which are decisive for the purchase, are associated with the psychological, motivational or emotional factors. Participants who expect that socioeconomic factors, such as maintenance costs, neighbourly relations, sense of security, sense of social connection and sense of suitable economic status, contribute highly to their decision to buy a home, have only one psychological factor expressed more : personal growth. This correlation is low.

In contrast, the living environment factors, such as proximity to public transport, transport accessibility, proximity to kindergartens and schools, proximity to employment opportunities, shops, health centres, cultural centres, etc. are associated with both motivational and emotional factors. The participants who decide to purchase real estate mainly based on the quality of living environment factors, i.e., who value proximity to schools, shops, health services, access to the home, proximity to public transport and good transport facilities and other infrastructure, better meet their basic psychological needs in all three dimensions: autonomy, competence, and connectedness. This means that they have a better sense of controlling tasks and accepting challenges, they see themselves more connected with the people around them and feel more independent and autonomous in taking important decisions.

Impact of living environment factors on the psychological well-being of potential home buyers are shown below. The main hypothesis that, in the decision to buy real estate there are two groups of factors: factors related to real estate - real estate factors and factors related to persons deciding to buy real estate - psychological factors, was confirmed in the survey. The potential decision to buy real estate is associated with both real estate factors and psychological factors. A further analysis of this hypothesis showed that not all real estate factors are associated with all psychological factors, but these connections are completely defined. Thus, it can be concluded that the main hypothesis in the further analysis is partially confirmed, namely: that in the decision to buy real estate there are two groups of factors, certain real estate factors and certain psychological factors. These results are consistent with the results of the study by Morita et al. (2010), who conclude that the decision to buy real estate is associated with the level of social support and a sense of trust in those around oneself. They also refer to studies, which examine the role of locus of control (Wang et al. 2008), wherein the importance of the internal point of control and a sense of autonomy and independence is a major factor in deciding to buy real estate.

Interestingly, these factors well discriminate also psychological characteristic of personal rivalry. According to the results, to the participants who believe that living environment factors are the most decisive factors when buying their own property, the purchase of their own real estate would also represent the feeling of personal progress and personal growth. The results also showed that those with higher demands in their own living environment factors have also higher self-esteem. This finding is confirmed as well by the results of the study by Pinto et al. (2004), who highlight the importance of a stable and high self-esteem also in the decisions to buy real estate. And they also have higher subjective emotional well-being, which is also confirmed by the results of the study by Avnet et al. (2012) and Caplin and Leahy (2001). Hereon, it can be concluded that to be satisfied with real estate or with living factors, in which a potential real estate is involved, high or optimally subjective emotional well-being is needed. At the same time, the collected results can be compared with the results of the examination of a relatively new phenomenon in the field of psychological factors when deciding about real estate, namely attachments or attachment to the real estate (Khozaei et al. 2012; Livingston et al. 2010). Attachment, which in psychology is a known and quite researched phenomenon, is acquiring a new dimension through research of the users' attitude toward real estate. It seems that people, who feel it is important in what infrastructural environment they live, or they would like to live, express constructive attachment to real estate also through higher subjective emotional well-being (Florek 2011).

From the real estate point of view, the above stated relates to findings by Luttik (2000), who listed the characteristic and attractiveness of environment, open view, peaceful environment, and good infrastructure to have the most important influence on the price, and the attractiveness of real estate. Anderson and Cordell (1988) in their research, like Morancho (2003) conclude that the proximity to educational institutions is essential. Similarly, as noted also by Munizzo and Virruso Musial (2009), more important factors are public transport accessibility, proximity to schools and important institutions (shops, cultural centres).

The analysis which covers the projection of psychological factors in the decision to buy real estate regarding changes in perception of the buyers' own social status and sense of independence has shown that correlations are namely low. But there is a certain trend which shows that, when participants with higher expectations acquire appropriate real estate, their social status would go up. They would feel more independent and they would maximize their self-satisfaction, express higher status motivation, and contingent self-esteem.

Rohe et al. (2001) studied social advantages of apartment owners and established that apartment owners compared to apartment tenants express higher satisfaction with their living environment, are socially more active in their living environment, change residence less often and more frequently contribute to the social stability of the neighbourhood. They note that the satisfaction level among apartment owners is higher. In the Baltimore case, apartment buyers and apartment tenants were observed and after a year and a half, it was concluded that the satisfaction of apartment buyers was higher than the satisfaction of tenants (Rohe & Stegman 1994). In a further three-year study, Rohe and Basolo (1997) determined that even after three-year ownership the owners of apartments were still more self-satisfied as the tenants. They defined this self-satisfaction as the combination of the general satisfaction with life, apartment, and neighbourhood. Kleinhans and Elsinga (2010) conclude that there is a strong correlation between owning a home and the feeling of independence and self-satisfaction.

Based on the analysis carried out we can assume about setting up a hypothetical model of psychological factors in the decision to buy real estate, which in an integrated and relational way clarifies the role of psychological characteristics of real estate buyers in their expectations regarding the decision to purchase. As shown in Figure 1, precisely the living environment factors are those which the psychological factors are most connected to. Model 4 points out four main psychological factors in the decision to buy real estate, which are: basic psychological needs, self-esteem, subjective emotional well-being, and personal growth. The model assumes that these same four psychological factors are those, which from a set of partial individual and social psychological factors integrate and connect psychological characteristics that connect potential buyers of real estate. All four factors significantly correlate with the living environment factors: basic psychological needs (r = .324), self-esteem (r = .242), subjective emotional well-being (r = .224) and personal growth (r = .256). It also shows that psychological factors are entirely independent of the financial and physical factors of real estate. It seems, therefore, that when buying real estate, the price, age, size, etc. are not as important as good infrastructure, quick access to everyday vital facilities, and other positive qualities of the living environment. With this decision are associated fulfilled basic psychological needs, stable self-esteem, subjective emotional well-being, and sense of personal growth.

It therefore appears that what potential buyers focus most on when buying real estate can be divided into two parts/phases. In the first phase, the greatest influence on potential buyers have physical factors of real estate (79% variance), where in the second phase, the decision to buy is influenced, in the largest part, by well-being, self-esteem, and feeling of personal growth, i.e., living environment factors. Together with physical factors they explain 92% of the variation.

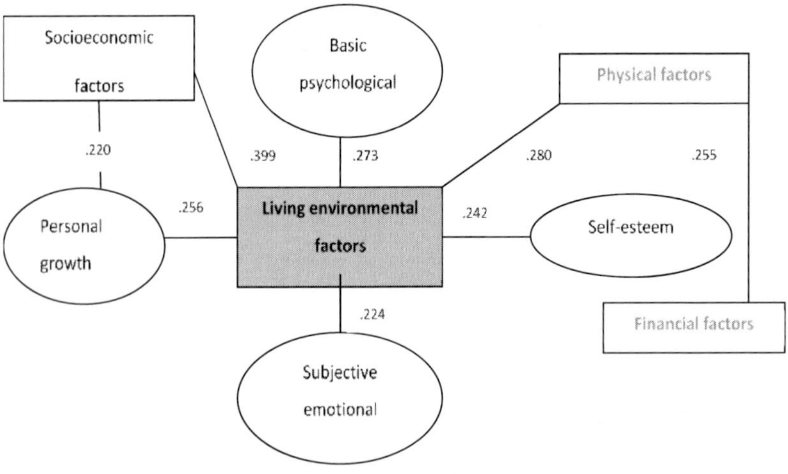

Figure 1. Model of interactions between psychological and living environment factors in the decision to buy real estate (Grum & Kobal Grum, 2015).

This is confirmed also by the survey, where results show that the biggest influence on the price of housing have the factors, which are linked to the neighbourhood (relations, origin, safety, tidiness, infrastructure, equipment) followed by location, financial and physical characteristics (Bourassa at al. 2003).

The results show how important influence have living environment factors (proximity to vital facilities, accessibility, substandard quality of the houses, waste management, agriculture, architecture, built environment). By merging variables (Table 1), the results show that among living environment factors the most pronounced factor expressed is waste management. According to the Zero Waste International Alliance (www.zwia.org), Zero Waste is a goal that is ethical, economical, efficient and visionary, to guide people in changing their lifestyles and practices emulating sustainable natural cycles, where all discarded materials are designed to become resources for others to use. Our results confirm the model of interactions between psychological and living environment factors in the decision to buy real estate. According to GURS (2016), last year Ljubljana recorded sales of about 2700 dwellings in multi-dwelling buildings, which is 10 percent more than in 2014, when their turnover compared to 2013 increased by about 30 percent. Markedly the number of executed real estate transactions also increased, implying a marked revival of the real estate market.

CONCLUSION

In the article, we have investigated sustainable interactions between psychological processes underlying human behaviour and the built environment: The Case of Ljubljana - Zero-Waste City. The main instruments for measuring the participants' expectations are questionnaires that we formed ourselves. A total of 1,270 participants took part in the survey. According to the results, we divide real estate factors into financial factors, physical factors related to physical characteristics of real estate, living environment factors and socioeconomic factors. Principles based on users' perceptions were measured by psychological scales, which had been tested in the existing, previously published studies. According to these measurements, we divided psychological characteristics into motivational and emotional characteristics. On this basis, we used a created model (Grum & Kobal Grum, 2015) where we assumed a hypothetical link between expectations of potential home buyers and their motivational and emotional characteristics.

The research showed that financial and physical factors are independent of psychological ones. Expectations about the price of apartment or house, location, size of the apartment, natural lighting etc. correlate with neither motivational nor emotional factors, but they form independent areas that are related to the real estate only. It seems that affordable price and good physical condition of real estate are the most important for buyers. It could be recommended to enhance financial politics to stimulate potential buyers to purchase a home. A living environment and socioeconomic factors both correlate with personal growth; which means that those participants who value most the following characteristics of real estate: proximity to vital facilities, substandard quality of the houses, waste management, sustainable agriculture, architecture, built environment, good neighbourly relations, feelings of safety, social belonging to the neighbourhood, etc. have higher motives of cooperation, self-improvement and self-growth than those with lower living environment and socioeconomic factors. It could be concluded that homeowners would be more satisfied and integrated into the living environment. The results could help the local governments to contribute to reducing climate change, protect the health, create green jobs, and promote local sustainability. The results are shown that the waste management (for example, Zero Waste Project) is a critical stepping-stone to other necessary steps in the efforts to protect the health, improve equity and reach sustainability. Zero Waste can be linked to sustainable agriculture, architecture, energy, industrial, economic, and community development (Zero Waste International Alliance, 2015). We confirmed the hypotheses that there is a strong sustainable interaction between the psychological processes underlying human behaviour and the built environment, and that among the sustainable built environment factors, the waste management expresses these interactions at night.

It is interesting, therefore, that the environmental factors with respect to real estate factors are associated only with socioeconomic and physical factors, but not with financial factors. Of all the real estate factors, the most associated with psychological factors is the environmental factor, which means that with the development of positive environmental factors we can increase the well-being or the sense of personal satisfaction with oneself. We note, however, that the finance is too much of an independent factor to be directly connected to psychological factors. But anyway, we believe that the results could be reached only with sustainable interactions between psychological processes underlying human behaviour and the built environment.

The results suggest that good living environment conditions and among them good waste management express positive interactions between psychological and living environment factors and lead to the decision to buy real estate. The Case of Ljubljana suggests that project Zero Waste City yields results in this direction: the satisfaction of the population is increasing, the supply of real estate is rising, and house prices are growing. If a purchase takes place and satisfies the buyer's needs, then it has fulfilled the buyer's expectations, and individuals' buying decisions result in their satisfaction, which becomes part of their experience.

ACKNOWLEDGMENTS

This study was partially funded by the Slovenian Research Agency (Development of social infrastructure and services for community based long-term care J6-9396; Psychological and neuroscientific aspects of cognition, P5-0110).

References

Andreson, L. M., & Cordell, H. K. (1988). Influence of trees on residential property values in Athens, Georgia (U.S.A.): A survey based on actual sales prices. *Landscape and Urban Planning. 15*(1-2), 153-164.

Avnet, T., Pham, M. T., & Stephen, A. T. (2012). Consumers' trust in feelings as information. *Journal of Consumer Research, 39*(4), 720-735.

Bourassa, S. C., Hoesli, M., & Peng, V. S. (2003). Do housing submarkets really matter? *Journal of Housing Economics*, *12*, 12-28.

Caplin, A., & Leahy, J. (2001). Psychological expected utility theory and anticipatory feelings. *Quarterly Journal of Economics, 116*(1), 55–79.

Cohen, D. H., Kozak, R. A., Vidal, N., Spetic, W., & Ide, R. (2005): Performance expectations and needs of the Japanese house consumer. *Forest Products Journal*, *55*(5), pp. 37−44.

Florek, M. (2011). No place like home: Perspectives on place attachment and impacts on city management. *Journal of Town & City Management 1*(4), 346–354.

Fobil, J., Juergen, M., & Kraemer, A. (2010*)*. Assessing the Relationship between Socioeconomic Conditions and Urban Environmental Quality in Accra, Ghana. *International Journal of Environment Research and Public Health*, 7(1), 125-145.

Gagné, M. (2003). The role of autonomy support and autonomy orientation in prosocial behavior engagement. *Motivation and Emotion, 27*(3), 199-223. Retrieved from http://www.springerlink.com/index/T2R181R81R8507W0.pdf.

Grum, B., & Kobal Grum, D. (2015). A model of real estate and psychological factors in decision-making to buy real estate. *Urbani izziv*, 26(1), 82-91.

GURS, (2015). *Poročilo o slovenskem trgu nepremičnin za leto 2015.* [*Report on the Slovenian real estate market for 2015.*]. http://www.e-prostor.gov.si/fileadmin/etn/Porocila/Letno_porocilo_za_leto_2015.pdf.

Heijs, W., van Deursen, A., Leussink, M., & Smeets, J. (2011). Re-searching the labyrinth of life-styles. *Journal of Housing and the Built Environment, 26*(4), 411-425.

Keats, D. M. (2000). *Interviewing, a practical guide for students and professionals.* (Buckingham, Open University Press, Celtic Court, Ballmoor).

Kernis, M. H., & Goldman, B. M. (2006). Stability and variability in self-concept and self-esteem. (In M. R. Leary & J. P. Tangney (Eds.), *Handbook of self and identity* (pp. 106-127). New York: The Guilford Press.

Khozaei, F., Ramayah, T., Hassan, A. S., & Suricnty, L. (2012). Sense of attachment to place and fulfilled preferences, the mediating role of housing satisfaction. *Property Management, 30*(3), 292-310.

Kleinhans, R., & Elsinga, M. (2010). Buy your home and feel in control: Do home ownership achieve the empowerment of former tenants of social housing? *International Journal of Housing Policy, 10*(1), 41-61.

Lewis, B. R., & Spyrakopoulos, S. (2001). Service failures and recovery in retail banking: The customers' perspective, *International Journal of Bank Marketing, 19*(1), 37-47.

Livingston, M., Bailey, N., & Kearns, A. (2010). Neighbourhood attachment in deprived areas: Evidence from the north of England. *Journal of Housing and the Built Environment, 25*(4), 409-427.

Luttik, J. (2000). The value of trees, water and open space as reflected by house prices in the Netherlands. *Landscape and Urban Planning, 48*(3-4), 161-167.

Morancho, B. A. (2003). A hedonic valuation of urban green areas. *Landscape and Urban Planning, 66*(35–41).

Morita, A., Takano, T., Nakamura, K., Kizuki, M., & Seino, K. (2010). Contribution of interaction with family, friends and neighbours, and sense of neighbourhood attachment to survival in senior citizens: 5-year follow-up study. *Social Science & Medicine, 70*(4), 543-549.

Munizzo, M. A., & Virruso Musial, L. (2009). *General sales comparison approach.* Canada, Cengage Learning.

Paradise, A. W., & Kernis, M. H. (2002). Self-esteem and psychological wellbeing: Implications of fragile self-esteem. *Journal of Social and Clinical Psychology*, *21*, 345–361.

Pinto, M. B., Mansfield, P. M., & Parente, D. H. (2004). Relationship of credit attitude and debt to self-esteem and locus of control in college-age consumers. *Psychological Reports*, *94*, 1405–1418.

Rohe, W. M., & Basolo, V. (1997). Long-term effects of homeownership on the self-perceptions and social interaction of low-income persons, *Environment and Behavior*, *29*(6), 793-819.

Rohe, W. M. & Stegman, M. (1994). The impact of home ownership on the social and political involvement of low-income people, *Urban Affairs Quarterty 3*, 152-172.

Rohe, W. M., Zandth, S., & McCarthy, G. (2001). The social benefits and costs of homeownership: A critical assessment of the research. *Joint Center for Housing Studies of Harvard Universitiy*, 1-31.

Ryckman, R. M., Hammer, M., Kaczor, L. M., & Gold, J. A. (1990). Construction of a hypercompetitive attitude scale, *Journal of Personality Assessment*, *55*, 630-639.

Shiller, R. J., Case, K. E., & Thompson A. (2010): What were they thinking? Home buyer behavior in hot and cold markets. *Brookings Papers of Economic Activity,* 265-298.

Tafarodi, R. W., & Swann, W. B., Jr. (2001). Two-dimensional self-esteem: Theory and measurement, *Personality and Individual Differences*, *31*, 653-673.

Temeljotov Salaj, A. (2005). The synergetic effect of the observer on the built environment. *Urbani izziv*, 16(2), 163-167.

Temeljotov Salaj, A., Gohari, S., Senior, C., Xue, Y., & Lindkvist, C. (2020), An interactive tool for citizens' involvement in the sustainable regeneration, *Facilities*, *38*(11/12), 859-870. https://doi.org/10.1108/F-09-2019-0099.

Wang, M., Chen, H., & Wang, L. (2008). Locus of control and home mortgage loan behaviour. *International Journal of Psychology*, *43*(2), 125–129.

Watson, D., Clark, L. A., & Tellegen, A. (1988). Development and validation of brief measures of positive and negative affect: The PANAS scales. *Journal of Personality and Social Psychology, 54,* 1063-1070.

Zero Waste Europe, (2015). *The story of Ljubljana.* https://www.zerowasteeurope.eu/downloads/case-study-5-ljubljana/.

Zero Waste International Alliance (2015). *What Does Zero Waste Mean? Zero is Zero.* http://zwia.org/standards/zero-is-zero/.

Reviewers:

Associate Professor Boštjan Kerbler, PhD
Urban Planning Institute of the Republic of Slovenia, Ljubljana, Slovenia.

Associate Professor Boštjan Aver, PhD
New University, European Faculty of Law, Ljubljana, Slovenia.

In: The Future of Real Estate
Editor: Jan Veuger
ISBN: 978-1-53619-414-2

Chapter 6

PROPERTY DEVELOPMENT VIABILITY AND COMMUNITY SPIRIT: RETHINKING THE SAFETY ANGLE

Tom Kauko*[*], *PhD
Independent scholar, Budapest, Hungary

ABSTRACT

What we in generic academic parlance refer to as "social factors" tend to have various major consequences for the built environment. For an individual property unit or site, its value development together with potential changes in the surroundings comprise such concerns, as do white flight at the level of neighborhood. This contribution addresses the symbiotic issue of property development viability and community spirit – including downsides, such as violent crime. How does property development viability depend on the community situation in terms of trust and social hazard? The problem is how to attract or retain property owners, private sector employers and employees, preferably within the

[*] Corresponding Author's E-mail: tomjkauko@gmail.com.

service sector, and customers for such service companies as well as other community members who would play by the rules of organized society. The livability and functionality of the built structures together with their on- and off-site circumstances depend, to a great extent, on the way the social environment relates to safety of these property owners, companies, their workforce, and spending customers. And this, in turn, has further implications for property development viability and community spirit, and, eventually, the real estate economy at large. The findings of this conceptual analysis pertain to the ability of real estate actors to make the most of these increasingly controversial relationships.

Keywords: community spirit, property development viability, real estate investment, safety

INTRODUCTION

Long before any sustainability science agenda, various theoretical and empirical literatures within economics, psychology, sociology, geography and planning have identified the importance of social factors in residential location choice. One could even argue that understanding the social aspects is a key issue for a successful analysis of how people move within an urban area (see e.g., Manzi et al. 2010, Ahmed 2011). Such thoughts also resonate with the corresponding original humanistic argument on emotional values, following Tuan (1974), that resident's choice of home environment depends on the relative evaluations of contradictory criteria: on one hand, people want safety, familiarity and avoidance of nuisance; on the other, they want grandeur, excitement and stimuli at the same time (see also Kauko 2004).[1]

Here several obvious questions arise. Do such desired residential environments exist, or could these be produced? And do similar perceptions exist for workplace environments – are they too caught in the

[1] One notices furthermore that, amidst the ongoing *discursive turn* in social sciences, this kind of seemingly schizophrenic rationalization of one's motivations can be fitted within a broader methodological view, following the philosophy of science of *relativism*, according to which the 'truth' does not exist in objective terms and is depending on particular narratives.

same choice dilemma? Furthermore, how would occupants of such ideal real estate feel, if their preferences become different than those of the developers? These speculations shift our analytical foci from the demand side towards the supply side. The issue then concerns property development and the production of apt vicinities, including the need to maintain vital communities in support of a continuing narrative of what is portrayed as "likable" in a place. Safe to say, in this context, that property development is not always portrayed as a technical exercise, in so far as social and cultural factors of the locality might have a surprisingly decisive influence on the decisions being made (see Guy et al. 2002).

Nevertheless, when examining the economic realities of a given project, financial stakeholders have a key role for the production of what is referred to as "sustainable built environment" (Lützkendorf et al. 2011). Indeed, it is the property developer and investor who are expected to come up with a lion's share of the financing of the sustainability elements. It is therefore essential that also these actors are represented in the participatory planning and development procedures. The extent to which the desired sustainability features can be approached as viable also depends on the economic cycles: at the time of financial downturn, original concepts based on large-scale developments may well have to be downshifted, and reworked as small-scale and refurbishment agendas. In such a situation, the local public economy furthermore needs a long-term "smartish" and spatially differentiated strategy, preferably with standards and protocols, to ensure an apt outcome in terms of livability as well as feasibility considerations.

So what then determines the approval of a given neighborhood? The affordability of the area or region is obviously a crucial factor – rents and prices of homes as well as nearby services may matter more than anything else for the prospective in-mover. Other absolute issues for average residents to tackle are of many kinds, and the space here is not sufficient to delve into all of them. Here one particularly important social factor is picked for scrutiny: the safety against physical violence and robbery; this can be approximated to whether one can easily avoid potential low-intensity danger. (In particular, in confrontations with street-gangs constituted of feral young men.) The problem might, for instance, be that, whilst I would accept living in a neighborhood dominated by ethnic group X, the members of that group might not accept my presence there (Kauko 2019a). In this arguably neglected problem area, the question is about the ability of the residents themselves, on one hand, and the public sector, on the other, to guard against these problems so that the area does not degenerate further into chaos and vulnerability. In this essay the focus is firmly on the former of the two aspects: the rationale for individual choice. (The other aspect involves public choice and would require more elaboration in a follow-up study.)

This chapter discusses the individual choice setting of the perceptions of a safe place. Reviewing the relevant features for these choices should also be seen as a first step towards developing a quantifiable research platform for the analysis of place safety. This kind of "place safety index" could also be seen as a potential innovation in terms of the set of elements included, in so far as these can be plugged into a property development viability approach. This index would be based on perceived threats to one's safety and thereby opposite to the already established "tolerance" indices. So an alternative measure to examine – and perhaps rank – place attractiveness for the prospective occupant, investor and developer as well as other stakeholders involved. Unfortunately, the problem here is that, while the safety angle is justifiable in both economic and social terms, it is also likely to offend some circles.

The research question is formulated as follows: How does property development viability depend on the community situation in terms of trust and social hazard? The problem is how to attract or retain property owners, private sector employers and employees, preferably within the service sector, and customers for such service companies as well as other community members who would play by the rules of organized society. The originality of this contribution is to adapt a *realist* approach[2] to socioeconomically sustainable development concerning real estate stakeholders (developers, investors, owners and occupiers).

[2] As in critical realism, social realism, race realism and so forth.

While universal by nature, this selection is made particular with a diagnose of recent socially hazardous, mostly urban events in mind. In the wake of violent riots and demands for police defunding, *who* will protect the law-abiding middle-class peoples? We are also living in the midst of a culture of blame, where everyone seems to be entitled to mudslinging and hypocrisy. The bottom-line is: the majority of us would like to generate trust in our communities, and to achieve that goal, also retain a strong law enforcement machinery (Kauko 2019a, 2020a,b).[3] Blunt as this sentiment may be, does it not make sense at a general level? Can we really judge this "silent majority" view from the narrow angle of what we, as supposedly "modern" persons, are being conditioned to believe? (Think of Tuan's wisdom above – primitive urges matter too.) Obviously, polite liberal viewpoints may, shockingly, vanish as quickly as they emerge; for example, according to a recent questionnaire survey, the majority of the population in the UK would have the death penalty reinstated (*Redfield & Wilton Strategies*, 2020).

At this stage a few words need to be said about methodology. As such, a discursive or multi-method approach does not need to subscribe to any fashionable political left-of-center logic at all. (This historically proven revelation may still be news to some younger scholars!) In response to the pupils of the Frankfurt School, who, in the name of "post-positivism" or related ideological acrobatics, might think they own all such positions by default (or simply because they do not care about statistics), we then need to shift into different, *pragmatic* – as opposed to *purist* – categories within the decision space of philosophies of science. Here it is to note that an essentially European critical theoretical tradition[4] existed long before the post-war cultural Marxism promoted by the Frankfurt School. This would enable applying the same methodologies the progressive liberal minded

[3] For anyone with very different opinion, I would suggest to self-critically analyze their own selections in terms of where they live, what kinds of neighbors they associate with, the schools they put their children in, and the areas they avoid walking through after dark, before accusing me of biased viewpoint (or worse).

[4] This is about Traditionalism (note the capital 'T'), as conceived by Julius Evola and René Guénon, and later followed by Oswald Spengler as well as many contemporary heavy weight thinkers such as Paul Gottfried.

scholars apply, be it with *realist* (as here) or *relativist* (i.e., social constructivist, post-structuralist or post-modernist) orientation. So, stated differently, those who claim to do critical social research cannot easily refute such research as "pseudo-science" anymore, if the methodological apparatus is largely the same – although now used in diametrically opposite fashion.

This chapter is organized as follows. After this introduction, the second section outlines the proposed *Islands of Property Management* approach. In the third section, the social side is reassessed. The fourth section deals with real estate analytics concerning crime and safety. The fifth and last section concludes the study.

THE ISLANDS OF PROPERTY MANAGEMENT APPROACH

Whereas urban planners tend to try to increase suburban densities, at the same time, developers can challenge planning principles related to urban form and function (Grant 2009). This results in friction between the two levels of analysis: one, individual buildings and property rights; and two, neighborhood and urban levels. The former analysis is simpler and familiar to real estate economists and probably to real estate appraisers too. The latter analysis is more complex and should be familiar for social scientists, geographers and, indeed, present day spatial planners. This is why a potential innovation referred to as the *Islands of Property Management approach* is proposed as a way to overcome – or at least substantially reduce – this friction (see Kauko 2019b). We can furthermore assume that analytical tools – and what is commonly referred to as Big Data – will help here.

The idea here is to look for common denominators – we are after all dealing with same ingredients, even if we use them in different order. Namely, variables relating to property price, area density and quality attributes of neighborhood revitalization have an effect on one another (e.g., Dunse et al. 2013). Management of individual buildings will inevitably result in the way the surrounding area is kept. On the other hand, neighborhood revitalization is likely to influence the price level of the property (total, per sqm. floor space, per sqm. land), either negatively or positively. If the intensified management of individual buildings leads to their improvement in quality, then the outcome also represents a gradual upsurge in the standing of the neighborhood – in environmental, social and economic terms. Here is also link to the more general spatial analysis literature as such "islands" of individual well-managed buildings can then act as "cells of development". This is based on an original idea by Wallner and colleagues (1996), but as modified to a smaller scale analysis.[5]

When the issue of improvement of an area is reduced to purely economic terms (i.e., the traditional mode of urban land and real estate economic analysis), the issue is about how a change in permitted area density (zoning) influences property prices (Dunse et al. 2013). The starting point is that a corresponding demand is required to induce that price increase. Then we experience an immediate effect: more floor-space (or higher plot-efficiency ratio) increases the total price increase, unless this is something akin to a trophy property with antiquarian value. Furthermore, this effect also increases the unit price for land. However, the same effect, when realized, due to decreasing marginal benefit, reduces the unit price for floor-space. These effects notwithstanding, improved on-site and off-site amenities as well as an upgrading the building quality (e.g., insulation) push all price measures upwards, as demand for the built-up property packages increases. The challenge however is to show all this empirically – and when possible, expand the analysis towards the important noneconomic dimensions.

From these more technical considerations, a number of questions arise. What would be the volume and number of property developments – both new and regeneration – as well (green spaces) as infrastructure concerns? What kind of buildings (both office and apartments) would be feasible? How would the necessary traffic arrangements be solved? Where and how

---

[5] In the original idea of Wallner and colleagues (1996) the scale was however different: it was suited for using small areas as "cells of development" to revitalize a whole urban area/region (see also Kauko 2015).

to provide sufficiently green spaces and public footpaths and communal areas? When attempting to answer these questions, we should develop well-founded arguments about economic, social, cultural and environmental long-term implications for the affected area and its current and future property stock. The successes then depend on how well the local conditions are understood by the analyst. Neighborhood revitalization is therefore ideally examined from the vantage point of individual real estate management plans and best practices.

As already suggested, this is a bottom-up approach based on improvement of individual buildings and sites, as opposed to a top-down approach typical for using the town-plan as a starting point (cf. Kauko 2015). The idea here is that by improving individual units of real estate, also the whole area will be improved as a consequence, although this will take time and proceed piece-by-piece. As units of real estate comprise both building and site, and as value is also derived from its immediate surroundings, this involves a three step thought procedure as follows:

1. How could the *building* be improved best, so as to facilitate an optimal functional aptness and maximization (or merely protection) of value? This might mean change in use and designing new features, or it might mean protection of existing use and features. And what about the security and safety aspect? Recently fear of crimes has grown and one main reason has to do with uncontrolled immigration, ghettoization and terrorism threats (Kauko 2018).
2. As *on-site* amenities are vital for the quality and value of any unit of real estate, how could the site (i.e., front garden and backyard for built property) be improved best, so as to enable swift logistics and also provide a pleasant recreational space for its occupants and users (without forgetting the above mentioned safety/security aspect)?
3. As also *off-site* location matters significantly for the ease of use and creation of value, how could the vicinity be improved as well? How this takes place is depending on the specific micro-location,

but here two main features can be singled out: amount of green space surrounding the site and the traffic arrangements leading to the site. Are there any kind of nuisance factors (i.e., negative externalities, as will be discussed further below)? If yes, can these be abated? And above all: how to coordinate the suggested improvements with neighboring property owners?

These three levels of analysis define the limits of a real estate oriented approach, where urban planning and policy processes constitute necessary constraints as well as opportunities. These processes, in turn, relate to a number of environmental, social, cultural, behavioral, economic, legal and administrative goals, at least partly uniting them. While this conceptualization takes its starting point in the individual property owner's choice, also neighborhood revitalization and urban regeneration initiatives, including decorations, planting trees and vegetation, partially pedestrian streets and similar small-scale measures, play an inevitable role in shaping the built environment at the micro-level. Many of these issues concern the balance of seemingly opposite ideals on how urban planning is meant for the common good; it can be about development or protection of something, and about tangible or intangible factors. In other words: we have to evaluate different arguments when looking at current and anticipated state of affairs. The following check list of sustainability criteria is suitable for our purposes:

- Environmental-ecologic[6]: modern or eco-certified buildings, durable construction materials, reuse of old building materials, brownfield site, recycling of waste, accessibility by bicycle and public transport, amount of green areas, car parks, clean premises and air, safety against threat from environmental hazards, walkability (on-site), and similar criteria.

---

[6] Whilst acknowledging that these two dimensions are essentially different, they tend to be "lumped together" in much of built environment studies.

- Economic-financial: Stable value uplift due to high quality, diverse or mixed character of functions, favoring local producers or artisans, use of *economies of scale* to promote affordable prices, *hi-tech* and ICT based convenience, transparency of the land and property development process, financial self-sufficiency, negotiation of lease terms (e.g., for sublets), and similar criteria.
- Cultural: Preservation and awareness of the local heritage and history, strong *sense of place,* aesthetic design or natural elements, fit with surroundings and the rest of the area in terms of style, supporting local artists and traditions, and similar criteria.
- Social: Social cohesion and inclusiveness (fit or isolation in demographic terms), asocial behavior, children's playgrounds, leisure and recreational opportunities, safety against crime and assault, security and surveillance measures, accessibility of transport links, and similar criteria.

From this list the social factors are singled out for particular focus in what follows. Within this group of attributes collected for empirical research purposes, the relatively straightforward local safety and security issues are often separated from the more nuanced understandings of "a sense of belonging to a place associated with the identity of the place" due to ostensibly different theoretical underpinnings (e.g., Del Giudice et al. 2019). However, as it stands, the amount of discussions surrounding this aspect is often contradictory and confused. Many viewpoints become quickly politicized, be it about followers of a mainstream liberal narrative of "business as usual" or a radical leftist vision of utopia. Against this backdrop, a valid analysis of what necessary needs to be done in a given location is elusive, albeit necessary.

The Social Side Reassessed

Apparently, the recent omnipresent push for increased "diversity and equality management" in both corporations and government has not yet been subject to rigorous scrutiny within academia.[7] At any rate, diversity is a complex feature, in relation to individuals and neighborhoods (Skovgaard Nielsen and Hedegaard Winther 2020). As we have seen in 2020 across American – and to a lesser extent Western European – cities, the manifestations of accelerated "diversity developments" are seen in massive conflicts and urban pathologies involving rioting, violence and looting. While some diversity and equality surely is beneficial, insofar as it enhances the adaptability of the business, it may be that investments in diversity promoting activities are taken from more productive investment areas. So, if that is the case, how to make sure that such actions do not hamper technological development? After all, some 50 years ago, NASA managed to get a man on the moon without diversity or equality policies. We have to accept that innovativeness cannot be forced by political actions. The cart should not be put before the horse here.

This example illustrates the latent perceptions of any kind of job environment. The real estate industry is no exception here; business functions rooted in tacit knowledge – as opposed to codified knowledge – inevitably need to be taken into consideration too, if corporate goals are to be met. So we need to find out what various core actors such as stakeholders and network strategists write, say and think about given issues, and how this can be framed in a favorable way. This exactly is the essence of social innovation also within the property development context.

As already stated, the broader methodological proposition here is structured around an alternative approach to real estate analysis. This approach is furthermore aimed at deconstructing the current hegemony of multiculturalism and racial egalitarianism.[8] This need arises from the apparent failures of this hegemony to recognize the relevant causalities and factual juxtapositions. When pursuing this research strategy, a realist

---

[7] Unfortunately, the fact is that we cannot find any egalitarian societies in the history of mankind, be it capitalist, socialist or ancient kinds. It is about sheer utopian egalitarian ideology, as part of the cultural subversion experienced in the last three or four decades in the West. (Social engineering of divisiveness, in the spirit of Marxism, of course.)

[8] Curiously, a recent study shows that leftist politics is positively correlated with mental illnesses (Kirkegaard 2020).

position is argued for, rather than an increasingly fashionable relativist one. This is motivated by the growing safety concerns in urban areas in both Europe and North America, under the threat of unhinged mass-immigration from developing countries. While lots of demographic, social and political processes – notably support for people-smugglers and leniency against perpetrators of violent crimes – are working against this concern, it is never too late to raise one's voice. Some urban scholars already foresee this change in attitudes of urban managers, who, in the wake of the "European immigrant crisis" 2015, increasingly have begun to contest and even reject multicultural promotion policies (Cianetti 2020)[9].

In general, the balance between surveillance technology and reasonable trust in government amid crisis situations much decides the way loyalties consolidate within diverse communities (cf. Harari 2020; Kotkin 2020). The real estate industry is by no means immune from these influences. Developers and appraisers need to tackle issues of social and behavioral character, in fact, by definition, as the valuation and development decisions are made by various groups of managers and experts. Several specific considerations must then be addressed, one of which refers to the safety of a given site or building. Of course, social innovations and digitalization are both needed to deal with security concerns. And in doing so, implications for both human and property rights emerge – with the former more abstract than the latter.

It is important to realize that even in the case of the social side of urban property development viability, any improvements do not happen quickly. The theoretical approach taken assumes that the spaces between individual sites or buildings would be transformed, on the basis of the people moving around there. And this, in turn, would be determined by the nature of the transactions taking place in the said sites or buildings. To a certain extent, this is of course optimistic thinking, in so far as the assumption is about a shared will to keep an area well maintained. Unfortunately, the scenario is

---

[9] As Cianetti (2020, 2709) puts it: '… from a supposed "multicultural consensus" to a refocusing on "community cohesion" and "diversity advantage" …'

likely to turn negative, if such an assumption does not hold. This delicate balance of issues is examined next.

REAL ESTATE ANALYTICS CONCERNING CRIME AND SAFETY

Fear of Safety

In general, social nuisance (negative externality), crime and immigrant ghettoes tend to have a negative impact on the way an urban area is evaluated by prospective in-movers, investors and tourists. The discourse surrounding these issues concerns the perceptions of safety of cities, and allows combining the real estate relevant analytics with views of the people affected. The issue of safety and security of our home environments is indeed vital, regardless of the stand taken by the analyst.

For example, considering some of the multicultural development in Western Europe, I feel rather safe in my country of residence, Hungary, which is a country where rather strict anti-immigrant rhetoric and policies are used (in particular, since the "immigrant crisis" begun in 2015). Part of the reason is, in fact, exactly about the need to protect the original citizens in the country. Besides the increased attractiveness of such an environment, the restrictive immigrant policies also tend to come with the added benefit of saving tax-payer's money from having to fund policies of preempting terrorism and combatting other violent threats.

Unless "actual thinking" is replaced by ideology, a safe living environment from which potential troublemakers are excluded would be a commonsense goal for most people. Is it not true that, despite the recent multiculturalist dogma, the ethnically homogeneous societies provide the safest environments for their residents? To guard such an environment, some degree of authoritarian state is required, which obviously then is bound to generate confrontations with those who have opposite opinions.[10] So the dividing issue is about which goal has stronger weight: the safety of the original residents or multicultural tolerance of prospective residents. The logical goal versus its utopian counterpart.

The current realist-pragmatist oriented theory on this issue is already sufficiently abundant to make claims on academic fora. Authoritarian regimes are typically also more ethnically homogeneous than their diverse libertarian – or just liberal – counterparts (cf. Putnam 2007; Dinesen et al. 2019; Kauko 2019a, 2020a,b). In the sense of Putnam's concept of trust, the more authoritarian, homogeneous environment has a greater degree of trust between its residents. And this implies a greater feeling of safety and security against theft and violence, too. The literature also suggests that a lesser racial or ethnic diversity tends to indicate locational desirability, and that the improved crime and community conditions that follow from this will further lead to increased residential satisfaction (e.g., Chapman and Lombard 2006).

In this vein, many predict that, in the foreseeable future of American social life and politics, race is going to be the main dividing issue (cf. Abrajano and Hajnal 2015; Jardina 2019). And indeed, distinctive "races" – including a self-conscious "white race" – whether offensive or not.When original residents move away of an area in fear of their safety (and property values), the phenomenon is known as *white flight*.[11] Tipping points for white flight from an area are said to occur when 20% of an area becomes populated by ethnic groups – this is known as the *Schelling hypothesis* (e.g., Fossett and Waren 2005). In USA this has been evident since the Civic Rights movement in 1960s, when blacks begun to move into hitherto white neighborhoods, thereby causing an unfavorable change in image, if not actual decline of the area, thereby scaring off some of the original residents.

---

[10] This characterization pertains to most of present day social science and humanities oriented academia, as MacDonald (2010) and Fosse and Gross (2012) testify.

[11] Wessel and Nordvik (2019) use the concept of "native out-mobility" as a broader category than "white flight" which they consider associated with cities in the USA.

In general, neighborhood factors influence the decision-making process of households in relation to the balance of "push" and "pull" factors. For example, housing choice voucher recipients (i.e., a federal low-income household mobility strategy in the USA) express concerns about the stress neighborhood violence places on them, and how neighborhood factors constrain their housing choice (Graves 2019). This phenomenon does not only cause a reduction of property value, but also a corresponding decrease in residential satisfaction with living in that place (cf. Chapman and Lombard 2006). In spatially oriented microeconomics, such issues can be put under the umbrella concept of "negative social externalities" contributed to poorly compatible adjacent or nearby land-uses.

Negative Social Externalities in Urban Areas

Urban economic theory has put a heavy significance on negative social externalities as a price influencing attribute since this research tradition begun in the 1970s. In principle, property valuation does involve identification and – whenever possible – quantification of social nuisance factors defined as nearby locations and aspects in the neighborhood that residents deem undesirable. The most usual approximations of negative social externalities in studies with economic and geographic foci cover social housing projects nearby (Laakso 1997), other perceived nuisance caused by antisocial behavior nearby (Kauko 2010; Kauko and d'Amato 2012) and share (in per cents) of ethnic and racial groups in an area (Smets and Kreuk 2008; Permentier et al. 2008; Wessel et al. 2017). In practice, these concerns are often related; for example, a local government might opt for a theoretically justified and ostensibly well-meaning socio-spatial mixing of different forms of housing, but end up with exodus of the original residents, combined with an erosion of value suffered by the adjacent property owners.[12] So this effect is broad and closely related to white flight.

Unfortunately, the kind of data required for such analysis is still not sufficiently openly accessible, even in the most advanced circumstances (e.g., Rokem and Vaughan 2019). Besides such more technical issues, the nature of these influences is still controversial, as many analysts argue that it is the general concentrated disadvantage that matters, rather than any kind of particular neighborhood factor (Lens 2013). Nevertheless, local experts tend to be familiar with the presence of such harms, one way or another, and also a prior study by this author showed that social factors at the neighborhood level, including negative externalities such as robbery and assault, were important for prospective residents in given market segments – this being in the Netherlands and Finland (Kauko 2006,a,b).

In this vein, we can make an empirical observation in relation to the prices of homes in disadvantaged neighborhoods populated with multicultural immigrants. Namely, some areas will have zero value, due to the fact that no prospective home buyer – or even renter – wants to live there anymore. Obviously, with luck, the owners can sell such flats as asylum centers, which is fair enough, but what is the new property value going to be then? Probably zero. The message to valuation experts here is that no valuation automata will help in valuing these cases. It is clear that this effect has the tendency to reduce property values – not just in the case of the subject property, but in the whole surrounding area. Such a detrimental effect on property value is real and can be analyzed in the context of both economics and psychology (Kauko 2019a, 2020a,b). Thus, this effect on property value is partly "purely" economic and partly psychological; in other words, determined on one hand by the market, and on the other hand by emotional and motivational factors (cf. Laakso 1998; Kauko and d'Amato 2012; Grum and Kobal Grum 2014; Forte et al. 2018).

[12] As such, this is the development in the City of Helsinki, Finland, since 1990s. More recently, the effect is exacerbated due to the strong advocacy of refugees and immigrants of African and Asian origin, and their relatively high share within the city's social housing sector. The relatively unconstrained spatial allocation of social housing is assisted by the high share of municipal landownership.

Asylum centers indeed comprise a special case in this set of social nuisance factors. Recent experiences at the external borders of Europe testify to this complex NIMBY problem (see Pechlidou et al. 2020). What matters here is how renters and buyers *perceive* this threat, rather than the factual situation. (So whether or not the occupants of the asylum center are harmless is irrelevant from a market point of view.) Demand falls as a result of unfavorable perceptions, and property prices are determined by demand in the short term. This reduction in nearby property values and rents is obvious, as this price change depends on preferences of potential buyers or renters for avoiding such locations.

Empirical studies on this particular effect are elusive, however. In a spatially extended hedonic study from the Netherlands, Theebe (2002) found that this effect was not generally significant, but that it showed up sporadically. So that the type of asylum center and particular location matter for whether such effect is identifiable or not. More recently, this negative externality effect was also noted in a questionnaire survey of real estate agents in Finland: 86 per cent of the respondents considered an asylum center the single most serious negative effect on property value (Talouselämä 2017). The reasons are obvious: Finland experienced an unexpected and unprecedented influx of 30,000 refugees via Sweden in 2015 (e.g., Viren 2017). We can speculate that this figure probably was lower earlier.

When evaluating the tradition of empirical property value impact analysis, a caveat is in place. It is namely possible that the hypothesized price effect is contributed to a more general latent influence than any particular negative externality. To give an example, Navarro and Ruther (2020) concluded that a general "social disorganization in the community" and unobserved neighborhood characteristics are more likely to influence the house prices than the particular hypothesized price effect, in this case, contributed to the presence of registered sex-offenders. It is also likely that, in circumstances where the influence of immigrants on the housing market is assessed, the observed price reduction may be a consequence of the low spending power of the occupants, rather than result of a socially determined effect (Forte et al. 2018).

Crime and Its Prevention

Evidently, even in comparatively safe circumstances crime rates and sense of security are connected (Hino et al. 2016). Nevertheless, traditionally crime used to be a neglected topic within real estate analysis. Therefore, Buck and Hakim (1990) set out to investigate if crime reduces property prices. For their case-study they picked a region known for its casino gambling industry, as this activity was seen as something that, despite its positive effect on prices via the amenity side of increased entertainment opportunities, has a dis-amenity side, via the tendency to increase crime or perceptions thereof – the net effect on price then being either positive or negative. Using statistics of property prices from 63 localities in the Atlantic City region, New Jersey, from a period of 15 years (five years prior to casinos and ten-years post-casinos), Buck and Hakim found out that this indeed was the case for all other crimes, except for larcenies. The suggested policy implication here was to intensify the use of resources to prevent crime, so that local economy would be strengthened. Thus, economic growth and crime reduction go hand in hand.

Unfortunately, not too much has changed since the findings by Buck and Hakim. While various design and management solutions for using the built environment have been tested to combat crime, this tradition promotes only "soft" approaches to tackle serious safety and security problems (see e.g., Hollander and Whitfield 2005; Kajalo and Lindblom 2015; Cozens and Tarca 2016). In this literature the issue is about finding acceptable means, rather than justifying the ends. (A sample of these studies is presented below.)

Chapman and Lombard (2006) carried out statistical analysis on fee-based residential communities based on the American Housing Survey (2003, more than 55,000 units). Some of this form of housing comprises gated communities which they compared with non-gated units. Their findings suggest that neighborhood satisfaction ratings depend, among others, on the lack of knowledge of crime by the residents in the neighborhood. The authors estimated the contemporary share of fee-based housing units in the USA as 10-18 per cent and growing. Chapman and

Lombard also suggested that crime is a recurrent theme, and that inhabitants do tend to consider added security measures. Part of this is about the amicability of neighbors too. As for policy implications of this literature, the issue is as to how the police force keep residents aware (but not fearful) of crimes in their area.

Youssef (2015) found that residents of single-access neighborhoods have a stronger "sense of seclusion" than their counterparts in open grid neighborhoods. His study based on interviews concluded that this further lead to stronger "sense of neighborhood cohesion" among the residents. He concluded that establishing a "sense of identity" depends on having "a clear boundary for a neighborhood", even though this ideal would contradict the officially promoted concept of local sustainability.

In general, a "sense of safety" is, as a rule, an important determinant of neighborhood satisfaction and housing choice for residents in present Western context, and controlling the access via the entry point to the neighborhood is here a relevant issue (Youssef, 2015). Other aspects exist too. While the existence of some aspect of negative social externality and problems of extreme diversity in urban populations is universal across larger cities in Western countries, this effect is however context dependent in terms of exact location within an urban area. To see the tipping point for white flight is difficult, when promoting inclusive diversification of communities (i.e., to strengthen their adaptability and innovativeness potential) towards a dangerous situation with establishing risky urban zones in combination with poorly thought policies (i.e., open border, allowing a parallel society with sharia law, police defunding, leaving juvenile perpetrators unpunished and the establishments of no-go areas). So here are several plausible trajectories and variables involved.

In this vein, the presence of low-income housing developments alone, as an isolated feature, is not responsible for high crimes; it is rather a mix of development and neighborhood characteristics (Skubak Tillyer and Walter 2019). Besides, whether design based solutions are appropriate is rather debatable, in so far as changing the layout and adding fencing can leave a more traditional urban environment disfigured (Beghdoud et al. 2018). Elsewhere, Coaffee (2017) advocates an inclusive "security-driven urban resilience" policy approach at the local level, rather than relying on design solutions or state-based solutions alone. This, at least, is a pragmatic (i.e., rather than purist) approach that captures the main issues at stake.

In the case of USA, after a decline in violent crime rate from the early 90s to the early 2010s, violent crime has begun rising again, and fear of crime and terrorism remains as high as ever (Sampson 2019). Moreover, various equal opportunity policies are likely to have devastating consequences for ordinary citizens, California's Proposition 47 being a case in point. This "public safety realignment" measure meant leniency in penalties for minor larcenies, but as a result, it increased property crimes during the four years observed after it was passed by the voters in 2014 (Bird et al. 2018).[13]

At any rate, the security situation cannot remain satisfactory as long as potentially dangerous groups are allowed to coexist in the spatial proximity of the law-abiding residential populace. Furthermore, as much of recent safety problems are commonly perceived to be a consequence of too lax immigration policy (e.g., van der Woude et al. 2017), best practices, essentially, would focus on immigration, and necessarily, race and ethnicity. The main message here is that we need policy about stemming unsustainable immigration streams; otherwise we find ourselves in the middle of serious problems – both social and economic ones. We also need to remind ourselves that residents tend to leave crime ridden areas, in accordance with white flight predictions, if they have the financial means to do so.

Non-White Overrepresentation in Crime

The way ethnic riots are being created and explained away by elites (i.e., the "grievance" culture traditions) provides backup for the realist argument of strenghtening the security apparatus. As the brief failed

[13] Again, one may predict heavy fallout from the law enforcement defunding tendencies being implemented.

CHAZ/CHOP experiment in Seattle in June 2020 proves, urban areas *do* need policing. Despite the goodwill of city management, there was no automatic "summer of love" (using Seattle Mayor Jenny Durkan's words), but chaos and violence (including a fatal shooting) erupted soon after the anarchist mob had declared the Capital Hill area in central Seattle autonomous. For a couple of weeks this six block area was declared off-limits for the police force, and guarded by external paramilitaries (presumably related to BLM movement, in itself controversial, of course). In the end, the police force was ordered to retake the lawless area. The liberal mass media endorsed the protest movement at first, but since then, to avoid further embarrassmcnet, decided to cover this incident sparsely. Interestingly, business owners in the area promptly sued the police for abandonment. This was an unprecendeted case.[14]

Especially in the USA ethnic violence is a persistent problem with longstanding institutional focus. The narratives are however of two different kinds, depending on the perspective one wishes to observe the violence from: political correctness requirements or what actually happens in reality. So if different racial groups are unable to live in total harmony, whose fault is it? Who is the perpetrator and who is the victim here? Curiously, unlike anti-minority hate-crimes which tend to occur in more advantaged and organized places, anti-white hate-crimes and motivations for anti-white victimization occur mostly in disorganized neighborhoods with high overall levels of violent crime and high proportion of black residents (Drakulich 2019).

Statistics on interracial violent crime incidents in USA are published by the Bureau of Justice Statistics (2018, table 14). The data is partitioned into six categories for all permutations between white, black and Hispanic populations, On the basis of this evidence, the reality of ethnic group-on-group violence is not what the mainstream media and liberal-leftist academia wants us to believe. Namely, the black group is nine times more likely to attack the white group, than *vice versa*. Because of the current trends in political correctness and constructed non-white victimhood, this

[14] Mayor Durkan was subsequently asked to resign due to incompetence.

fact is not heard often. Instead, the false claim of blacks being overrepresented in violence is upheld.

In USA, blacks are, indeed, overrepresented in general crime statistics, too (Cooper and Smith 2011; Rubenstein 2016). Based on statistics from over a decade ago, despite only comprising 13% of the population, blacks commit over half of the crimes in the USA (Cooper and Smith, 2011). Now ten years later, in the wake of the BLM initiated defunding of police, crime in biggest American cities is going up dramatically. The threat of violent black gangs and criminals is more real than ever in many urban areas there. Americans also fear for the increased arming of BLM, considering all the financial support transferred to them by multinational corporations recently. However, these concerns are not aired in mainstream media or academia, as the spirit is that we should not let the truth distort a good narrative.

Immigrant Overrepresentation in Crime

As scholars and researchers, we should acknowledge that both *pro* and *con* views against the ongoing "immigrant crisis" are legitimate, and that the reason this contribution subscribes to the latter has to do with recent well-documented experiences in support of such a stance.[15] Given the rise in anti-immigrant sentiments in Europe, whether or not ethnic diversity represents a tangible threat to the existing residents of neighborhoods, remains a research topic of urgency (van Heerden and Ruedin 2019). Arguably, these sentiments are justified by the fact that immigrants are overrepresented in violent criminal activity. The reality is that the mostly uneducated economic migrants from countries in Africa and Middle East are overrepresented as perpetrators of violent and sexual crime by a factor of up to 40 depending on specific circumstances and ethnic background

[15] We could perhaps add here that, according to this line of argumentation, the right to safe living environment is universal and therefore trumps United Nation's limited human rights declarations.

(Jonasson 2017; Kauko 2019a, 2020a,b; cf. Salmi et al. 2015). It is also to note that, in some European countries, this overrepresentation of ethnic immigrant groups, including those of second generation, has increased strongly in the last decade or two – Sweden being worst hit in this respect (Bergman 2019).

In the case of Sweden, even the absolute number of crimes committed by first or second generation immigrants has exceeded the corresponding figure of native perpetrators, despite the latter group still representing approximately two-thirds of the total population (Engellau 2019). Malmö, where gang related shootings and explosions have become worryingly frequent, is often seen as the worst city in whole Europe in this respect, even if having only 320,000 inhabitants (Jönsson 2019).[16] We may also explain this trend by the increase in refugees – as opposed to immigrants in general – as evidence from comparable situations elsewhere (Lower Saxony in Germany) suggests (Pfeiffer et al. 2017). Generally speaking, especially immigrants from Middle East and Africa, many of whom are of "refugee" or "unauthorized" status, are far more likely to commit violent crimes than what the indigenous population of their host countries in Europe are. In what follows, we examine some of the implications of this overrepresentation.

Obviously, juvenile crime and violent street gangs have existed long before any mass migration begun (at least, when speaking about modern day volumes). However, in those days just about everyone, at least in public, shared the values of the society at large, as communities were structured in a strongly mono-cultural fashion. Currently, the situation is completely the opposite, as gangs roaming the streets are composed of people of rather different ethnic background and, in some cases, religion. In brief, juvenile perpetrators of crime do not have the same moral standards as the majority of the community any more. This means unavoidable social conflicts and socially unsustainable urban communities.

---

[16] The corresponding situation in neighboring countries is none too different: Denmark (Danmarks statistik (2018); Norway (Andersen et al. 2017).

And with changing demographics, the white indigenous populations are increasingly becoming the underdogs in these conflicts.

The cases of violent crimes perpetrated by immigrants from developing countries, including terrorism, have in recent years reached such an extent that this problem is impossible to brush under the carpet anymore. Furthermore, second generation immigrants of certain ethnic groups tend to have a higher crime rates than their first generation immigrant counterparts of same ethnicity (Vazsonyi and Killias 2001; Cho 2019). When looking at specifically European cities with high levels of immigrant crime (Paris, Brussels, Malmö, in particular), the perpetrators can even be third – and probably even fourth – generation immigrants. And often these populations comprise only Muslims from Africa and Asia. Inevitably, the increasing presence of such a population then leads to white flight out of the neighborhood and, eventually, the whole urban area.

The facts listed above indeed suggest a bleak prognosis for urban safety at large. However, the possibilities of correcting the trend are not totally diminished yet; we can still find optimistic reasons for turning the course. At the neighborhood level, the collective effects of immigration on violence are complex and mediated by the strength of friendship and kinship networks, showing both positive and negative influences (Feldmeyer et al. 2019). While the effects described above, in many cases, are associated with real harms, it may well be that in some circumstances the specific influences of ethnicity and immigration are drowned out by the more general, classical location-based influences on urban residential mobility and property value such as accessibility and physical qualities. Nonetheless, certain presumptions tend to hold, for example, that the racial and ethnic demographic composition and the socioeconomic ascent of neighborhoods are found to be associated features in the USA (Owens and Candipan 2019). It can also be noted that, in the wake of the contested US election 2020, concerns about how liberal immigration restrictions are likely to deteriorate public safety are apparently as topical as ever (Herman 2020).

CONCLUSION

One's preferred living environment may or may not be multicultural, but it has to be safe and secure enough. This chapter has dealt with how individual residents and occupants of workplaces can feel safe in their everyday life. Ideally, neighbors share community values, and it is in everyone's interest to reproduce a safe inclusive space[17]. However, in the current situation of social and political chaos this might require a strong institutional security apparatus, after all, instead of any defunding of police. If necessary, potentially violent criminals and rioters should be excluded from such a community. This requires a relatively authoritarian approach, regardless of its current meta-political unfashionability.

The *Islands of Property Management* approach singles out the relevant influences and scales of market transaction related to (re)development or refurbishment – and more broadly: the management of built structures and their adjacent space. Of all such possible influences, a contribution that earnestly deals with social factors is still an undertheorized topic in this field. None the less, real estate values do fall, to a great extent, because of social factors. White flight and urban decay occur because of social factors. That prices and rents fall, and prosperous inhabitants move out of urban areas, reduce the attractiveness of such places, and inevitably, lead to the erosion of tax revenue of the local government.

The social factors brought up here are, depending on the circumstances, usually understood as compromised safety concerns related to a place-specific combination of black ghetto culture and mass immigration from the developing world. In this context non-whites are a real threat for whites, and not *vice versa*. To say this openly is politically incorrect, of course, even blasphemous, so we need courage to point this out. (One might even be tempted to draw parallels with Galileo here.)

Evidently race is going to be the main dividing socio-political issue of our times. What it boils down to is the ability of someone to fit in with the

---

[17] Not to be confused with the "new left lingua" concept of "safe spaces".

dominant community – or, without looming conflicts, communities – in a given neighborhood. The groups with the biggest difficulty to integrate into a functional Western society are the blacks (in the USA) and the Muslims (in Europe). The former due to their victimization status in current establishment-driven progressive liberal discourse; the latter due to their fanatic nepotism. We can therefore argue that it is the minorities who should accommodate themselves to majorities; not *vice versa*. This argument used to be completely common sense, and should still be, but is not anymore.

Considering the rising tensions between different racial and ethnic communities, and contrary to the politically correct declarations we have to face, diversity – currently an euphemism for forced increasing of the amount of people of color – is not a strength. At least not unconditionally. Namely, different races tend to have rather different endowments, interests and expectations. White people thrive in a society established by themselves. The same applies for other races. Because of this omnipresent preference for similarity, mixing can only work as long as major conflicts and scarcity situations can be avoided. Therefore, to establish a threshold point for "optimal diversity", akin to *Pareto optimality* in welfare economics, could be helpful in solving these problems.

The main issue here is that diversity does not improve societies, if promoted to an untenable point. The untenable point is where the Putnamian trust within a given community of neighbors or coworkers ceases to exist. This is because, past this point, the shared values among the members of the community have been eroded, due to mixing groups that are too different. In other words, the "glue" that is keeping the trust in place: family, religion, ethnicity, race or similar socio-cultural category, has lost its binding power, if not disappeared altogether. Why is that the case? Are we not equal, after all, and therefore able to live together trustfully and in great harmony?

The problem is the loss of sense of familiarity, which, by implication, also means a loss of trust. And the loss of trust might also escalate to a loss of safety, so to an increased feeling of insecurity. A law-abiding person is well adviced to avoid potential encounters with hoodlums, especially where these form groups. We have seen in the news lately what gangs of frustrated angry young men can do. In the final analysis, the ones who have the most to lose have the most reason to fear; and *vice versa*, those who are desperate, and do not have much to lose, may have a great enough incentive to commit crimes, to ofset the risk of being caught. This sense of group-oriented danger is something that also statistical data can corroborate, but for that we need to be able to approximate socio-economic status with ethnicity and race.

This chapter has also offered a starting point for a larger research undertaking on security concerns, where both social innovations and digitalization are addressed. In doing so, effects on both human and property rights need to be examined. Ideally, this quantifiable info – safety index composed of approximations for actual violent crime rate as well as percentages of certain ethnic or immigrant groups who are overrepresented in violent crime – could also be plugged into an alternative property development viability approach. Thus, to enable a socially innovative platform for "place livability", where the set of elements included – safety, security, trust, homogeneity, perception of crime, lack of nuisances and so forth – would replace their established, corporate counterparts based on promotion of tolerance, diversity and multicultural mixing.

The research also aspires to contribute to new urban theory where safety aspects and crime prevention is at the core. Such an endeavor would incorporate both territorial competition and social sustainability discourses. It would also generate a number of policy suggestions about how the urban safety of existing residents and businesses could be ensured amid a situation of potentially hazardous in-moving patterns. And once more, we must recognize that, on both sides of the Atlantic, crime indeed has an ethnic – and racial – dimension.

However, at the same time, we must bolster our thesis against the typical lazy accusations of "racism" or "white supremacy" which, unfortunately, serious minded academics today have to confront. This can be done conveniently by pointing out that such accusations would be moral, as opposed to scientific, rational or factual evidence based. As such, how the right to a safe place would relate to judgements of "racism" is not clear-cut at all. While the concept of "racism" is morally suspicious and metaphysical, rather than scientific, biologically this whole critique is point-less; indeed, what we today call "racism" might even be necessary for the survival of any organism, including humans.

In the spirit of Jardina's (2019) eloquent argumentation, humans are tribal creatures, when push comes to shove.[18] We cannot ignore deeper instincts programmed into us, despite our cognitively developed brain functions. In a crisis situation, cognitive higher level "learnt" behavior is forgotten, and replaced by simpler neural processes. So the thin crust of altruism disappears; instead, we just favor our own kin, or reasonable similarity, the very least. By implication, what by today's standards is "racism", becomes the norm, as with all animals including humans. From a public choice perspective, the logical assertion [sic] would then be that, if we really live in a "racist" reality, as so often heard, we would need representatives of this "silent majority" of "racist" communities to decide about how we develop our built environments – and not just physically, but socially too.

REFERENCES

Abrajano, M., and Hajnal, Z. (2015). *White Backlash: Immigration, Race, and American Politics*. Princeton: Princeton University Press.

Ahmed, K. G. (2011). Evaluation of Social and Cultural Sustainability in Typical Public House Models in Al Ain, UAE. *International Journal of Sustainable Development Planning*, 6(1): 49–80.

Andersen, S. N., Holtsmark, B. and Mohn, S. B. (2017). "*Kriminalitet blant innvandrere og norskfødte med innvandrerforeldre En analyse av registerdata for perioden 1992-2015,*" (in Norwegian) Statistics

[18] This principle of "favoring one's own kin" applies also conversely. For example, recent Jewish gentrifiers in New York would, wishfully, consider themselves socially constructed non-whites, but, nevertheless, end up being physically attacked by local black street-gangs – because of their visible "whiteness".

Norway, https://www.ssb.no/sosiale-forhold-og-kriminalitet/artikler-og-publikasjoner/_attachment/332143?_ts=16035d6f0d8 [accessed 18 November 2019].

Beghdoud, L. Kh., Kacemi, M., Tewfik Bouroumi, M. and Walid, H. (2018). Problems of urban violence: The case of Boulevard Macta in Sidi Bel Abbes. *Urbanism Architecture Constructions*, 9(1): 23–38.

Bergman, J. (2019). *Sweden Spinning out of Control*, Gatestone Institute, https://www.gatestoneinstitute.org/14819/sweden-crime [accessed 18 November 2019].

Bird, M., Lofstrom, M., Martin, B., Raphael, S., and Nguyen, V. (2018). "*The Impact of Proposition 47 on Crime and Recidivism*", PPIC, July, https://www.ppic.org/wp-content/uploads/r_0618mbr.pdf [accessed 3 December 2019].

Buck, A. J. and Hakim, S. (1990). Are Property Values Being Adversely Affected by Crime? *Journal of Property Valuation & Investment*, 9: 37–44.

Bureau of Justice Statistics (2018). *National Crime Victimization Survey,* USA.

Chapman, D. and Lombard, J. (2006). Determinants of Neighbourhood Satisfaction in Fee-Based Gated and Nongated Communities. *Urban Affairs Review*, 41(6): 769–799.

Cho, J. Y. (2019). Latino Nativity Variations Link to Street Violence in Drug Markets. *Crime & Delinquency*, 65(1): 69–93.

Cianetti, L. (2020). Governing the multicultural city: Europe's 'great urban expectations' facing austerity and resurgent nativism. *Urban Studies*, 57(13): 2697–2714.

Coaffee, J. (2017). A Balanced Response? The Quest for Proportionate Urban Security. *International Journal of Urban and Regional Research*, 41: 1–6.

Cooper, A. and Smith, B. L. (2011). "*Homicide Trends in the United States, 1980-2008,*" U.S. Department of Justice, https://www.bjs.gov/content/pub/pdf/htus8008.pdf [accessed 11 July 2020].

Cozens, P. and Tarca, M. (2016). Exploring housing maintenance and vacancy in Western Australia – Perceptions of crime and crime prevention through environmental design. *Property Management*, 34(3): 199–220.

Danmarks statistik (2018). *Invandrere I Danmark 2018*, (in Danish) https://www.dst.dk/da/Statistik/Publikationer/VisPub?cid=29445 [accessed 18 November 2019].

Del Giudice, V., De Paola, P., Torrieri, F., and Nijkamp, P. J., and Shapira, A. (2019). Real Estate Investment Choices and Decision Support Systems. *Sustainability*, 11, 3110.

Dinesen, P. T., Schaeffer, M. and Sønderskov, K. M. (2019). Ethnic Diversity and Social Trust: A Narrative and Meta-Analytical Review, Preprint version. *Annual Review of Political Science*, 23.

Drakulich, K., Fay-Ramirez, S. and Benier, K. (2019). The Neighborhood Context of Perceived and Reported Anti-White Hate Crimes. *Race and Justice*: 1–19.

Dunse, N., Thanos, S. and Bramley, G. (2013). Planning policy, housing density and consumer preferences. *Journal of Property Research*, 30(3): 221–238.

Engellau, P. (2019). *Invandring och brottslighet – et trettioårsperspektiv,* (in Swedish) Stiftelsen Det Goda Samhället, https://detgodasam halletdotcom.files.wordpress.com/2019/06/rapport-om-invandring-och-brottslighet.pdf [accessed 18 November 2019]. [*Immigration and crime - a thirty-year perspective*]

Feldmeyer, B., Madero-Hernandez, A., Rojas-Gaona, C. E. and Copley Sabon, L. (2019). Immigration, Collective Efficacy, Social Ties, and Violence: Unpacking the Mediating Mechanisms in Immigration Effects on Neighborhood-Level Violence. *Race and Justice*, 9(2): 123–150.

Forte, F., Antoniucci, V. and De Paola, P. (2018). Immigration and the Housing Market: The Case of Castel Volturno, in Campania Region, Italy. *Sustainability*, 10: 343.

Fosse, E. and Gross, N. (2012). Why are Professors Liberal? *Theory and Society*, 41: 127–168.

Fossett, M. and Waren, W. (2005). Overlooked Implications of Ethnic Preferences for Residential Segregation in Agent-based Models. *Urban Studies*, 42(11): 1893–1917.

Grant, J. L. (2009). Theory and Practice in Planning the Suburbs: Challenges to Implementing New Urbanism, Smart Growth, and Sustainability Principles. *Planning Theory and Practice*, 10(1), March: 11–33.

Graves, E. (2019). Moving to Improve? A Qualitative Meta-analysis of Neighborhood Violence and Residential Decision-making among Housing Voucher Holders. *Journal of Planning Literature*, 34(1): 19–37.

Grum, B. and Kobal Grum, D. (2014). A model of real estate and psychological factors in decision-making to buy real estate. *Urbani izziv*, 26(1): 82–91.

Guy, S., Henneberry, J. and Rowley, S. (2002). Development Cultures and Urban Regeneration. *Urban Studies*, 39(7): 1181–1196.

Harari, Y. N. (2020) "The world after coronavirus," *Financial Times* (20 March), https://www.ft.com/content/19d90308-6858-11ea-a3c9-1fe6fedcca75 [accessed 23 May 2020].

Herman, M. (2020). "Biden's Immigration Policies Could Threaten Public Safety," *Newsmax* (25 November), https://www.newsmax.com/platinum/biden-immigration/2020/11/25/id/998748/ [accessed 28 November 2020].

Hino, K., Uesugi, M. and Asami, Y. (2016). Official Crime Rates and Residents' Sense of Security Across Neighbourhoods in Tokyo, Japan. *Urban Affairs Review*: 1–25.

Hollander, J. B. and Whitfield, C. (2005). The appearance of security zones in US cities after 9/11. *Property Management*, 23(4): 244–256.

Jardina, A. (2019). *White Identity Politics*. Cambridge, United Kingdom & New York, NY, USA: Cambridge University Press.

Jonasson, J. P. (2017). *Sexualbrottslighet bland män födda i Sverige och i utlandet – en medborgarstudie*, (in Swedish) https://pjjonasson.files.wordpress.com/2017/10/sexualbrottslighet_bland_man_fodda_i_s

verige_och_i_utlandet.pdf. [accessed 15 May, 2018]. [*Sexual crime among men born in Sweden and abroad - a civic study*]

Jönsson, H. (2019). "Abandoning Malmö to Its Criminals," *Quillette* (15 November), https://quillette.com/2019/11/15/abandoning-malmo-to-its-criminals/ [accessed 25 November, 2019].

Kajalo, S. and Lindblom, A. (2015). Creating a safe and pleasant shopping environment: a retailer's view. *Property Management*, 33(3): 275–286.

Kauko, T. (2004). Sign value, topophilia and house prices, *Environment and Planning A*, 36:5: 859–878.

Kauko, T. (2006a). What makes a location attractive for the housing consumer? Preliminary findings from metropolitan Helsinki and Randstad Holland using the analytical hierarchy process. *Journal of Housing and the Built Environment*, 21: 159–176.

Kauko, T. (2006b). Expressions of housing consumer preferences – a proposition for a research agenda, *Housing, Theory and Society*, 23(2): 92–108.

Kauko, T. (2010). Sustainable urban property development and neighbourhood dynamics, *The Open Urban Studies Journal*, 3: 103–111.

Kauko, T. (2015). Finding an apt strategy for (what we currently believe is) sustainable urban land use and area development. *Urbanism. Architecture. Constructions*, 6(3): 11–34.

Kauko, T. (2018). Time for the Urban Safety Discussion to Move On? *International Journal of Current Advanced Research*, 7:5(I): 12799–12800.

Kauko, T. (2019a). *Decline and Fall... or survival of Western Urbanity. Some thoughts on urban safety in a warming political climate*. Riga: LAP.

Kauko, T. (2019b). How to pick relevant sustainability criteria for the built environment: A bottom-up approach, *Urbanism. Architecture. Constructions*, 10(1): 5–16.

Kauko, T. (2020a). In search for a realistic perspective on urban safety: The attractiveness concerns caused by mass-immigration, *Urbanism. Architecture. Constructions*, 11(1): 17–32.

Kauko, T. (2020b). *Illusions of Wokeness and Western Urbanism. Some ruminations*. Riga: LAP.

Kauko, T. and d'Amato, M. (2012). "Neighbourhood effects." In *International Encyclopedia of Housing and Home,* (e-book) Elsevier, MS 166, 50–54.

Killias, M. (1989). Criminality among Second-Generation Immigrants in Western Europe: A Review of the Evidence. *Criminal Justice Review*, 14(1): 13–42.

Kirkegaard, E. O. W. (2020). "Mental illness and the left," *Mankind Quarterly* (February), (preprint).

Kotkin, J. (2020). "Viral Politics," *Quillette* (18 April), https://quillette.com/2020/04/18/viral-politics/ [accessed 28 April 2020].

Laakso, S. (1997). "*Urban Housing Prices and the Demand for Housing Characteristics*," Helsinki, The Research Institute of the Finnish Economy (ETLA).

Lehti, M., Salmi, V., Aaltonen, M., Danielsson, P. and others (2014). *Maahanmuuttajat rikosten uhreina ja tekijöinä,* [*Immigrants as crime victims and offenders in Finland, in Finnish*, with English summary] Oikeuspoliittisen tutkimuslaitoksen tutkimuksia 265.

Lens, M. C. (2013). Subsidized Housing and Crime: Theory, Mechanisms, and Evidence. *Journal of Planning Literature*, 28(4): 352–363.

Lützkendorf, Th, Fan, W. and Lorenz, D. (2011). Engaging financial stakeholders: opportunities for a sustainable built environment. *Building Research & Information*, 39(5): 483–503.

MacDonald, K. (2010). Why are Professors Liberals? *The Occidental Quarterly*, 10(2): summer: 57–87.

Manzi, T. Lucas, K., Lloyd-Jones, T. and Allen, J. (2010b). "Understanding Social Sustainability: Key Concepts and Developments in Theory and Practice." In Manzi, T., Lucas, K., Lloyd-Jones, T. and Allen, J. (eds.), *Social Sustainability in Urban Areas*, 1–28. London and Washington D.C.: Earthscan.

Marshall, I. H and Marshall, Ch. E. (1997). Immigrants, Crime and Prison Commitments in the Netherlands: A Time Series Analysis (1952-1988). *Criminal Justice Policy Review*, 8(1): 25–55.

Navarro, J. C. and Ruther, M. (2020). A geospatial analysis between the sale prices of single-family properties and the presence of registered sex offenders in Jefferson County, Kentucky. *Urban Studies*, 57(5): 944–958.

Owens, A. and Candipan, J. (2019). Racial/Ethnic Transition and Hierarchy Among Ascending Neighborhoods. *Urban Affairs Review*, 55(6): 1550–1578.

Pechlidou, E., Frangopoulos, Y. and Hatziprokopiou, P. (2020). "The spatial management of the "migration crisis" and local opposition: Public discourse, actors and reactions against refugee accommodation in Thessaloniki." In Markou, A. S. and Zlatkova, M. (eds), *Post-Urbanities, cultural reconsiderations and tourism in the Balkans*, 139–160. Athens: Hêrodotos.

Permentier, M., Van Ham, M. and Bolt, G. (2008). Same Neighbourhood … Different Views? A Confrontation of Internal and External Neighbourhood Reputations. *Housing Studies*, 23(6): 833–855.

Pfeiffer, Ch., Baier, D. and Kliem, S. (2017). *Erhebliche Sicherheit-slücken im deutschen Asylsystem*, (in German), BAMF. [*Considerable security gaps in the German asylum system*]

Putnam, R. (2007). *E Pluribus Unum*: Diversity and Community in the Twenty-first Century the 2006 Johan Skytte Prize Lecture. *Scandinavian Political Studies*, 30(2): 137–174.

Redfield & Wilton Strategies (2020). "A Majority of Britons Support Reinstating the Death Penalty for Terrorism Convicts," (17 July) https://redfieldandwiltonstrategies.com/a-majority-of-britons-support-reinstating-the-death-penalty-for-terrorism-convicts/ [accessed 27 July 2020].

Rokem, J. and Vaughan, L. (2019). Geographies of ethnic segregation in Stockholm: The role of mobility and co-presence in shaping the 'diverse' city. *Urban Studies*, 56(12): 2426–2446.

Rubenstein, E. S. (2016). *The Colour of Crime. Race, Crime and Justice in America*. Rev. ed. Oakton, VA: New Century Foundation.

Salmi, V., Kivivuori, J. and Aaltonen, M. (2015). Correlates of immigrant youth crime in Finland. *European Journal of Criminology*, 12(6): 681–699.

Sampson, R. J. (2019). *Neighbourhood effects and beyond:* Explaining the paradoxes of inequality in the changing American metropolis. *Urban Studies*, 56(1): 3–32.

Skovgaard Nielsen, R. and Hedegaard Winther, A. (2020). The complexity of diversity in reality: Perceptions of urban diversity, *Urban Studies*, 57(14): 2817–2832.

Skubak Tillyer, M. and Walter, R. (2019). Low-Income Housing and Crime: The Influence of Housing Development and Neighborhood Characteristics. *Crime & Delinquency*, 65(7): 969–993.

Smets, P. and Kreuk, N. (2008). Together or Separate in the Neighbourhood? Contacts Between Natives and Turks in Amsterdam. *The Open Urban Studies Journa*l, 1: 35–47.

Talouselämä (2017). *Kiinteistövälittäjille suunnattu kysely kertoo: Asunnon sijainti vastaanottokeskuksen lähellä voi pienentää myyntihintaa*, (in Finnish) (1 September) http://www.talouselama.fi/uutiset/kiinteistovalittajille-suunnattu-kysely-kertoo-asunnon-sijainti-vastaanottokeskuksen-lahella-voi-pienentaa-myyntihintaa-6673006 [accessed 13 September 2017]. [*A survey of real estate agents says: The location of an apartment near a reception center can reduce the selling price*]

Theebe, M. A. J. (2002). *Housing Market Risks*. PhD Thesis, University of Amsterdam. http://dare.uva.nl/search?arno.record.id=106654 [accessed 16 January 2017].

Tuan Y.-F. (1974). *Topophilia: A Study Of Environmental Perception, Attitudes, And Values*. PrenticeHall, Englewood Cliffs, NJ.

van der Woude, M, Barker, V. and van der Leun, J. (2017). Crimmigration in Europe. *European Journal of Criminology*, 14(1): 3–6.

van Heerden, S. and Ruedin, D. (2019). How attitudes towards immigrants are shaped by residential context: The role of ethnic diversity dynamics and immigrant visibility. *Urban Studies*, 56(2): 317–334.

Vazsonyi, A.T. and Killias, M. (2001). Immigration and crime among youth in Switzerland. *Criminal Justice and Behaviour*, 28(3): 329–366.

Viren, M.(2017). *Maahanmuutto – Talouden ongelma vai ongelmien ratkaisu?* (In Finnish), Suomen Perusta. [*Immigration - An Economic Problem or a Problem Solving?*]

Wallner, H.P., Narodoslawsky, M. and Moser, F. (1996). Islands of sustainability: a bottom-up approach towards sustainable development. *Environment and Planning A*, 28(19): 1763–1778.

Wessel, T., Andersson, R., Kauppinen, T. and Skifter Andersen, H. (2017). Spatial Integration of Immigrants in Nordic Cities: The Relevance of Spatial Assimilation Theory in a Welfare State Context. *Urban Affairs Review* 53(3): 812–842.

Wessel, T. and Nordvik, V. (2019). Mixed neighbourhoods and native out-mobility in the Oslo region: The importance of parenthood. *Urban Studies*, 56(5): 885–905.

Youssef, K. (2015). Single-Access Neighbourhoods and Neighbourhood Cohesion. *Critical Housing Analysis*, 2(2): 1–10.

In: The Future of Real Estate
Editor: Jan Veuger
ISBN: 978-1-53619-414-2

Chapter 7

IMPLEMENTATION OF LAND POLICY AT LOCAL LEVEL, AND IMPACTS OF THE FUNCTIONING OF THE REAL PROPERTY MARKET

Božena Lipej**, *PhD and Nastja Mihelj
European Faculty of Law, New University, Ljubljana, Slovenia

ABSTRACT

The central question of the research was whether land policy impacts the operation of the real property market at local level in Slovenia, specifically in the City Municipality of Nova Gorica (MONG). The research found that land policy is an important integral part of the social and economic system and the spatial planning policy; and it should function in conformity with other policies. When defining the land policy, its principles, objectives and instruments need to be taken into account. However, in this respect, it is required to make an analysis of the situation

---

* Corresponding Author's E-mail: bozena.lipej@gmail.com.

and trends in the areas of spatial planning, land transactions and land management. The research presents the results of the analysis of several spatial planning and real property market aspects over the period of the last 13 years in the MONG and its surrounding area of Gorica. They confirmed the research dilemma.

Keywords: building land compensation, City Municipality of Nova Gorica, construction permit, land policy, municipal spatial plan, public utility charge, real property market, Slovenia

INTRODUCTION

Land policy or land management is one of the key levers that enable the execution of spatial strategies and development programs. Land policy is important in creating spatial conditions for efficient real property management; it encourages a sustainable spatial development, and thereby ensures conditions for a coherent and comprehensive development of cities, towns and other residential areas. It constitutes an initial implementation policy of spatial planning in the territory of the municipality, and reduces unpredictable land management, which may be reflected in unpredictable spatial or socio-economic development. The purpose of land policy is to find a balance between public benefits and private interests (Ministrstvo za okolje in prostor, 2020b). Land policy is the initial implementing policy of spatial planning. If we wish to define land policy, we must consider its fundamental principles, objectives and instruments. Land policy implementation involves several measures which are used by municipalities and the state.

One of the professional bases for the making of land policy is the municipal spatial plan (MSP). In addition to the MSP, public utility charges and compensation for the use of building land are also relevant in this context. With the purpose of determining the volume of real property transactions and the realized sales prices of real property, we have also analyzed the real property market and the related issue of building permits.

The MONG is one of eleven urban municipalities in Slovenia, and the largest municipality in the Gorica region. In mid-2018, the MONG had a population of 31,690 and covered an area of 279 km^2 (Statistični urad Republike Slovenije, 2018).

LAND POLICY

Land policy refers to the organization and direction of specific circumstances in the area of land management and use, while also covering the decision-making about the measures required and their implementation, for the purpose of spatial management policy implementation as well as for the purpose of defining the rules and conditions for the operation of entities in the real property market. Land policy is an intervention of the state in the area of spatial policy implementation (such as urban and regional planning) or in the area of regulating conditions in the real property market (Virtanen, Verlaat, 1999). According to the UNECE (2005), land policy is concerned with using and conserving land so as to meet social and economic objectives. It works by establishing tangible private and public objectives for example by promoting equal access to property for all people while respecting the sensitivity of local needs and requirements. Land policy influences the ways in which the development of land is regulated, the revenue derived from the land (through sale, lease, taxation, fees, etc.), and how conflicts concerning the ownership and use of the land can be resolved. Deininger (2003) even discussed that, given the long-term nature of interventions in the area of land policy, integration into the broader development strategy is particularly relevant to provide a basis for relating land policy to other interventions. As presented by Davy (2012), land policy is the result of the choices and actions of policymakers, who contemplate land uses, public interests, and rights. The technical term for what connects the land uses, planning, and property is land policy.

Land policy may also create spatial conditions for efficient property management, and encourage prudent spatial development, thereby ensuring conditions for a compliant and comprehensive development of cities, towns and other residential areas. There is no comprehensive system for the implementation of land policy established in Slovenia, but there are specific, predominantly administrative, spatial measures. An active land policy may be implemented only if supported by mutually coordinated administrative, legislative, financial and spatial planning measures. (Kralj, 2014). Something similar was discovered by Palmer et al., (2009) recognizing that many countries do not have a comprehensive land policy; rather, they have different policies for different types of land and other natural resources: urban, agriculture, forestry, water, etc. As presented by Lipej (2015), the development of effective real estate management systems supports national and regional development and policies, including land policy, related to sustainable development and economic growth.

There are two approaches to the formation of land policy objectives. In the first approach, all possible objectives are systematically defined or at least identified, while in the second approach more specific problems that have been detected in the area of spatial and land management are identified at first. The first approach is more applicable at the macro level (strategic, political, national), and the second one fits more to the micro level (implementing, local) (Virtanen, Verlaat, 1999).

Land policy objectives are both specific and general. While specific objectives are subject to the space and time in which they are created, general objectives have a longer-term character and are not linked to the state, region or local community. The objectives which are directly connected to the growth and development of cities, may be (Weiβ, 2000):

- to obtain in a timely way appropriate land for the construction on behalf of the public or private interest;
- to ensure at minimum a quality and reliable supply of utilities for the population, conditions for a rational construction of municipal infrastructure, and for the provision of public utility services;
- to impact the direction of land settlement by direction and regulation of the real property market.

The way policy instruments are activated to achieve a certain policy goal can be conceived strategies of land policy. A strategy is thereby considered as a deliberate way of using (i.e., activating) instruments of land policy to achieve the policy goal. Strategies of land policy are often classified into passive and active land policy (Hartmann, Spit, 2015; Shahab et al., 2020). Municipalities have different instruments of land policy at their disposal, such as land readjustment, transferable development rights, private law instruments (such as contracts), or strategic land banking (Shahab et al., 2019; Gerber, J. D. (2018). The choice of policy instruments depends on the strategies decision makers adopt. Kobetic (2016) adds that land policy is a set of administrative and financial instruments intended for the implementation of emerging and valid spatial acts and other spatial development documents and efficient spatial management, especially by providing a sufficient fund of accessible building land and supporting public utility infrastructure.

The Ministry of Environment and Spatial Planning of the Republic of Slovenia develops instruments for the implementation of land policy, which observes and carries out spatial development and planning decisions through administrative and financial measures by ensuring efficient management with land as a resource. This enables satisfaction of the needs of the population, economy and other interests (Ministrstvo za okolje in prostor, 2019). With land policy measures, the state and the municipality, or several municipalities together, carry out the activities that enable the realization of spatial development objectives and steer the development of residential communities (ZureP-2, 2017).

There are several measures for the implementation of active land policy which municipalities and the state can use (gov.si, 2019):

- building land development: development stages, land development and land consolidation;
- land protection: construction works and consent to change the boundary of the plot;
- land acquisition and rights: supply plan, pre-emption right and expropriation;

- financial resources of the land policy: municipal contribution and tax for unused land;
- renovation and arrangement of the space: measures for renovation and maintenance order;
- use of public areas and built public good.

The MONG Municipal Spatial Plan

The MSP is the fundamental spatial implementing act of the municipality. With regard to the MSP, and within the scope of spatial planning, the municipality is authorized to determine the objectives and starting points of the spatial development of a municipality, defining spatial use and the conditions for spatial interventions, and planning of spatial arrangements that have a local significance (Ministrstvo za okolje in prostor, 2020a).

The strategic part of the MSP comprises the starting points and objectives of the municipality's spatial development. On the basis of the guidelines related to housing development, landscape development, and public infrastructure works layout, the strategic part presents the directions for the definition of land use. The implementing part specifies: land use, public infrastructure works, spatial implementing conditions and the areas for which they are prepared, as well as the guidelines for their making (Odlok o OPN, 2018). Pursuant to the directions contained in spatial strategic acts, and taking into account the regional regulations, land use is specified according to the physical properties of the land, and the planned use (ZUreP-2, 2017). Construction is only permitted on building plots. Outside the area of a building plot, construction is only possible to the extent permitted by law and decree (Odlok o OPN, 2018).

The implementation part of the MONG MSP must be taken into account when issuing building permits for the construction of facilities, in spatial planning and construction of less complex and complex structures, in changing the purpose of facilities and land use, and in other interventions (Odlok o OPN, 2018).

Table 1. Comparison of areas of basic land use in the MONG

Basic land use/Category	Municipal spatial plan in force until 2012		MSP since 2012	
	Area (ha)	Share (%)	Area (ha)	Share (%)
Building land	1,571.12	5.62%	1,788.53	6.40%
Agricultural land	6,650.43	23.79%	6,665.80	23.85%
Forest land	19,492.06	69.73%	19,231.29	68.80%
Water land	205.41	0.73%	214.12	0.77%
Other land	33.33	0.1%	52.62	0.19%
Total	27,952.35	100.00%	27,952.36	100.00%

Source: MONG, 2012.

We analyzed the situation relating to basic land use, according to the previous spatial plan of the MONG, which was in force until 2012, and with regard to the MSP, which is still in force today, complete with all the amendments since 2012.

As can be seen from the Table 1, by 2012, agricultural and building land came second and third respectively to forest land, which covered the majority of land, i.e., 69.73%. According to the MSP, there are predominantly forest areas, which reduced by 260.77 hectares. Agricultural land covers 23.85%, and has slightly increased. This is followed by building land, which has increased by 6.40% in comparison to the previous plan, e.g., by 217.41 hectares.

Functioning of the Real Property Market in the Mong

The basic purpose of the real property market is to inform about real property values and changes of ownership between the real property seller and the real property buyer. Real property demand is created on the basis of the preferences and purchasing power of the population, and the state of the economy. Consequently, local real property markets are formed, which are linked to a smaller geographical area (Finančni slovar, 2019). Grum and Temeljotov Salaj (2010) clarified that the expectations of potential real estate buyers are diverse and differ according to the buyers' needs, wishes, interests, legal options and material ability. And that the external expectation factors involved in the residential property market mainly include those that describe housing and tax legislation, regulatory measures and the economic situation. As defined by the UNECE (2005), an efficient real property market involves regulating institutions that ensure a stable and transparent framework within which transactions take place. It should provide easy access to the market for all participants including landowners, tenants and corporate bodies such as banks and lending institutions, and representatives of those with third party and minority rights. According to Lipej (2008), the real estate market needs access to basic data and information, in particular to market prices and time trends.In order for the market to be successful, it is necessary to ensure transparency, security of ownership, efficient cadastral and land registration systems that provide fast, reliable and affordable access to real estate data for users. It is evident, and noted by Wallace and Williamson (2006), that a complex real property market involves a complicated set of interrelated activities and outcomes. FAO (2012) recommended that the state should recognize and facilitate fair and transparent sale and lease markets as a means of transfer of rights of use and ownership of land; and that all actions should be consistent with national and international law. Taking into account that national authorities are politically open to new financial investment models, which could contribute to economic sustainability, Temeljotov Salaj et al., (2018) discussed a new land investment model for value capture strategy that could be attractive for a wider group of private investors. And well noted by Veuger (2017) that the financial and real estate markets are markets that exaggerate through irrational behavior. Fear of 'eat or be eaten' determines people's behavior. Financial and thus real estate markets are always unstable and must always be regulated by people and organizations.

The functioning of the real property market was examined in the MONG and across the Gorica area, for residential real property (apartments and residential houses), and agricultural and forest land in the period from 2007 to 2019. For this purpose, we used the available real property market data of the Surveying and Mapping Authority of the Republic of Slovenia, which enables systematic monitoring of the resulting sales prices (Geodetska uprava Republike Slovenije, 2020).

Firstly, we analyzed average prices of sold apartments. As can be seen from the Table 2, the most apartments were sold in the year 2017 (117), and the least apartments were sold in 2018 (76). The average surface area of apartments ranged between 51 and 58 m^2; the average years of construction ranged between 1972 and 2009; and the prices ranged between 1,400 and 2,195 EUR/m^2.

Next, we analyzed the average prices of sold residential houses in the Gorica area, because we were unable to obtain any filtered data for the MONG.

Table 2. Overview of apartment transactions, MONG 2007–2019

Sold apartments/Year	Number of transactions	Average surface area (m^2)	Average year of construction	Average price (EUR/m^2)
2007	97	57	No data	1,770
2008	104	57	1983	2,195
2009	80	56	1972	1,850
2010	95	51	1976	1,930
2011	79	56	1976	1,760
2012	89	54	1975	1,610
2013	81	55	1975	1,510
2014	83	54	1975	1,460
2015	91	52	1975	1,480
2016	91	58	1973	1,400
2017	117	54	1975	1,560
2018	76	56	1975	1,620
2019	96	54	1972	1,800

Source: Geodetska uprava Republike Slovenije, 2007–2019.

Table 3. Overview of residential houses transactions, Gorica area 2007–2019

Sold residential houses/Year	Number of transactions	Average surface area (m^2)	Average year of construction	Average land surface (m^2)	Average price (EUR)
2007	103	160	No data	704	129,000
2008	66	157	1956	529	156,638
2009	38	178	1937	811	164,800
2010	91	136	1928	537	121,700
2011	109	143	1923	575	115,500
2012	89	145	1928	664	101,800
2013	76	149	1964	650	112,000
2014	121	140	1921	650	73,000
2015	104	150	1948	620	78,000
2016	154	150	1946	720	81,000
2017	176	145	1943	790	84,000
2018	139	149	1922	640	82,000
2019	168	159	1930	620	87,000

Source: Geodetska uprava Republike Slovenije, 2007–2019.

As can be seen from the Table 3, the largest number of residential houses in the Gorica area were sold in the year 2017 (176), and the least in 2009 (38). The average surface area of residential houses ranged between 136 and 178 m^2. The prices of residential houses with associated land ranged between EUR 73,000 and 164,000.

We also analyzed the transactions of agricultural and forest land in the Gorica area in the period from 2014 to 2019. For the period before 2013, data was not available either for the MONG, nor for the Gorica area.

As shown in the Table 4, in the period 2014 – 2019, the largest number of transactions of agricultural land (permanent crops excluded) in the Gorica area were carried out in 2019 (150); the least in 2015 (108). The average area of the sold agricultural land ranged between 3,500 and 5,700 m^2. And the average price ranged between 1.30 and 2.11 EUR/m^2.

Table 4. Overview of agricultural land transactions, Gorica area, 2014–2019

Sold agricultural land/Year	Number of transactions	Average price (EUR/m^2)	Average surface area (m^2)
2014	129	1.30	5,700
2015	108	1.57	4,200
2016	127	1.77	3,500
2017	143	2.11	4,400
2018	137	1.62	4,500
2019	150	2.03	4,300

Source: Geodetska uprava Republike Slovenije, 2014–2019.

Table 5. Overview of forest land transactions, Gorica area, 2014–2019

Sold forest land/Year	Number of transactions	Average price (EUR/m^2)	Average surface area (m^2)
2014	111	0,36	17,500
2015	97	0.37	13,600
2016	100	0.32	18,100
2017	105	0.40	19,300
2018	91	0.49	10,700
2019	174	0.42	18,400

Source: Geodetska uprava Republike Slovenije, 2007–2019.

The largest number of transactions of forest land in the Gorica area (Table 5) were carried out in 2019 (174); the least in 2018 (91). The average area of the sold forest land ranged between 10,700 and 19,300 m^2. And the average price ranged between 0.32 and 0.49 EUR/m^2.

Issuing Building Permits in the Mong

A building permit is the basic permit that enables an investor to execute construction. A legally valid building permit is required for a new construction, for reconstruction and for a change in intended use of structure. A building permit is not required if the project involves a less complex and temporary structure, maintenance and removal of works, maintenance works for public benefit, or enforcement of an imposed inspection measure. A building permit ceases to be valid if an investor fails to reports the commencement of works within five years from the date the permit became final (Gradbeni zakon, 2017).

Because the number of issued construction permits impacts the operation of the real property market in the MONG, we analyzed construction permits in the period from 2007 to 2019, based on the available data.

Table 6. Positively resolved applications and building permits, MONG 2007 - 2019

Applications and building permits/Year	Granted applications for less complex and complex structures	Building permits for all structures per 1,000 inhabitants
2007	372	2.0
2008	273	1.9
2009	321	2.6
2010	255	1.3
2011	210	1.0
2012	217	1.0
2013	212	1.4
2014	176	0.9
2015	182	1.0
2016	181	1.8
2017	165	1.6
2018	172	1.0
2019	162	2.0

Source: Statistični urad Republike Slovenije, 2020.

The Table 6 shows the total number of granted applications for the issue of a building permit for construction of less complex and complex structures. The largest number of positively resolved applications was in 2007 (372); the least in 2019 (162). As can be seen, the number of issued building permits per 1,000 inhabitants varied. The number of issued building permits was the highest in 2009 - specifically, 2.6 per 1,000 inhabitants - and the least permits were issued in 2014, only 0.9 per 1,000 inhabitants. On average, 1.75 building permits per 1,000 inhabitants were issued per year.

We further obtained data and analyzed apartments and buildings for which building permits were issued, and the share of issued buildings permits for residential and non-residential buildings.

The average surface area of apartments and buildings, for which building permits were issued varies, as shown in the Table 7. Average apartment surface area ranges between 71 and 174 m^2. In buildings, the lowest average surface area was 122 m^2; and the highest 2005 m^2. In the period between 2007 and 2014, the most building permits were issued for residential buildings, while in the period 2015 - 2017 the situation turned for the better in respect of non-residential buildings.

Table 7. Apartments and buildings, and the share of issued buildings permits, MONG 2007 - 2019

Apartments and buildings/Year	Apartments – average surface area (m^2)	Buildings – average surface area (m^2)	Residential buildings - share (%)	Non-residential buildings - share (%)
2007	85	536	72.3	27.7
2008	71	2005	76.3	23.7
2009	112	557	81.7	18.3
2010	130	645	76.7	23.3
2011	111	794	69.7	30.3
2012	114	554	84.8	15.2
2013	135	293	93.2	6.8
2014	138	319	92.6	7.4
2015	127	183	43.2	56.8
2016	159	167	38.3	61.7
2017	120	122	27.5	72.5
2018	132	224	60.6	39.4
2019	174	259	49.2	50.8

Source: Statistični urad Republike Slovenije, 2020.

Building Land Development Program and Compensation for the Use of Building Land in the MONG

Building Land Development Program

Building land is land which is intended for building works on the basis of spatial acts. Building land development covers the design engineering and construction of utility equipment and facilities, and networks of other public service infrastructure needed for the spatial arrangements or facilities designed in the MSP or in a municipal detailed spatial plan to be executed and to serve their purpose. Building land is communally developed when access to the public road network is constructed, and when it can be connected to the public electricity, public water supply and public sewage networks. In municipal spatial acts, a municipality defines the type of municipal utilities that need to be built or completed. (ZUreP-2, 2017).

The building land development program discusses the following existing municipal utilities: transport network, sewerage system, water supply network, remote heating network, open public areas network, and waste management facilities network (MONG, 2013).

Compensation for the Use of Building Land

Compensation for the use of building land is a levy paid for indirect burden on the land as a limited asset through the land on which the structure is built or planned. Within the financial measures of the land policy, the compensation remains in force until the enforcement of the real property tax. (Ministrstvo za finance, 2015). It is defined by the municipality and represents an important source of municipal budgets, because it can achieve as much as 10% of the value of the total municipal budget and accounts for the highest municipality's own revenue (Odlok o odmeri NUSZ, 2014). The compensation is payable for unbuilt and built building land (Odlok o ureditvi NUSZ, 2017).

The areas that are subject to the assessment of the compensation are defined on the basis of specific criteria. Within the MONG, there are six areas defined that are subject to the assessment of compensation. To determine the amount of compensation for built and unbuilt land, the prescribed criteria are followed (Odlok o ureditvi NUSZ, 2017). We were unable to obtain the amounts of collected compensations.

Assessment of the Public Utility Charge in the Mong

The public utility charge is one of the financial resources for implementing the land policy measures. It is the only system resource for financing the construction of municipal utilities. The public utility charge for new municipal utilities is the contribution to reimbursing partial costs of construction of municipal utilities which the person liable is to pay the municipality. The public utility charge for existing municipal utilities is the contribution charged in respect of the existing municipal utilities which the person liable is to pay the municipality. By paying the public utility charge, the person liable obtains the right to connect to or use municipal utilities (Ministrstvo za okolje in prostor, 2020).

This research has focused on the amount of annual public utility charge in the MONG in the period 2016 - 2019, where the data was available. The Table 8 shows that the calculated municipal charge for residential buildings (single-dwelling, two-dwelling and multi-dwelling) was the highest in 2018; and the least in 2017, in the amount of EUR 114,983.70. The table shows further the amount of the calculated public utility charge for non-residential buildings (industrial, agricultural, garages, stores, warehouses, healthcare buildings, institutional care buildings, office buildings, restaurants, administrative buildings, fire stations). It mainly increases from EUR 44,834.05 in 2016 to EUR 157,201.30 in 2019.

Table 8. The amount of calculated public utility charge with regard to the type of buildings, MONG 2016 - 2019

Public utility charge buildings/ Year	Single-dwelling residential (EUR)	Two-dwelling residential (EUR)	Multi-dwelling residential (EUR)	Non-residential (EUR)	Total (EUR)
2016	139,954.26	792.41	No data	44,834.05	185,580.72
2017	84,398.40	184.03	30,401.27	87,953.79	202,937.49
2018	178,851.26	No data	82,645.35	159,440.85	420,937.46
2019	201,881.09	14,168.75	43,791.45	157,201.30	417,042.59

Source: MONG, 2019.

CONCLUSION

Land policy is an important integral part of the social and economic system and the spatial planning policy. It must function in conformity with other policies, such as residential, agricultural and environmental. Land policy is directly connected to spatial planning, and also, to the real property market. The most important factors that impact the prices of real properties in the market are supply and demand. In the MONG, and in the broader Gorica area, the real property market has been developing in a relatively stable way. This can be seen in the context of residential property, as well as in agricultural and forest land, displaying a trend of increased prices of apartments in recent years, and fluctuations in other real property types. The intensity of issuing building permits with a time delay results in larger supply and greater activities of the real property market.

One of the important professional bases for the making of land policy is the MSP which, in addition to the intended land use, by means of which the municipality plans and directs the development, provides the framework for the issue of building permits, spatial placement and construction of simple and less complex structures, change of intended use of buildings and land use, and for other projects, and specifies the conditions regarding the construction of municipal utilities. The areas in the MSP earmarked for building land have increased by over 200 hectares in comparison to the previous spatial plan, which represents an increase of land earmarked for future building development.

The existing two mechanisms of land policy implementation, which ensure a portion of financing for local self-governing communities, and which local self-governing communities may make use of, are the public utility charge and compensation for the use of built and unbuilt land, which have been analyzed on the basis of the available data. The MONG ranks third among city municipalities in Slovenia in the volume of income arising from the public utility charge, which indicates its significant role in the city municipality's budget.

References

Davy, B. (2012). *Land Policy: Planning and the Spatial Consequences of Property*. Farnham: Ashgate.

Deininger, K. (2003). *Land Policies for Growth and Poverty Reduction. A World Bank Policy Research Report*. The World Bank and Oxford University Press. Accessed March 14, 2019. https://documents.worldbank.org/en/publication/documents-reports/documentdetail/485171468309336484/land-policies-for-growth-and-poverty-reduction

FAO (2012). *Voluntary Guidelines on the Responsible Governance of Tenure of Land, Fisheries, and Forests in the Context of National Food Security*. Rome: Food and Agriculture Organization of the United Nations (FAO). Accessed May 10, 2019. http://www.fao.org/nr/tenure/voluntary-guidelines/en/

Finančni slovar (2019). *Nepremičninski trg*. [*Financial Dictionary* (2019). Real Property Market]. Accessed June 17, 2019. http://www.financnislovar.com/definicije/nepremicninski-trg.html

Geodetska uprava Republike Slovenije (2007–2019). *Letna poročila o slovenskem trgu nepremičnin* [*Surveying and Mapping Authority of the Republic of Slovenia (2007–2019). Annual Reports on the Slovenian*

Real Property Market.] Accessed July 14, 2020. http://www.e-prostor.gov.si/zbirke-prostorskih-podatkov/etn/#tab5-970

Geodetska uprava Republike Slovenije (2020). *Evidenca trga nepremičnin.* [*Surveying and Mapping Authority of the Republic of Slovenia (2020). Real Property Market Record.*] Accessed July 10, 2020. http://www.e-prostor.gov.si/zbirke-prostorskih-podatkov/etn/

Gerber, J. D. et al., (2018). *Instruments of Land Policy: Dealing with Scarcity of Land.* New York: Routledge.

Gov.si (2020): *Zemljiška politika.* [*Land Policy.*] Accessed September 19, 2020. https://www.gov.si/teme/zemljiska-politika/

Gradbeni zakon (2017). *Uradni list Republike Slovenije, št. 61/2017 s spremembami.* [*Building Law (2017). Official Gazette of the Republic of Slovenia, no. 61/2017 with amendments.*]

Grum, B. and Temeljotov Salaj, A. (2010). The External Expectations of Potential Real Estate Buyers in Slovenia and Japan. Urbani izziv, Vol. 21, no. 2, p. 37-47. December 2010. Ljubljana, Urban Planning Institute of the Republic of Slovenia. [*Urban Challenge Journal*, Vol. 21, no. 2, p. 37-47. December 2010.].

Hartmann, T. and Spit, T. (2015). Dilemmas of Involvement in Land Management – Comparing an Active (Dutch) and a Passive (German) Approach. *Land Use Policy*, Vol. 42, p. 729 – 737. doi: 10.1016/j.landusepol.2014.10.004.

Kobetič, L. (2016). Instrumenti in ukrepi zemljiške politike na območjih stavbnih zemljišč. Stavbe in stavbna zemljišča. Podjetje in delo: revija za gospodarsko, delovno in socialno pravo, let. 42, št. 6/7, str. 36–39. [Land Policy Instruments and Measures in Building Land Areas. Buildings and Building Land. Company and Work: Magazine for Economic, *Labor and Social Law*. Vol. 42, no. 6/7, p. 36-39.]

Kralj, K. (2014). *Delovna skupina za področje aktivne zemljiške politike in širša delovna skupina, področje aktivne zemljiške politike. Ljubljana: Inženirska zbornica Slovenije.* [*Working Group for Active Land Policy, and Wider Working Group for Active Land Policy. Ljubljana: Chamber of Engineers of Slovenia.*] Accessed April 18, 2019. http://www.izs.si/fileadmin/dokumenti/Zakonodaja/spremembezakonodaja-2014/Izhodisca)-MzIP-podrocje-aktivne-zemljiske-politike-20-1-2014.pdf

Lipej, B. (2015). *Benchmarking sistemov za upravljanje nepremičnin. Geodetski vestnik*, let. 59, št. 2, str. 262 – 274. [*Benchmarking Land Administration Systems. Geodetski vestnik, the publication of the Association of Surveyors of Slovenia*, Vol. 59, no. 2, p. 262 – 274.] http://www.geodetski-vestnik.com/59/2/gv59-2_lipej.pdf.

Lipej, B. (2008). *Razvojna perspektiva nepremičninskega področja. Geodetski vestnik*, let. 52, št. 4, 625 – 638. [*Development Perspective of the Real Estate Field of Work. Geodetski vestnik, the publication of the Association of Surveyors of Slovenia*, Vol. 52, no. 4, p. 625 – 638.] http://www.geodetski-vestnik.com/52/4/gv52-4_625-638.pdf.

Mestna občina Nova Gorica – MONG (2012). *Občinski prostorski načrt Mestne občine Nova Gorica. Bilanca površin stavbnih zemljišč za OPN Nova Gorica.* Predlog 5. [City Municipality of Nova Gorica - MONG (2012). *The MONG Municipal Spatial Plan. Balance of Building Land Areas.* Draft 5.]

Mestna občina Nova Gorica – MONG (2013) *Program opremljanja stavbnih zemljišč za območje Mestne občine Nova Gorica.* [City Municipality of Nova Gorica – MONG (2013). *Building Land Development Program for the MONG.*]

Mestna občina Nova Gorica – MONG (2018). *Napoved za odmero nadomestila za uporabo stavbnega zemljišča, Priloga, Karta območij.* [City Municipality of Nova Gorica – MONG (2018). *Forecast of Assessment of Compensation for the Use of Building Land. Map of Areas.*] Accessed April 22, 2019. http://www.nova-gorica.si/za-obcane/postopki-in-obrazci/2011110115044 16/

Mestna občina Nova Gorica – MONG (2019). *Komunalni prispevek.* [City Municipality of Nova Gorica – MONG (2019). *Public Utility Charge.*] Accessed April 18, 2019. https://www.nova-gorica.si/za-obcane/postopki-in-obrazci/2011102714313160/

Ministrstvo za finance (2015). *Nadomestilo za uporabo stavbnega zemljišča.* [Ministry of Finance (2015). *Compensation for the Use of*

Building Land.] Accessed April 3, 2019. http://www.fu.gov.si/fileadmin/Internet/Uvodne_strani/Prebivalci/davki123.pdf#page=10.

Ministrstvo za okolje in prostor (2019). *Zemljiška politika.* [Ministry of Environment and Spatial Planning (2019). *Land Policy.*] Accessed April 9, 2019. http://www.mop.gov.si/si/delovna_podrocja/urbani_razvoj_in_zemljiska_politika/.

Ministrstvo za okolje in prostor (2020a). *Občinski prostorski akti.* [Ministry of Environment and Spatial Planning (2020a). *Municipal Spatial Acts.*] Accessed July 20, 2020. https://www.gov.si/teme/obcinski-prostorski-akti/

Ministrstvo za okolje in prostor (2020b). *Zemljiška politika.* [Ministry of Environment and Spatial Planning (2020b). *Land Policy.*] Accessed July 19, 2020. https://www.gov.si/teme/zemljiska-politika/.

Odlok o občinskem prostorskem načrtu (OPN) Mestne občine Nova Gorica (2018). *Uradni list Republike Slovenije*, št. (no.) 13/2018. [Decree on the Municipal Spatial Plan of the MONG (2018). *Official Gazette of the Republic of Slovenia*, no. 13/2018.]

Odlok o odmeri nadomestila za uporabo stavbnega zemljišča (NUSZ) v Mestni občini Nova Gorica (2014). *Uradni list Republike Slovenije, št.* 95/2014. [Decree on the Assessment of Compensation for the Use of Public Land in the MONG) (2014). *Official Gazette of the Republic of Slovenia,* no.95/2014.]

Odlok o ureditvi nadomestila za uporabo stavbnega zemljišča (NUSZ) v Mestni občini Nova Gorica (2017). *Uradni list Republike Slovenije*, št. 79/2017. [Decree on the arrangement of compensation for the use of public land in the MONG (2017). *Official Gazette of the Republic of Slovenia*, no. 79/2017.]

Palmer, D. et al., (2009). *Towards Improved Land Governance. Land Tenure Working paper 11.* Food and Agriculture Organization of the United Nations, United Nations Human Settlements Programme. Accessed July 20, 2020. http://www.fao.org/3/a-ak999e.pdf.

Shahab, S. et al., (2019). An Analysis of the Factors Influencing Transaction Costs in Transferable Development Rights Programmes.

Ecological Economics, Vol. 156, p. 409–419. doi: 10.1016/j.ecolecon.2018.05.018.

Shahab, S. et al., (2020). *Strategies of Municipal Land Policies: Housing Development in Germany, Belgium and Netherlands.* https://www.tandfonline.com/doi/full/10.1080/09654313.2020.1817867

Statistični urad Republike Slovenije (2018). Občina Nova Gorica. [Statistical Office of the Republic of Slovenia (2018). *Municipality of Nova Gorica.*] Accessed July 8, 2020. https://www.stat.si/obcine/sl/Municip/Index/112

Statistični urad Republike Slovenije (2020). *Gradbena dovoljenja - izbrani kazalniki po občinah.* [Statistical Office of the Republic of Slovenia (2020). *Building Permits – Selected Indicators by Municipalities.*] Accessed July 06, 2020. https://pxweb.stat.si/pxweb/Database/Ekonomsko/19_gradbenistvo/06_19707_dovoljenja/06_19707_dovoljenja.asp

Temeljotov Salaj, A. et al., (2018). Land Value Strategies in PPP – What Can FM Learn From it? *Facilities*, Vol. 36, No.1/2, p. 24-36. doi: https://doi.org/10.1108/F-03-2017-0033.

United Nations Economic Commission for Europe - UNECE (2005). *Land Administration in the ECE Region. Development Trends and main Principles.* New York, Geneva: UN.

Veuger, J. (2017). *A viable Real Estate Economy with Disruption and Blockchain.* Saxion University of Applied Sciences. Groningen. Facilities, December 2017. https://www.researchgate.net/publication/321921870_Trust_in_a_viable_real_estate_economy_with_disruption_and_Blockchain. doi: 10.1108/F-11-2017-0106.

Virtanen, P., Verlaat, J. (1999). *Urban Land Policy-Goals and Instruments.* London: International Federation for Housing and Planning.

Wallace, J., Williamson, I. (2006). Building Land Markets. *Land Use Policy* 23, p. 123-135, Elsevier.

Weiβ, E. (2000). Bodenordnung in Stadtischen Verdichtungsgebieten der Bundersrepublik Deutschland. In: *Aktuelle Probleme der Stadt- und Landplanung*, Peter Lang AG, Bern. [Land order in urban densely populated areas of the Federal Republic of Germany. In: *Current problems in urban and rural planning*]

Zakon o urejanju prostora - ZUreP-2 (2017). *Uradni list Republike Slovenije*, št. 61/2017. [Law on Spatial Planning - ZUreP-2 (2017). *Official Gazette of the Republic of Slovenia*, no. 61/2017.]

In: The Future of Real Estate
Editor: Jan Veuger
ISBN: 978-1-53619-414-2

Chapter 8

WORK FROM HOTELS: IS HYBRID THE FUTURE?

Hester van Sprang*[*] *and Brenda Groen, PhD
Saxion University of Applied Sciences, Deventer, The Netherlands

ABSTRACT

Already before but especially during the Covid-19 pandemic, working remotely and working from home increased. However, not every knowledge worker can and wants to work from home. Before the crisis, e.g., business travelers, independent professionals, small business, and freelancers already looked for flexible workspace. This group has now been joined by those who look for an alternative to working from home. This provides opportunities for coworking spaces and organizations that traditionally do not focus on providing workplace: hotels. Besides hospitality, they may also offer workplaces: hybrid hospitality. This chapter discusses alternative workplaces' market; it examines coworking spaces, working-from-hotels, and hybrid hospitality. Furthermore, the chapter discusses what hybrid means. It may be a diversification of the offer, using existing rooms for another purpose, and intensifying space

* Corresponding Author's E-mail: h.vansprang@saxion.nl.

use by enabling an easy conversion of a room depending on the function needed. Moreover, the chapter discusses the hybrid trend for hotels is there to stay.

Keywords: hospitality industry, remote working, flexible offices, coworking, hotels, Work-From-Hotel, hybrid hospitality, business models, resilience

1. Introduction

The COVID-19 pandemic has resulted in a dramatic drop in occupancy in hotels in the major cities. Due to travel restrictions, tourists cancelled holidays, international business travelers switched to online meetings, and parties, events and conferences were either postponed or became online events. Organizations sent their knowledge workers home, leading to a surge in online working. Working from home became more feasible than organizations ever imagined, and individual workers experienced the benefits (and the downsides) of working from home.

But every crisis offers new opportunities. Major hotel chains were quick to innovate and recognized the opportunity to bring back some business to their hotels, by catering to those workers who find themselves needing an alternative to the "home" in "work from home." Hyatt was first out of the gate with its 'Work from Hyatt' program, and then Marriott and Hilton followed with packages of their own, from day-passes to "workstations" in resorts. Some hotel groups offer guest rooms as makeshift daytime offices; other hoteliers offer quarantine packages to individuals who need to isolate themselves, have planned a staycation or are working from home indefinitely. Thus, a new addition to the as-a-service workspace market: Work-From-Hotel (WFH) is a hybrid between leisure and work.

Whereas for traditional hotels that entered this track, this was a response to the crisis, innovative brands, like CitizenM, Zoku and TheStudentHotel, already catered for this group before the pandemic.

These hybrid hotels focus on business nomads, people that have made working anywhere anytime into a lifestyle. On top of the traditional offer of lodgings, food & beverage, they offer a place for social and cultural exchange with likeminded people in a setting of elevated hospitality (see 6: hybrid hospitality). They blend work, home and leisure, blurring the boundaries between the three. Why go to a traditional office if hotels, experts in hospitality, offer you fun, a flexible office, in, if necessary, a place to stay away from home?

To what extent may hotels profit from this development? Airbnb disrupted their hotel market by turning private homes into hotels, could hotels and hybrids do the same to the (flexible) office market by offering flexible and hospitable workplaces?

2. Workplace Is Not Limited to Traditional Offices

Back in 2013, FMN and CoreNet Global predicted that by 2020 the work environment would no longer be limited to the traditional office but would exceed building boundaries and includes multifunctional areas that combine work, housing and leisure (FMN & CoreNet Global, 2013, p. 6). In the same period, Termaat, Van Sprang & Groen (2014) identified the future potential of five workspace concepts based on a two-year study into new workspaces' business models:

1) Club: organizations' headquarters aimed at organizations' core business; internal focus, facilitating collaboration and knowledge sharing (part of former traditional office).
2) Campus: a collection of offices centered around a Club, focused on task performance (former traditional office).
3) Hub: regional office for short/mid-term uses of space, focusing on task performance (solo or team). Compared to the former satellite concept in 2013, this concept is more user-centered, and facilities

possibly shared with other (external) companies to improve occupancy rates.

4) Coworking space: regional work and meeting space (formerly known as ‘third space’), commercial short/mid-term term rent of workspace, added value: high accessibility and network centered.
5) Home-office (as an explicit place of work): since 2015, the ‘hoffice’ concept started, where people, like in coworking spaces, work together, in members’ homes (Rossitto and Lampinen, 2018).

All but the home office and 'hoffice' have a business model. Now, in 2021, we can conclude that these business models for workspace have become omnipresent. Coworking spaces are booming (Ng, 2016; Deskmag, 2019). The flexible space sector has accounted for a substantial share of net absorption in global gateway cities in recent years (JLL, 2020). One of the driving forces is the changing labor market, with a growing number of independent professionals and distributed work. The Global Coworking Growth Study 2020 estimates the number of coworking spaces to reach 40.000 by 2024, with 5 million users globally, almost doubling the 2020 numbers.

As the above shows, the commercial real estate office market underwent rapid changes since 2014, with the transition from ownership to availability for end-users as an underlying core theme. Rosa (2010, cited in Scullica & Elgin, 2020) defines three distinct categories—technological acceleration, acceleration of social change and acceleration of the life rhythms—that have completely transformed the perception and organization of space and time in collective life. New lifestyles based on work flexibility, a temporariness of interpersonal relationships, frequent travel and discontinuity of living have repercussions on the spaces and the ways they are operated.

3. The COVID-19 Pandemic as a Wake-up Call: Do We Need Our Offices?

And then the COVID-19 pandemic pushed this development further than anyone could have foreseen. Global research by JLL (2020) indicates that demand for flexible space has come to a virtual halt with most deals representing a spillover from last year. Coworking space is the most impacted due to its high exposure to freelancers (17%), start-ups (27%) and SMEs (38%). The other user groups are remotely working entrepreneurs (8%), remote corporate workers (5%), digital nomads (3%) and large-scale corporations (2%) (coworkinginsights.com, 2019). In the long term, however, businesses will have a greater need for flexible space to accommodate shifting workforce practices and to provide varied workplaces for employees.

JLL (2020) mentions in its corporate real estate perspective that COVID-19 has served as the ultimate accelerant to corporate transformation, speeding up many trends evident before the pandemic and pushing organizations towards change. These developments lead to a reduced need for office space, as shows clearly in the banking industry. A global survey among 800 senior financial services executives (Deloitte, 2020) revealed that about one-third of the banking, insurance, and investment management respondents say their companies plan to rationalize their CRE footprint over the next six to twelve months. For example, ABNAMRO has decided to sell its landmark head office in the Amsterdam Business District, stating: ‘We will redevelop one of our locations in Amsterdam into a Paris-proof workplace designed to facilitate the trend of remote working. Alongside this, we will sell our head office building and lease back part of it’ (DutchNews.nl, 30 November 2020). Likewise, ING announced plans to close offices in The Netherlands, South America and Asia.

Worldwide, this virus forced people to work remotely, which in most cases means working from home. Before the COVID-19 pandemic, the proportion of home-based workers across the world was relatively low, a mere 3% of employees were working exclusively or mainly from their home (ILO, 2020a). Since the beginning of 2020, the percentage of teleworkers has risen tremendously. For example, Bick et al. (2020) document that more than one-third of the US workforce worked entirely from home in May 2020, as did 46% of the UK workforce during lockdown (The Guardian, 20 September 2020). Many studies show that workers value working from home and want to maintain this post-COVID for at least part of the week. According to ILO calculations, around 30% of North American and Western European workers are in occupations that allow home-based work (ILO, 2020b). A survey by Gartner (2020) showed that 82% of 127 company leaders, representing Human Resource, Legal and Compliance, Finance and Real Estate, intend to allow employees remote working parttime even when buildings will reopen for workers. Nearly half (47%) said they even plan to enable employees to work remotely full time going forward. For some organizations, flex time will be the new norm as 43% of survey respondents reported they would grant employees flex days, while 42% will provide flex hours. So, a combination of onsite and offsite working will most probably become the norm.

For many organizations with employees working both onsite and remotely, adapting to a new, more complex hybrid workforce is the challenge, as to how people work together to get their job done. As stated in the introduction, working from home also has downsides. Shareena & Sahid found that willingness to work from home is entirely dependent on the presence of children, of having a quiet and comfortable space to work, as well as good internet connectivity. Employees that lack these conditions may seek alternative workspaces to get out of the house, looking to get some temporary separation from housemates or simply to experience a change of scenery. That implies that working in third places is no longer limited to independent workers, frequent (business) travelers and digital nomads. Even the ‘anchors’ and ‘connectors’ in the typology of knowledge workers presented by Greene and Myerson (2011), workers that used to work primarily in their office, may now feel the need a third workplace. The question is, what type of workplace will they use? Club, Hub, Campus, or Coworking space? Could hotels offer a suitable alternative?

3.1. Digital Nomads and Their Alternative Offices

Whereas most remote workers have a stable place to live and work from home (and possibly also other places), digital nomads take this location independence further. 'They travel and do so frequently; both domestically and internationally. They select their location choice based on leisure and lifestyle expectations, not work. Therefore, they often choose comfortable, warm, scenic places that are also quite affordable and welcoming to Westerners' (Thompson, 2018, p.3). Mobile lives demand flexibility, adaptability and reflexivity to be ready for the unexpected and embrace novelty (Bauman, 2004, p.4), not only for the individuals but also for those and the real estate that host them. Though free to go wherever they want to go, digital nomads tend to visit exiting locations that host a community of likeminded people. Because, even in these beautiful places, people need social interaction and a sense of belonging. In places that accommodate digital nomads, the boundaries between the first place (home), the second place (work), and the third-place (public space) blur. The emergence of such a fourth place, that often merges elements of two or more places leads to new spatial categories such as co-living, coworking, and co-mingling spaces. The function of such a fourth place is to foster networking, to promote mingling, and to favor collaboration, face-to-face interactions, and the exchange of tacit knowledge, making it the place for the knowledge economy (Morisson, 2019, p.449).

But networks are only of value when relevant others participate. To attract the right target groups, staging an experience that reflects the brand image is increasingly important. Following Berry et al. (2006), Pijls et al. (2017) define an experience as the interaction between the individual and its environment, containing functional, mechanical and humane clues, and the inner responses to this interaction. Both the physical environment and staff behavior design deliver 'clues' that together conjure an image of the brand and the hospitality offer. In the hospitality industry, customer satisfaction and loyalty are influenced by the hospitality experienced during a stay. The overall experience of hospitality of a person results from the performance on the experiential dimensions Inviting, Care, and

Comfort (Pijls et al., 2017). Inviting relates to openness and experience of freedom during a visit (Pijls et al., 2020). Aspects that contribute to the feeling of welcome of the guest are friendliness, inviting, warm, home-like, openness, sincerity and generosity (Brotherton & Wood, 2008; Hemmington, 2007; Clapp & Ridge, 2016). Care is associated with providing support, taking care of a person, relieving him/her of tasks or worries, and taking an interest. Comfort is associated with feeling at ease, relaxed and comfortable (Pijls et al., 2020). Workplaces were traditionally not focused on hospitality the way the hospitality industry is. Hangouts for digital nomads and coworking spaces already realized that hospitality and fostering a community are indispensable for becoming the place to be. The next paragraph will zoom in on the hotel industry, an industry traditionally focused on providing hospitality.

4. The Hotel Industry

The hotel industry is a subdivision of the hospitality industry that specializes in providing customers with lodging services. The first hotel chains were formed during the first half of the 20th century in the United States and now dominate the market (Melissen et al., 2018). In 2018, the global hotel industry was a $525bn industry, consisting of 18 million rooms. 54% of rooms were affiliated with a worldwide or regional chain ('branded'), up from 50% in 2012, and 46% are unaffiliated ('independent'). Table 1 shows the global top 10 largest hotel chains. Each chain encompasses multiple brands to target specific market segments. The top 5 hotel groups accounted for 25% of the market share in 2018 (IHGPLC, 2019).

The hotel industry is a rather traditional industry; since ancient times, the core offering consists of lodging, food & beverages. Hotels operate in a fiercely competitive market, in which the guest experience is key to business success. On the one hand, because potential guests orient themselves by other guest's reviews of their experiences, on the other hand, because services, like goods before them, have increasingly become commoditized and experiences emerged as the next step in the progression of economic value (Pine & Gilmore, 1988).

Table 1. 10 largest hotel chains worldwide (as of June 2020)

Hotel chain	Number of properties	Number of guest rooms
Wyndham Worldwide	9,280[1]	697,607[2]
Mariott International	7,484[1]	1,400,693[2]
Choice Hotels	7,118[1]	597,018[2]
Hilton Worldwide	6,160[1]	974,508[2]
InterContinental Hotels Group	5,895[1]	881,562[2]
AccorHotels	5,100[3]	704,000[4]
Best Western Hotels	4,131[1]	380,165[2]
G6 Hospitality	1,392[1]	118,356[2]
Aimbridge Hospitality	1,261[1]	179,821[2]
Radisson Hotel Group	1,183[1]	226,473[5]

Hotels can be categorized by size, function (business, leisure), service, and cost. The level of luxury is generally indicated by service-levels (limited-service, mid-range service, and full-service), a star rating system (1-5 stars), or the American diamond classification (1-4 diamonds). Most hotels cater to both business guests and leisure guests as their demand is complementary in time. To attract business guests, many hotels offer services like conference rooms, banqueting and printing services. To improve the financial return on shared amenities most hotels make a conscious effort to welcome non-guests to their properties with upscale drinking and dining outlets, spas and pool facilities, and open-up lobbies and ground floor areas for remote working and meeting. This did not change the offer itself but is merely an attempt to attract a different customer segment to bring in extra revenues.

---

[1] https://www.statista.com/statistics/197869/us-hotel-companies-by-number-of-properties-worldwide/.

[2] https://www.statista.com/statistics/197859/total-number-of-guestrooms-of-us-hotel-companies-worldwide/.

[3] www.group.accor.com.

[4] Accor-Wikipedia.

[5] https://www.radissonhotelgroup.com/development_our-portfolio.

However, the guest and the use of facilities are subject to change. Travel is faster and more accessible, leading to more frequent but shorter stays (Gaggi and Narduzzi 2006). This mixture of business and leisure is referred to as 'bleisure' by Raymond (2013, cited in Scullica & Elgin, 2020), which characterizes the aforementioned digital nomads. For this reason, accommodation facilities must be more flexible in their offer of space-services for new travelers. However, traditional hotel real estate is inflexible, as is the design of guest rooms with beds dominating the space.

4.1. Hotel Business Models

Hotel chains operate hotels in four different ways: franchised, managed, leased (e.g., Zoku), and owned/operated (vertical integrated, like citizenM and The Student Hotel). The choice depends mainly on market maturity, owner preference and, in some cases, brand strategy. Hotel companies are rarely owners of the property. Owners and shareholders demand quick returns on investment, especially in times of increased market uncertainty, which leads to limited planning and pricing horizons and a predominantly short-term profit focus (Melissen et al. 2018). This short-term profit-driven focus has increased pressure on margins worldwide.

Derived from Porter's (1995) generic strategies, hotels can follow three generic strategic pricing strategies:

1) Cost-based pricing – adds a profit margin to the cost base to generate a positive financial return.
2) Competitive pricing - following the competition to protect or grow a company's market share at the risk of vicious negative price development.
3) Customer-driven pricing or value-based pricing – the opposite of cost-based pricing- follows the customer's willingness to pay for a hospitality experience.

Within the hotel industry, the easiest way to measure success is by monitoring its key performance indicators. These include revenue per available room (RevPAR), average daily rate (ADR), and occupancy rates, all of which have seen growth over the past decade (Statista.com). Average Daily Rate (ADR) is a commonly used financial indicator in the hotel industry to measure a hotel's statistical performance compared to competitors and to benchmark the performance of a hotel to itself over time. The number represents the average rental income per paid occupied room per period. ADR, along with the property's occupancy, are the foundations for the property's financial performance. The RevPAR is an indication for thc financial health of the business based on the ADR multiplied by the occupancy rate. It can also be determined by dividing the total room revenue by the total available rooms.

The demand for hotel rooms is subject to fluctuation. Therefore, in their operational pricing, hotels use yield management practices to optimize RevPAR and occupancy rates. Yield management (or revenue management) is defined as 'the art and science of optimizing the total contribution of an organization's multiple revenue streams by controlling price and availability of products in line with the organization's strategic direction' (Josephi, 2015, p185.) These practices show from dynamic pricing, whereby different customers pay a different price for the same room to generate the best possible financial return. Thereby, hotels aim to maximize their income. However, one should note that RevPAR focusses on revenue per room, which may become a less interesting measure when hotels diversify the use of their spaces - in such case revenue per square meter might be more interesting than RevPAR.

4.2. How Hotels Adapt to the COVID-19 Pandemic

While the global hotel industry has been thriving over the past years, the coronavirus's impact on the lodging industry has been severe. Monthly hotel revenue per available room worldwide showed a sharp decline across all regions, like average daily rates and occupancy (Statisa.com, 2020a).

In May 2020, the RevPAR in Europe saw the most dramatic effects of the virus, dropping by 85.33 US dollars to 11.35 US dollars compared to the previous year (Statista.com, 2020b).

The unprecedented low occupancy rates of hotels encouraged hotel operators to be more creative in attracting guests and diversifying revenue streams by, for example, the use of a quiet guestroom as a private office for locals looking for some extra space during the workday. Guestline (2020) developed a guideline for hotels that want to offer their lobby and business center facilities as coworking space. Based on a survey of 2,000 business professionals, they advise hoteliers to see to the needs of business people by offering high-speed internet and enough charging outlets; a distraction-free space; comfortable seating arrangements; a clean and accessible refreshment area; acoustic privacy; and (data-)security. This offer mimics the offer of coworking spaces but lacks the community aspect.

5. Coworking Spaces

A coworking space is a combination of the second place (work) and the third place (public space). In contrast with traditional café place (third place), where the primary function is to enjoy each other's company, the coworking place' function is to work and network (Morisson, 2019, p.447). What Morisson calls 'the fourth place', Niewiadomska (2013) labels as a third way of working, between the traditional office and home office. Chegut and Langen (2019) describe coworking spaces as offices where the users share amenities and form a community. According to Waters-Lynch and Potts (2017), coworking spaces focus on social and collaborative activities. Work in coworking spaces is quintessentially mobile, enabled by the diffusion of digital communication infrastructure. Coworking spaces also favor autonomous work in that it is neither exclusively dependent on employer-owned tools nor entirely beholden to employer-determined schedules (De Preuter et al., 2017).

The difference between shared (serviced) office and coworking space is the difference between monetizing merely the use of space versus the access to an appealing community with coworking culture (Zhou, 2019). To develop such a sense of community, of shared values, people need to encounter each other. The propinquity effect states that distance is related to the chance people will develop relationships (Gullahorn, 1952). Shared services and events can enable impromptu encounters among workers, leading to socialization and cooperation (Hua et al., 2010).

Coworking spaces are regarded as 'serendipity accelerators', designed to host creative people and entrepreneurs who wish to break isolation and find a convivial environment favoring meetings and collaboration (Moriset, 2014). Coworking spaces with a livelier community are generally characterized by the organization of many activities and by sharing values and principles related to knowledge sharing and community building (Capdevilla, 2013). However, as private offices generate increased revenues, the share of private space in coworking spaces is increasing: every tenth coworking space is now made up of 60% or more private offices (Deskmag, 2018). As their walls can hinder a collaborative atmosphere and therefore threaten the conditions that encourage coworking and new encounters, these concepts now start to resemble serviced offices.

Table 2. Examples of coworking brands

Coworking	Number of locations
Regus coworking (part of IWG)	2,600 locations in 106 countries[6]
WeWork	828 locations in 120 cities in approximately 32 countries[7]
Spaces (part of IWG)	429 city center locations[8]
Uncommon	5 locations in London[9]
B.	3 locations in Amsterdam[10]

[6] https://www.linkedin.com/company/regus/.
[7] https://en.wikipedia.org/wiki/WeWork.
[8] https://franchise.iwgplc.com/en-gb/iwg-franchise-business-model.
[9] https://uncommon.co.uk/.
[10] https://b-buildingbusiness.com/.

A literature review by Kojo & Nenonen (2017) suggests that mobile multi-locational workers typically use coworking spaces with a need for on-demand workplaces, like young professionals, freelancers and business people who prefer working in a place where people will communicate, collaborate and share knowledge (Parrino, 2015; Capdevila, 2013; Gandini, 2015). According to De Peuter et al. (2017), the key users of coworking spaces are self-employed media- and cultural workers.

5.1. Coworking Business Models

As a business model, coworking spaces are an exponent of the 'as-a-service' economy, as they provide workspace as a service on demand. Coworking spaces may be publicly supported, whereas others are entirely privately owned. The dominating model is for-profit (83% of coworking spaces; Deskmag, 2019). Market research shows that in 2019, most of this industry's growth came from brand-new businesses (65%) while chains and second or more locations make up the remaining 35% (Zuckerman, 2020). 65% of properties are rented or leased, 19% of properties are owned, 7% are managed under contract, 7% a joint venture with the owner (Deskmag, 2019).

The size of coworking spaces varies from several dozen square meters to entire buildings (Bates 2006, cited in Kojo & Nenonen, 2017). According to Deskmag (2019), 49% of coworking locations is under 500 m^2, 14% is 500-100 m^2, 20% is 1000<2000 m^2 and 17% is over 2000 m^2. A typical coworking space has around 80 members, working at 70 desks spread over an area of around 800 m^2. An average member churn-rate of between 2-9% leads to the highest chance on financial profitability (Deskmag, 2018; Deskmag, 2019). Coworking spaces may constitute a network in which each space that belongs to the network adopts more or less the same brand image and operational model (Olma, 2012).

The contracting commitment of independent coworking spaces is typically flexible, short and membership-based. When the coworking space allows pay-per-use, the rotation speeds tend to be high, with weak ties in the community.

5.2. Coworking in Hotels

Not only real estate companies, but also hotels capitalized on the booming coworking industry. Brands such as Sir Hotels and Ruby Hotels created dedicated coworking spaces on their sites. Ennismore's The Hoxton group also launched their own coworking concept, Working From_, at their Southwark site in London as well as in Fulton Market in Chicago (Stay The Night, 2020).

6. Hybrid Hospitality

In the contemporary, globally interconnected, continually moving and accelerating world, hospitality and "feeling welcomed" become central themes of our daily lives. The office is no longer the only place for (knowledge) work, the home is no longer our central focus of living, and hotels, cafes and restaurant no longer only serve as a place to eat, sleep and relax. We increasingly dwell in collective and shared spaces for progressively shortened and discontinuous times, and these places may offer a combination of functions (Scullica & Eleganti, 2020). Innovative entrepreneurs cleverly developed mixed-use properties previously dedicated to one kind of use only. Besides coworking facilities, hybrids offer a form of what Morisson (2019) calls co-living: the combination of the first place (home) and the second place (work). The function of co-living is to create an atmosphere conducive to living and working under the same roof.

Before the COVID pandemic, front-runners in the hotel industry (see Table 2) developed concepts that provide a place for remote working and living for an extended period of stay. It is an additional business model that reflects the peak and off-peak rhythm of hotels. The same spaces are used more intensively for different guests. To enable this, hotels must adapt their rooms and policies because many traditional hotels are not suitable for this purpose. Core characteristics of the hybrid hospitality hotel are (Colliers International, 2020):

- Pleasant workspaces such as enclosed focus rooms, meeting and event rooms and coworking spaces
- A general living space suitable for collaboration and togetherness
- Good facilities such as restaurants and bars that are affordable and suitable for (small-scale) events
- Providing day flexibility for workplaces
- A 'hospitality first' experience with a personal and high-quality service
- An inspiring and dynamic environment with international allure
- Without the bed as the room's centerpiece, rooms can be used as a hotel room, serviced apartment, workspace, meeting room and event space (private restaurant, private theatre).

When this last characteristic is not present, the hotel applies mixed-use as it is a diversified offer of rooms that enables multiple uses on property-level, whereas hybrid concepts use multifunctional spaces.

In hybrid concepts, the sense of community is an essential aspect of the value proposition. Interaction between users is supported by shared space where people can connect, collaborate and feel at home (Stay The Night, 2020), just like coworking spaces do, but with the difference that digital nomads do not have another place to go home to at night. Therefore, according to the experts interviewed, the community's ties are strong.

The added value of hybrid hospitality for companies and employees is the maximum flexibility in workplaces and meeting rooms, without the need to engage in long-term commitments with guarantees. A high initial investment in terms of design can thus be avoided. It also reduces accommodation costs when used for a maximum of two to three working days in addition to working from home. Finally, hybrid hospitality also has added value to society. With a mixed-function, the hotel will have a better connection to the city and the neighborhood, instead of only serving tourists and business travelers from outside the town (Colliers International, 2020).

Table 2. Examples of innovative hybrid brands

Hybrid brand	Activities	Number of properties
CitizenM	Work-sleep-meet-entertain	21 (+16 in development)[11]
TheStudentHotel	Stay – Work – Meet - Entertain	13 locations in 5 countries[12]
Selina	Hotel-hostel-coworking	81 in 13 countries (expanding to 400 locations in 2024)[13]
Zoku	Home-office hybrid with hotel services	1 (+3 opening 2021)[14]

6.1. Hybrid Business Models

Hybrids operate in similar ways to hotels, being franchised, managed, owned or leased (see 4.1). Industry leaders indicate the owned and leased properties may be more common than in the traditional hotel industry, but this may be an effect of the dominance of American hotel chains and their preference for franchised and managed business models. Hybrid business models focus on maximizing revenues by minimizing unused capacity. This strategy is referred to as 'intensifying' (increased use of, or greater productivity within properties), as opposed to 'densifying' strategies that focus on reducing the amount of space per user (which is the rationale behind many open-plan offices). As hybrids operate 24/7, they have roughly twice as much time to cover their fixed costs than coworking spaces. However, it does require the last characteristic of hybrid hotels mentioned above: a room that is not solely focused on sleeping, like in the

[11] https://www3.citizenm.com .
[12] https://www.thestudenthotel.com/coworking-space/.
[13] https://www.selina.com/all-locations/.
[14] www.liveZoku.com.

traditional hotel. A hybrid business needs a design that enables multifunctional uses of the rooms.

The other cornerstone in the hybrid business model is resilience. Hybrid business models and properties are designed for maximum flexibility and multifunctionality. The combined revenue streams (short stay, extended stay, remote working, events, and even residential) increase resilience and reduce unused capacity. The most profitable combination of target groups is travel and work, as this combination allows for (almost) 24/7 use of the same space. For example, a room used for an overnight stay between 19.00h and 08.00h, can -after cleaning- be available for daytime workers from 9.00h. The sleeping area is closed off, and overnight guests can store their personal belongings securely. At the end of the day, the room is again cleaned and available for overnight stay once more. So far, Zoku is the only hotel where this is possible. To compensate overnight guests for the inconvenience of clearing the room, guests sometimes receive a share of the extra revenues. By combining restaurant functions, events and coworking, common space occupancy could be stretched for up to 16 hours a day.

7. Methods

As a first step, four expert interviews were held to gain first-hand insights into the respective markets, the business models, challenges and prospects. Two experts were GMs in the international hotel industry in the past; one expert is co-founding father of multiple hybrid concepts (i.a.. Zoku), one is a research professor. Next, desk research was conducted to compare the offer of hotels, coworking spaces and hybrids. Five international city hotels from the top 10 hotel chains (Table 1), five coworking brands depicted in Table 2 (of which three are global market leaders), and four hybrid models (Table 3), were included in the analysis. The hotels included were selected based on the availability of a workspace offer for remote working, 4-5 stars, metropolitan locations, international spread (Amsterdam, Singapore, Washington, Paris, Brussels). The analysis included: target groups (freelancers, (business)travelers, remote workers, start-ups, SME, corporates), type of space (office, hotel room, loft, common space), functions (hot desk, designated desk, private serviced office, customized private office, overnight stay, residential), operating hours, contract, price category, the presence of community and type of amenities.

8. Results

8.1. Hotels

Hotels that offer Work-From-Hotels focus on B2B target groups (businesses that want employees to work in a representative environment away from the office), and B2C (people who need an alternative for work from home). Resort hotels also offer 'workcations', but this falls out of the scope of this chapter. Many hotels offer day rates for the use of common spaces for coworking and meeting, and guest rooms for remote work in a private setting, much like activity-based work concepts, as predicted by Lub et al. (2016) in their study on the future of hotels. Rates for coworking are comparable to those in the coworking market: on average €15 per day. Rates for day use of guest rooms varies from €50 per day for standard rooms to €200 per day for suites. When the use of hotel amenities like spa's, pools and fitness rooms is allowed, this is reflected in the price. Most hotels allow 10 to 12 hours between check-in and check-out for daytime use. Hotels do offer loyalty programs, but no sense of community. Users are regarded as individuals; any form of social interaction is up to the individuals themselves.

Suites are better suited for work (but rather expensive) than standard hotel rooms, which commonly have large beds dominating the space and, in most cases, small, unergonomic desks. Therefore, *without* an upgrade of the guest rooms, the former GM-respondents expect this offer to be a temporary phenomenon to make money in slow times. However, some of the high-end top-10 hotel chains take targeting the B2B sector serious, by transforming meeting rooms into shared offices for several dozens of people, e.g., enabling teams to work together. Moreover, some hotels convert guest rooms into private offices for 1-3 people. Accor, for example, has converted hotel rooms in 320 hotels to daytime' hotel office': hybrid rooms with an upgrade of the office facilities with spacious desks, wireless keyboards and mouse, ergonomically furniture and stationery. In these rooms, the sleeping arrangements have been made less prominent. The research professor explains: "Now that hotels are generally owned by investors, the turnover per square meter has become much more important than the room occupancy rates. And hotels typically have a lot of unused capacity due to large common areas and the rather long time between check-out and check-in. Remote working and coworking are ways to optimize the turnover per m2 as it provides a stable customer and revenue flow that is independent of travel." The fact that platforms like MEOW (My Extraordinary Workspace) jump in this development seems to support his vision. Like desk booking platforms, they could become a vital channel to connect to the market, and like these, take a relatively large share of the rates in return. For example, MEOW takes 20% of the coworking fee, and 10% of any additional booking of hotel rooms and meeting rooms (NRIT Media, 2020).

8.2. Coworking Spaces

Coworking spaces, in general, have a broad target group: freelancers, remote workers and SMEs. Or, as WeWork states on its website: “businesses of all sizes - from freelancers to Fortune 500’s.”

Their memberships and contracts cater to the need for flexibility of these target groups: day passes, hot desks memberships, dedicated desks in shared offices memberships, and private office space. Rates vary and depend among others on location, the standard, and amenities. Coworking spaces depend on communities for customer loyalty, and the community is of added value to users for social and business reasons. The strength of community ties depends on the member churn rate and the type of users.

Memberships allow the use of space for several days per month up and until full access. In general: private office space has contract terms from 3 months to 1 year, with 30 days or more notice, whereas coworking spaces commonly apply one moth for dedicated desks.

In general, dedicated desks and office members have 24/7 access to their space, whereas access to shared desks in coworking spaces is limited to operating hours and staff presence. All coworking spaces have community managers and organize events to stimulate a sense of community. Some add development programs to the menu. Speedy and secure WIFI, phone booths for private calls, common space for interaction combined with F&B/kitchenettes and network events is always provided. Some have extras included in the fee, like fitness centers, yoga classes, showers, shared bikes, bring your dog, reception services, and limited use of meeting rooms. Also, coworking spaces with attractive bar/restaurant facilities often open these up to the public to generate traffic.

But, the 'co' in coworking refers to working together, not to the combination of different kinds of use. Coworking spaces have one focus, supplying a workplace, whereas hybrids supply for different kinds of functions.

8.3. Hybrids

Hybrids combine more than two functions and tap into different target groups by definition; however, they differ in the combinations they make. The desk research showed that some organizations profile themselves as hybrids. In contrast, on second look, they are 'just' coworking spaces or regular hotels that brand themselves as vibrant communities, to become more attractive to Millennials.

According to the co-founder of Zoku, 'community ties are stronger in hybrids than in coworking spaces, as people do not have a home to go to at night. (Digital) nomads need the community to feel at home, and thus they actively seek ways to connect to others.

The common spaces, including active management to facilitate effortless connections in hybrids, are essential for making a home.'

Community-building is supported in three ways: by the membership (no free use of space or facilities), by active community management, and by scheduled events. Co-living-travel hybrids actively connect to local communities, as this adds to their members' travel experience. Hybrids that are more focused on work actively help members establish local networks for business or for an extended stay.

Hybrid business models have flexibility and community-building at heart. Spaces are designed in such a way that multifunctional use is always possible. This means that they can breathe with market demand and that spaces are suitable for multiple functions without adaptions. This makes hybrid concepts the most robust business model of the three included in this analysis.

8.4. Combined Findings from a Guest Perspective

The main activities in peoples' lives can be summarized as sleeping, working, socializing, nourishment (Food & Beverages), sports & leisure. If we depict the different functions that accommodate people's multifaceted lives as modules, we can map and compare the offer of regular offices, residential facilities, hotels, coworking spaces, and hybrid hospitality. The relevant modules for different types of workers are printed in bold; the non-relevant modules in normal font.

Type of guest: the average knowledge worker, the 'anchor' in Greene & Myerson's typology, uses the regular office and his/her residential housing to facilitate a clearly separated work and private life (Greene & Meyerson, 2011). Whenever (s)he is working, (s)he can be found in his/her room at the office.

Regular office – work as a primary function – long-term contracts

sleep	**work**	F&B	**business meetings**	community and events	sports & leisure

Residential properties – long stay

sleep	work	**F&B**	business meetings	**community and events**	sports & leisure

During (short) holidays, the (s)he may go to a hotel, as a leisure guest.

Hotel – primary function short-stay lodgings, meetings & events

sleep	work	F&B	**business meetings**	community and **events**	sports & leisure

Type of guest: the independent professional. Independent professionals or freelancers need short-term/flexible office spaces as their contracted work is dynamic. Furthermore, they require a social function to mingle and share experiences with peers. They spend the night at their private homes. Coworking spaces fit this need.

Coworking space – flexible memberships and community

sleep	**work**	F&B	**business meetings**	**community and events**	sports & leisure

Type of guest: digital nomads. For digital nomads frequently change their location, mostly travel solo and have a lower income from gig-work. They look for interesting places to stay: a temporary home-base with likeminded others, affordable and attractive comfort on an exciting location, and flexibility. Fun first, work to live, not live to work.

Hybrid hangout – initiatives like Selina

sleep	**work**	**F&B**	business meetings	**community and events**	**sports & leisure**

Type of guest: the frequent business traveler. This person frequently travels for meetings and projects, matching the navigator type according to Greene & Meyerson (2011). The business traveler wants decent facilities for concentration work in between meetings. The business traveler is 'a rolling stone' but enjoys the company of like-minded people. Or people in general. Options for stay:

- a hotel with common coworking space, social interaction but unfortunately also distraction.
- a hotel that offers hybrid rooms for working and sleeping. More studio than a bedroom, with comfortable seating arrangements, a form of social contact, and ideal if one visits the same place frequently, or for an extended stay too short for residential hires.
- options to have meetings in the hotel
- go to the gym and relax

Hotel office hybrid

sleep	**work**	**F&B**	**business meetings**	community and events	sports & leisure

Genuine hybrid hospitality - combining stay, work and community like Zoku

sleep	**work**	**F&B**	**business meetings**	**community and events**	**sports & leisure**

This description is based on the guest perspective. From the owner's perspective, it makes a big difference whether different functions are in different rooms, or whether the spaces are versatile enough to enable multiple functions. Not necessarily by offering all necessary amenities in one space, but by easily selecting what amenities should be present when as a guest, you get what you pay for. Reminiscent of a small apartment where the bedroom turns into workspace because the convertible bed disappears into the wall; a guest that does not pay for sleeping cannot 'unlock' the bed. The same room may function as a workplace and as a bedroom. That's a true hybrid concept.

Conclusion and Discussion

The pandemic has proven to be a powerful driver for societal change. It has accelerated trends, changed people's behavioral patterns and has forced society at large to adapt to digital and remote working. This makes corporates shift priorities and rethink their real estate strategies. It is generally understood that part-time remote working is here to stay and that home working alternatives have market potential. From a corporate perspective, hotels and hybrid brands can provide flexible rent rates that are particularly attractive during uncertain economic times and no large up-front investments or lengthy contract obligations, just like operators of flexible office space can, but with elevated hospitality. Therefore, hotels and hybrids present an attractive alternative for companies transitioning to a model in which their employees mainly work remotely.

Furthermore, although the travel industry expects to bounce back in time, our respondents expect that travel behavior will change. Short international trips for business meetings are not expected to return. Also, the number of expatriates is expected to reduce and replaced by extended business trips of several weeks (slow travel), bringing opportunities for extended stay and co-living functions.

The coronavirus has taught us that resilience is key for businesses to survive. To build resilience, forward-thinking companies across the industry have found effective ways to innovate, take risks and merge concepts. They have redesigned their spaces and added functions, and made their business models more robust while increasing the turnover per square meter. Spaces may be used for different functions, or spaces are dedicated to new or even innovative functions. In the case of hybrid hospitality, spaces can change use from one kind into another, even on one day, allowing an intensified use. The four experts agree that hybrid models are flexible enough to evolve alongside shifting consumer needs while accommodating their multifaceted lives. This is confirmed by our desk research results; a hybrid model provides investors with a more guaranteed base income by an intensified use of square meters and generates a higher return in peak periods. The base income should cover a large percentage of fixed costs, while the flexible costs can vary as demand does. All in all, we conclude that hybrids and hotels that offer dedicated workspace will be a permanent addition to the flexible office market. As the market demand for flexible solutions is expected to rise too, only time can tell if their presence will be disruptive or cater to a particular customer segment outside the scope of the regular coworking spaces.

DISCUSSION

This study took place during the second wave of the coronavirus and the subsequent repeated lockdown measures. Predicting the future is always hard, but in times like this, the dynamics are unprecedented. Furthermore, it is a small and non-representative sample of the industry. However, we tried to compare apples to apples as much as possible by including a similar range of stars in the hotels and selecting hotels that belong to the market leaders, so that concepts developed are not limited to one hotel but implemented at least regionally, preferably globally.

Finding enough truly hybrid concepts with an international presence that include serious work facilities proved a challenge. We ended up with four instead of five, with the Selina concept bordering what we found acceptable (as they provide only coworking spaces to their overnight guests and not much information was publicly available). Furthermore, one might discuss whether these concepts have mixed use of rooms or hybrid rooms. For comparing coworking spaces, we selected brands with more than one location in metropoles that had considerable size. Three of the top 5 market leaders were included, with the addition of Uncommon and B. as the major brands that border serviced office space. Community and collaboration seem to be there for marketing purposes mostly. The draft version of this chapter was reviewed by two of the interviewed experts. We gladly used their input to improve the literature review, findings and conclusions.

References

Bauman, Z. (2004). *Waste Lives: Modernity and Its Outcasts*. Cambridge, UK: Polity Press.

Berry, L. L., Wall, E. A., & Carbone, L. P. (2006). Service clues and customer assessment of the service experience: lessons from marketing. *Academy of Management Perspectives*, *20*(2), 43-57. https://doi.org/10.5465/AMP.2006.20591004.

Bick, A., Blandin, A., & Mertens, K. (2020). *Work from home after the COVID-19 Outbreak*. London, Centre for Economic Policy Research. https://cepr.org/active/publications/discussion_papers/dp.php?dpno=15 000.

Brotherton, B., & Wood, R. C. (Eds.) (2008). *The SAGE Handbook of Hospitality Management*. London, U.K.: Sage Publications Ltd.

Capdevila, I. (2013). *Knowledge dynamics in Localised Communities: Coworking Spaces as microclusters*. http://dx.doi.org/10.2139/ ssrn.2414121.

Chegut, A., & Langen, M. (2019). The Financial Impacts of Coworking: Rental Prices and Market Dynamics in the Commercial Office Market.

Clapp, J., & Ridge, E. (2016). *Security and Hospitality in Literature and Culture: Modern and Contemporary Perspectives*. New York, U.S.A.: Routledge.

Colliers International (2020). *Hotels om in the werken - hybrid hospitality is de toekomst* [whitepaper]. [Colliers International (2020). *Hotels to work from – hybrid hospitality is the future* [whitepaper]].

Deloitte (2020). Deloitte Insights: 2021 *Commercial Real Estate Outlook – rebuilding to enhance resilience.*

De Peuter, G., Cohen, N. S., & Saraco, F. (2017). The ambivalence of coworking: on the politics on an emerging work practice. *European*

Journal of Cultural Studies, *20*(6), 687-706. http//doi.org/10.1177/1367549417732997.

Deskmag (2019). *The 2019 Global Coworking Survey.*

Deskmag (2018). *The 2018 State of Coworking Spaces.* https://www.deskmag.com/en/coworking-spaces/the-state-of-coworking-spaces-in-2018-market-research-development-survey.

FMN & CoreNet Global (2013). *Wat wil de eindgebruiker? Op naar een vraaggestuurde kantorenmarkt. Samenvatting resultaten fase 1.* [FMN & CoreNet Global (2013). *What does the end user want? Towards a demand-driven office market. Summary of results phase 1*].

Gaggi, M., & Nardzzi, E. (2006). *La fine del ceto medio e la nascita della società low cost.* Einaudi, Turin [Gaggi, M. & Narduzzi, E. (2006). *The end of the middle class and the birth of the low-cost society.* Einaudi, Turin].

Greene, C., & Myerson, J. (2011). Space for thought: Designing for knowledge workers. *Facilities*, *29* (1/2), 19–30. http://doi.org/10.1108/02632771111101304.

Gandini, A. (2015). The rise of coworking spaces: A literature review. *Ephemera*, *15*(1), 193–205.

Guestline (2020). *A hotelier's guide: Designing the ideal coworking space.* https://www.guestline.com/nl/a-hoteliers-guide-on-coworking/.

Gullahorn, J. (1952). Distance and friendship as factors in the gross interaction matrix. *Sociometry*, *15* (1-2), 123-134. https://doi.org/10.2307/2785450.

Hemmington, N. (2007). From Service to Experience: Understanding and defining the hospitality business. *The Service Industries Journal*, *27*(6), 747-755. http://doi.org/10.1080/02642060701453221.

Hua, Y., Loftness, V., Kraut, R., & Powell, K. M. (2010). Workplace collaborative space layout typology and occupant perception of collaboration environment. *Environment and Planning B: Planning and Design*, *37*, 429- 448. http://doi.org/10.1068/b35011.

Josephi, A. (2015). *The phenomenology of Revenue Management: Explorations in the Hotel Industry.* Maastricht, The Netherlands: Maastricht School of Management.

IHGPLC (2019). *Strategic Report – Industry overview.*

ILO (2020a). *The home as workplace: Trends and policies for ensuring decent work.*

ILO (2020b). *Working from Home: Estimating the worldwide potential, ILO policy brief.*

Jakonen, M., Kivinen, N., Salovaara, P., & Hirkman, P. (2017). Towards an economy of encounters? A critical study of affectual assemblages in coworking. *Scandinavian Journal of Management, 33*(4), 235–242. http://dx.doi.org/10.1016/j.scaman.2017.10.003.

JLL (2020) *Global Real Estate Perspective – Highlights Investor and Corporate*, Global Research, November 2020.

Kojo, I., & Nenonen, S. (2017). Evolution of coworking places: drivers and possibilities. *Intelligent Building International*, *9*(3), 164-175. https://doi.org/10.1080/17508975.2014.987640.

Lub, X. D., Rijnders, R., Niño Caceras, L., & Bosman, J. (2016). The future of hotels: The Lifestyle Hub. A design-thinking approach for developing future hospitality concepts. *Journal of Vacation Marketing*, *22*(3), 249-264. http://doi.org/10.1177/1356766715623829.

Melissen, F., Van der Rest, J. P., Josephi, S., & Blomme, R. (eds.) (2018). *Hospitality Experience*. Groningen/Utrecht, The Netherlands: Noordhoff Uitgevers.

Moriset, B. (2014). Building new places of the creative economy. The rise of coworking spaces, *Paper presented at the 2nd Geography of Innovation International Conference, Utrecht University, The Netherlands.* Available at https://halshs.archives-ouvertes.fr/halshs-00914075.

Ng, C. F. (2016). Public spaces as workplace for mobile knowledge workers, *Journal of Corporate Real Estate, 18*(3), 209-223. http://doi.org/10.1108/JCRE-10-2015-0030.

Niewiadomska, E. W. (2013). *Marketing Strategies to Grow Your Coworking Business!* http://www.deskmag.com/en/8-marketing-strategies-to-grow-your-coworking-business-791.

NRIT Media (2020). *Mix hotel en werkplek – hotels anders inzetten en ontwikkelen in 6 trends*. https://www-nritmedia-nl.saxion.idm.oclc.org/

kennisbank/43438/mix-hotel-en-werkplek/?topicsid=[NRIT Media (2020) *Mix hotel and workspace – a different use and development of hotels in 6 trends*].

Olma, S. (2012). *The Serendipity machine – A disruptive business model for society 3.0.* Amersfoort, The Netherlands: VLDB.

Pijls, R., Groen, B. H., Galetzka, M., & Pruyn, A. T. H. (2017). Measuring the experience of hospitality: scale development and validation. *International Journal of Hospitality Management, 67*, 125-133. http://doi.org/10.1016/j.ijhm.2017.07.008.

Pine, B. J., & Gilmore, J. H. (1988). Welcome to the Experience Economy, *Harvard Business Review*, July-August. https://hbr.org/1998/07/ welcome-to-the-experience-economy.

Parrino, L. (2015). Coworking: assessing the role of proximity in knowledge exchange. *Knowledge Management Research Practices, 13,* 261-271. https://doi.org/10.1057/kmrp.2013.47.

Porter, M. (1995). *Competitive Advantage: Creating and sustaining superior performance*. New York, USA: The Free Press.

Rossitto, C., & Lampinen, A. (2018). *Co-Creating the Workplace: Participatory Efforts to Enable Individual Work at the Hoffice. Computer Supported Cooperative Work (CSCW), 27*, 947–982. http://doi.org/ 10.1007/s10606-018-9319-z.

Scullica, F., & Elgani, E. (2020). Time. Hybrid Spaces for Users-Bodies between Work and Hospitality. In: Anzani A. (eds.) *Mind and Places.* Springer Series in Design and Innovation, 4. Springer, Cham. https://doi.org/10.1007/978-3-030-45566-8_19.

Shareena, P., & Shahid, M. (2020). Work from home during COVID-19: employees' perceptions and experiences. *Global Journal for Research Analysis, 9*(5). http:doi.org/10.36106/gjra. https://www.worldwide journals.com/global-journal-for-research-analysis-GJRA/article/work-from-home-during-covid-19-employees-perception-and-experiences/ MTQ2ODE=/?is=1&b1=5&k=2.

Statista.com (2020a). *Hotel industry worldwide - statistics & facts* December 2020. https://www.statista.com/topics/1102/hotels/.

Statista.com (2020b). *Monthly hotel revenue per available room worldwide from 2018 to 2020, by region*. https://www.statista.com/statistics/206844/hotel-revpar-by-region-worldwide/.

Stay The Night Ltd. (2020). *The Future of Hospitality – Why 2021 is the Year of the Hybrid* [whitepaper].

Termaat, W. A., Van Sprang, H., & Groen, B. H. (2014). Workspace 2020 - Club, Hub and Cowork space: business models for optimal FM support for office workers in the future, in *Proceedings of the 13th EuroFM Research Symposium*. http://doi.org/10.13140/2.1.2537.2963.

The Guardian (20 September 2020) *Another day not at the office: will working from home be 2020's most radical change?*

Thompson, B. Y. (2018). Digital nomads: employment in the online gig economy. Glocalism: *Journal of Culture, Politics and Innovation*, 1, doi: 10.12893/gjcpi.2018.1.11.

Waters-Lynch, J., and Potts, J., and Butcher, T., Dodson, J., & and Hurley, J. (2016). *Coworking: A Transdisciplinary Overview*. SSRN: https://ssrn.com/abstract=2712217.

Zhou, Y. (2019). *A Taxonomy of Coworking Space: Manhattan, NYC*. https://ecommons.cornell.edu/bitstream/handle/1813/70837/14_A_Taxonomy_of_Coworking_Space_Manhattan__NYC.pdf?sequence=1&isAllowed=y.

Zuckerman, A. (2020). *Coworking statistics 2019/220: Market share & Industry Growth*. Available via: https://comparecamp.com/coworking-statistics/.

In: The Future of Real Estate
Editor: Jan Veuger
ISBN: 978-1-53619-414-2

Chapter 9

Real Estate as a Service

Jan Veuger[1,*], Joris Winters[2], Herman J. Kok[3] and Paul Wessels[4]

[1]Saxion University of Applied Sciences, The Netherlands
[2]Arcadis Nederland B.V.
[3]MARK Capital Management Ltd
[4]Chairman RICS working group Research & Innovation

Abstract

When looking at the expertise in the RICS Research Group and Development in The Netherlands and a holistic approach to the possible relevant developments in the field of the built environment - whether or not influenced by COVID-19 - an integral approach is of great importance for the raison d'être of real estate. A long-term approach to real estate will increasingly play a role in which the boundaries between construction and management of the built environment are blurred, but where there is still a long way to go to bring service to a higher level. We therefore look from three different perspectives by experts from this

* Corresponding Author's E-mail: j.veuger@saxion.nl.

group at (1) Corona crisi accelerates the green blue revolution in real estate (2) Perspectives of Urban Mixed Use in Post-Corona Central Urban Areas and (3) cooperation in new coalitions.

Keywords: flexibility, service, urban locations, digitization, other infrastructure and new alliances

INTRODUCTION

As a globally recognised professional body, everything the Royal Institution of Chartered Surveyors (RICS) do is designed to effect positive change in the built and natural environments. Through our respected global standards, leading professional progression and our trusted data and insight, we promote and enforce the highest professional standards in the development and management of land, real estate, construction and infrastructure. Our work with others provides a foundation for confident markets, pioneers better places to live and work and is a force for positive social impact.

With over 134,000 highly qualified trainees and professionals, and offices in every significant financial market, we are ideally placed to influence policy and embed our standards within local marketplaces in order to protect consumers and businesses. In doing so, we can innovate and progress the development of spaces and places so they are fit for future generations, in addition to the challenges faced in the present.

Surveyors keep traffic flowing, water running and people moving. They shape our roads, bridges and tunnels, our skyscrapers, stations and stadiums. They work in mines and in fields, on cliffs and on beaches. They value the houses we live in and the places we work in. They create safer homes and happier communities. And they're busy shaping our future too: helping to regenerate deprived areas and planning smart cities connected by the Internet of Things, while pioneering safer, more sustainable and more environmentally friendly building methods.

Name	Role	Organization
Robert Dackus MIM MRICS	Head Reserach and Concepts	3W Real Estate
Kay Deana MRE MRICS	Manager Portfolio Strategy and Research	Heimstaden
Dr. Herman Kok MRE MRICS	Vice President, Head of Research	MARK Capital Management Ltd
Dr. Ir. Gert Joost Peek MRICS	Owner and professor Applied Sciences	SPOTON and Rotterdam University of Applied Sciences
Paul Wessels MSc MRICS	Chiarman Working Group Research and Innovation	RICS
Joris Winters MSc MRICS	Sector Leader Property and Investment	Arcadis The Netherlands BV
Machiel Wolters MSc MRICS	Senior Director	CBRE The Netgerlands
Dr. Ing. Jan Veuger MRE FRICS	Professor Blockchain and Real Estate	Saxion University of Applied Sciences.

Figure 1. Expertise in the Research Group and Development RICS Netherlands.

Surveyors work closely with a wide range of people: architects and engineers, bankers and ecologists, town planners and property developers. And they use the latest technologies: flying drones to map land and measure buildings, creating virtual reality models of buildings, and using Big Data to tackle global issues like climate change, migration and urbanisation. There are more than 100 varied career roles across the surveying profession in three main sectors: construction and infrastructure; property; and land.

The Research and Development Group of the Royal Institution of Chartered Surveyors (RICS) In the Netherlands, the main focus is on developments affecting the real estate market. From this working group regular publication (Kok et al. 2020) is provided whether or not in combination with webinars, the two most recent of which are 'Webinar Real Estate as a Service' (October 22th 2020) and 'Webinar Samenwerking als medicijn tegen een verstolde huizenmarkt' (Webinar Collaboration as a medicine against a clogged up housing market) (December 9th 2020).

1. Real Estate as a Service

When looking at the expertise in the RICS Research Group and Development in The Netherlands (Figure 1) and a holistic approach to the possible relevant developments in the field of the built environment - whether or not influenced by COVID-19 - an integral approach is of great importance for the raison d'être of real estate. A long-term approach to real estate will increasingly play a role in which the boundaries between construction and management of the built environment are blurred, but where there is still a long way to go to bring service to a higher level. We therefore look from three different perspectives by experts from this group at (1) Corona crisi accelerates the green blue revolution in real estate (2) Perspectives of Urban Mixed Use in Post-Corona Central Urban Areas and (3) cooperation in new coalitions.

2. Corona Crisis Accelerates the Green Blue Revolution in Real Estate (by Paul Wessels)

The corona crisis is further accelerating awareness of how much our built environment contributes to well-being and health. It will also accelerate building and area standards that are evidence-based and supported by peer-reviewed science.

The American futurist Rex Miller recently put it this way: 'We've all been caught in a convulsion of historic dimensions. We didn't ask for it, see it coming, or know what to do when it arrived. We will collectively be dealing with months and perhaps years of collateral damage to our economy, employee mental health and the psyche of our nation.'[1]

The rise in health care costs is certainly not a new phenomenon. For example, look at practice in the Netherlands: Between 1972 and 2018, health care expenditure in the Netherlands rose from 6 billion to 100

[1] Rex Miller, Strategy in Rebuilding: Principles to Build Post Traumatic Growth (2020).

billion euros. The National Institute for Public Health and the Environment (RIVM) estimates that the costs will rise to € 291 billion in 2060. The vast majority (€ 96 billion) will go to hospital care. Expenditure on care for the disabled, elderly care and mental health care will then probably amount to € 30 billion.[2] Based on an average annual real growth of the economy of 1.7 percent up to 2060, we see that health care expenditure as a percentage of the gross domestic product will increase from 12.7 to 19.6 percent between 2015 and 2060. This would mean that health care expenditure per capita would increase from more than € 5,100 to almost € 15,800: a tripling.[3]

The same trend is present in all Western countries. In the United States, the situation is even more serious: If the current rate keeps up, by 2050 almost 40% of GDP will be required to cover health costs.[4]

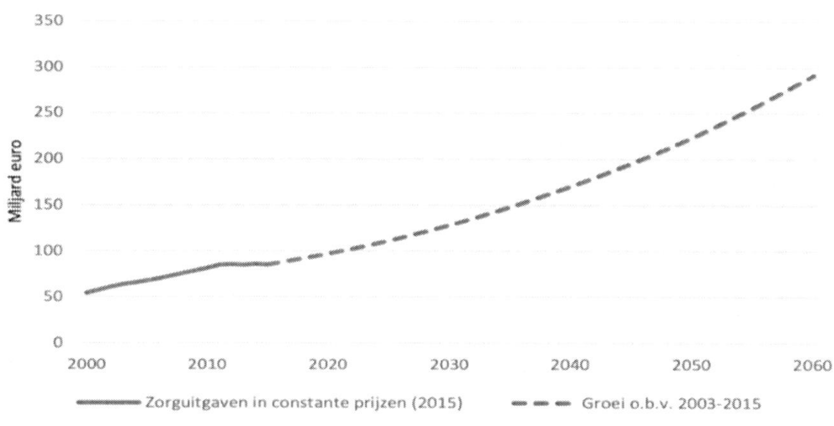

Source: RIVM.

Figure 2. Healthcare expenditure Netherlands, projection based on diagnosis-specific long-term growth.

[2] Outlook for health care expenditure 2015-2060, Quantitative preliminary research commissioned by the Scientific Council for Government Policy, RIVM, page 3.

[3] Outlook for health care expenditure 2015-2060 (2020), Quantitative preliminary research commissioned by the Scientific Council for Government Policy, RIVM, page 11.

[4] Rex Miller, Phillip Williams, Michael O'Neill, Michael O'Neill (2018), The Healthy Workplace Nudge How Healthy People, Culture, and Buildings Lead to High Performance, page 22.

2.1. Corona Accelerates the Health Crisis

The corona crisis is exacerbating the situation. A Commonwealth Fund study concluded in the summer of 2020 that a third of adults in the US had suffered from a powerful cocktail of stress, anxiety and sadness since the start of the pandemic. The rapid spread of COVID-19, the tidal wave of information and misinformation, along with the feeling of isolation from physical distancing and quarantine measures, demands a high price. And it will not be over by the beginning of 2021.

Here too the US scores higher than many other countries, especially in northwestern Europe. For example, the Netherlands scored low in that study compared to other Western countries, with only 14% of the population reporting similar complaints.[5]

But for all countries, the COVID-19 trauma is putting pressure on a population already dealing with chronic health issues and thus the accumulating effect on mental health. The main cause is stress, a factor that multiplied significantly in 2020. It is estimated that in the US alone, 90 million people in this country are currently experiencing Level 1 or 2 trauma as a result of the pandemic.'[6]

2.2. Re-Humanizing the Workplace

A person's mental health is uncertain: it can be influenced - for better or worse - by work and social conditions, environmental factors, lifestyle and health behavior. From a business perspective, mental health care is often viewed as something outside of employers' remit - and seen as a 'nice to have', rather than an essential element. But as the evidence mounts, CEOs realize that investing in the mental health and resilience of

[5] https://www.commonwealthfund.org/publications/ issue-briefs / 2020 / aug / americans-mental-health-and-economic-consequences-COVID19.

[6] Rex Miller, Strategy in Rebuilding: Principles to Build Post Traumatic Growth (2020).

their employees is more than altruistic; it has a direct impact on productivity and profitability.

When organizations focus on employee health, it is now more important than ever to pay attention to people. Right now, we have the opportunity to be there for other people in a way that may not have seemed important prior to the pandemic. Check in with your colleagues with a simple 'Are you okay?' is a good place to start.

The environments we create to facilitate work become proxies of how well we work and live together. Re-humanizing the workplace is the first bridgehead to avert the threat of runaway health costs. Knowing that more than 80% of a company's exposure is the cost of its people and that people spend more than 90% of their lives in buildings, what does it take to turn every building into a platform that supports the health and well-being of its residents?

David Radcliffe, vice president of real estate and workplace services for Google, put it this way: 'Are we squeezing pennies to reduce building cost and losing dollars of engagement?'[7]

One of the most difficult things for leaders during periods of recovery from major disasters is to adapt to the reality that this is not an event, but a process. We are entering the stage of disillusionment and must immediately prepare for reconstruction. The pandemic exposed many structural deficiencies in the health system, the inequalities in our economy, the lack of clear governance, an unprepared and unequipped education system, a lack of emergency preparedness, as well as the health and well-being of our employees.[8]

2.3. The Rise of the Chief Wellness Officer

Before COVID19, companies were already on an unsustainable path in terms of health and health costs. For example, one of the best-known

[7] Rex Miller, Phillip Williams, Michael O'Neill, Michael O'Neill (2018), The Healthy Workplace Nudge How Healthy People, Culture, and Buildings Lead to High Performance,

[8] Rex Miller, Strategy in Rebuilding: Principles to Build Post Traumatic Growth (2020).

human wellness researchers, Dr. Michael Roizen, wellness officer of the Cleveland Clinic, argues that business leaders should become their own chief wellness officers; they cannot delegate supervision of this to HR departments alone. Companies have a unique opportunity to reverse this trend because of the millions of people they directly affect and then indirectly affect when employees return home. Dr. Roizen summarizes it in one mission: "Our task is to give healthy employees the energy to work. That's the only way the company can survive.[9]

This has a major impact on the way we judge the built environment. In addition to 'green' certification, 'blue' certification is becoming increasingly important. A certificate for green buildings has evolved from a 'nice-to-have' to a 'baseline must-have' among many progressive tenants, landlords and investors. The implementation, validation and communication of some concept of Healthy Buildings is expected to become an even more important differentiator for advanced companies in the future.

Buildings and portfolios are compared on these aspects and this has dramatic economic consequences. An important reason for this is that many of the 'clients' of these buildings are institutional investors, who typically spend 5-10 percent of their portfolios on real estate through direct investment or real estate investment funds. Many investors have also expressed their preference for green buildings in recent years. The theme of health has now been added to this.

2.4. Test, Verify and Certify

One of the main criticisms of green building certification systems is that they largely represent the design and performance of a building at any given time. Does the BREEAM certification of an office from 2010 really tell us anything about the performance of that building today, a decade later? The answer is largely no. Fortunately, just as there has been a

[9] Rex Miller, Strategy in Rebuilding: Principles to Build Post Traumatic Growth (2020).

movement in education towards 'lifelong learning', there is an outgrowth of buildings as we try to move from static assessments to dynamic assessments, where building performance is continuously measured and verified.[10] In short, this comes down to the continuous testing, verification and certification of buildings and portfolios when it comes to health and well-being.

This is what a good healthy building certification protocol looks like according to Harvard researchers Joseph G. Allen John D. Macomber (2020): Evidence based and backed by peer-reviewed science. Is flexible and can include evolving research and new technological advances. Is standardized, consistently defined and verifiable. Is cost effective (and with a cost-benefit analysis that includes human health and performance). Is not only defined at one point in time. Is managed and verified with on-site testing by experts trained in the anticipation, evaluation, management and control of hazards. Enables performance verification, including monitoring of health performance indicators such as real-time indicators of the quality of the indoor environment in spaces that are representative of where people spend their time. Has been developed in close collaboration with end users and building health experts (e.g., engineers, health scientists and medical professionals). Is recognized by the market and investors in providing commercial value. Encourages shared value between stakeholders (e.g., investors, owners and tenants).[11] It is not without reason that we see the rise of health standards such as WELL, Fitwell and others. And existing 'green' standards such as BREEAM and LEED are also being added with new health characteristics.

Science has known for a long time, but accelerated by the corona crisis, the realization breaks through how much our built environment affects our well-being and our health. The breakthrough from green to blue buildings, and the transparency in information required for this, is the biggest revolution in real estate in living memory.

---

[10] Joseph G. Allen John D. Macomber (2020), Healthy Buildings, How Indoor Spaces Drive Performance and Productivity, page 148.

[11] Joseph G. Allen John D. Macomber (2020), Healthy Buildings, How Indoor Spaces Drive Performance and Productivity, Page 173, 174.

3. Perspectives of Urban Mixed Use in Post-Corona Central Urban Areas (by Herman Kok)

While Covid-19 is unlikely to stope the ongoing urbanisation, it is likely to have a substantial influence on the built environment. Preference for living, working, consuming, and socialising are changing because of Covid-19 related restrictions. Part of these changes will be structural, affecting the demand parameters for real estate in different asset classes. A good share of all retail, office, and residential is likely to be improved for health and space quality reasons, ranging from a limited adjustment to a full repurposing or redevelopment. Mixed use real estate in central areas of dynamic cities may be in an advantageous position, as mixed use offers the opportunity to combine functions and shift between them. Mixed use areas also tend to reduce mobility, especially car mobility and can result in shorter commuting distances. Mixed use areas also contribute to the liveability of urban areas as there is a greater variety of use and negative impacts of deserted office areas and bedroom communities can be prevented.

3.1. Urbanisation to Continue

The world is going through an unprecedented wave of urbanisation. More than half of the world population lives in cities, a share that is expected to grow to two-thirds by 2050 [1]. Urbanisation rates also continue to increase in Europe. Large cities function as cradle for ideas, innovations, and relations. For people moving to the city, enrolling in higher education, and starting their career are key motives. And people tend to find partners and initiate household formation in the large cities. Large cities and their agglomerations in Europe have been enjoying higher rates of economic growth and stronger demographics than the country's average, resulting in larger gap between large cities on the one hand and rural and peripheral areas on the other.

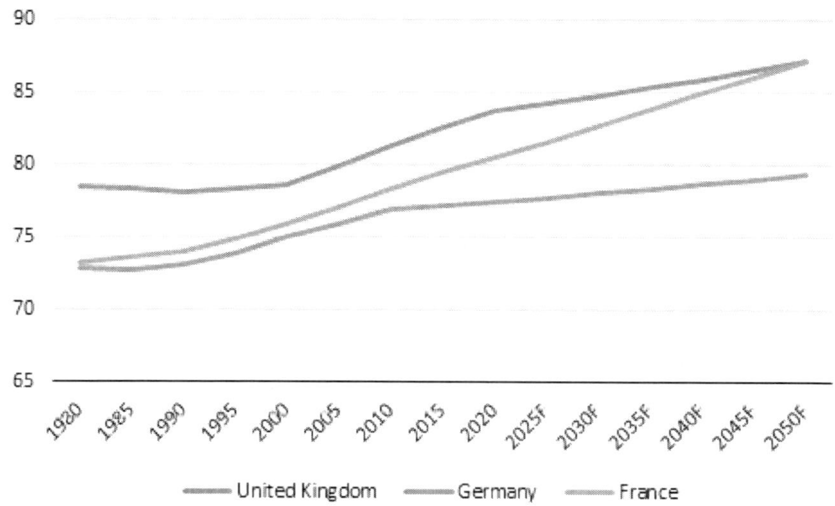

Source: Oxford Economics, December 2020 [2].

Figure 3. Urbanisation rate 1980 – forecast 2050.

In Europe, many capital cities and large secondary cities were hubs of economic growth outperforming the country's national average thanks to diverse economies and high degree of diversity in the urban population. Many central urban areas have beein undergoing massive reviatlisations since the 1980s. Urban planning policies shifted from a doctrine of separating functions to a model of mixing functions. Urban planner Jane Jacobs favoured already a mixed-use urban development model in the 1960s [3], based on mixing residential with workplaces in a quality walkable public space setting. This with services, retail, and food & beverages embedded in the area to serve the needs of the neighbourhood.

The appeal of mixed use is strong in Europe's large cities partly because of the urban patterns grown historically, and cities experience an ongoing economic transition towards the services and experience economy.

Among all age groups, expectations are growing for dense, vibrant, mixed use urban locations that enable a 'live work play' lifestyle. These demands are especially high in inner cities that have become safer, with improved schools and hospitals, access to green space and a high standard of public services and infrastructure [4].

Europe's cities are in an advantageous position, as their compact city centres, established networks of public transport, and dense clusters of infrastructure and institutions mean there is experience withy and a strong starting point for creating and managing mixed-use environments.

Urban innovation has been a strong driver for mixed use environments. Technological advances were often thought to reduce the value of agglomeration effects and the prospects of large cities. However, digital technologies only increased the value of clustering, proximity, and the mixture of functions. Combining uses and systems in mixed-use locations serves the purposes of human interaction, production, and consumption in the new economy. This in a context where boundaries between work, leisure, social life and family life are becoming increasingly hybrid. Technological innovation helps to reduce the impacts of noise and air pollution, reuse and recycle assets and repurpose facilities for multiple uses.

However, high land prices and development cost, combined with restrictive urban planning, often resulted in a reduction of sqm space per capita for living spaces, workplaces, and public space. In some cases, the result was a too dense urban environment with a modest quality public space. One of the assumptions was that people would spend more time in public places such as restaurants, café's and fitness clubs – so called 'third places [5]' – and would therefore need less private space for a certain quality of life.

3.2. The Impact of Covid-19

Though Covid-19 has affected cities dramatically, Covid-19 is unlikely to reverse the continuing urbanisation but will change the way cities are being organised.

Besides the strong negative impact on the economy, one of the main consequences of Covid-19 is an acceleration of ongoing mega-trends affecting society and urban development [6]. These include a growing importance of the circular economy, a rapidly progressing digitalisation, an increased focus on health and wellbeing, and a stronger need for inclusion. Despite the phenomenal growth of cities, cities tended also to experience major problems. Widening income and wealth gaps within the city as well as between the large cities and the rest of the country are an increasing source of polarisation and political tension. High land and real estate prices put increasing pressure on the quality of developed buildings and public space, with the amount of available space per person, decreasing substantially over the last decades with smaller dwellings, more crowded offices, and less public space as outcome. Covid-19 emphasized these problems: the larger these problems in cities, the more these cities were impacted by Covid-19 and related lockdown measures.

Covid-19 has a massive impact on almost all aspects of consumer behaviour [7], which in its turn will impact the way consumers use real estate and function in the city. It affects the way we shop, the way we socialise, the way we work, the way we live, and the way we move. Many of these changes are there to stay. For instance, the accelerated growth of online sales in the retail trade and the increased possibilities to work from home are there to stay. Also, people in the city realise that a dwelling is more than just a place to sleep. Our home is our Castle [8], a home that should provide space to work and to socialise, should have some outdoor space like a garden or balcony, and should be designed in such a way to prevent nuisance between neighbours.

Retail real estate, both highstreet properties and shopping centres, are strongly affected by Covid-19, and many of these are expected to undergo functional changes. The increase of online shopping, a structural phenomenon in the last 10 years, accelerated substantially because of Covid-19. While physical stores were closed during lockdown periods, overall retail sales hardly declined. Online sales volumes increased while physical sales decreased. Also, not being able to go to restaurants or to the workplace, sectors like grocery, do-it-yourself and home sports and entertainment traded very well, while sectors like fashion and shoes & leather were suffering. Covid-19 is to accelerate the process of repurposing of retail space. For many retail locations to stay relevant, downsizing, integrating additional functions in the area, and repurposing surplus space into another use like services, workplaces, or residential are essential.

The lockdown is also changing the view on the use of office space. The longer the lockdown periods too, the more one realised how to work from distance and how to upkeep productivity. While offices will continue to be the heart of organisations, 93% of corporate decision makers expects working from home and remote working to increase. Pre-Covid, this was only 31% [10]. This will impact the office stock dramatically, with decline in demand for space, but an increase in demand for quality. Also, smaller, and well managed core cities like Amsterdam and Stockholm seem to be in an advantageous position compared to the largest core cities such as London and Paris. Also, business clusters away from the main CBD might be preferred. For investors and developers this implies that there will be a growing need for upgrading and reformatting office buildings in line with post-Covid-demand, as well as a further increasing need for repurposing office premises into other uses, such as student housing or other forms residential.

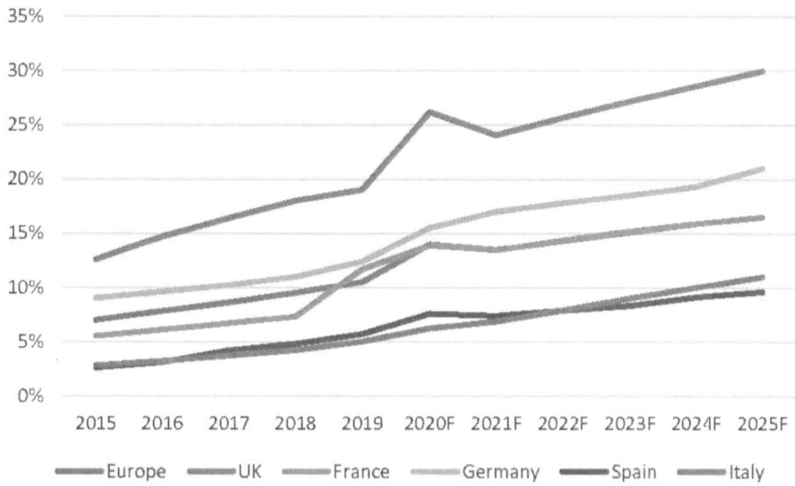

Source: Mintel, August 2020 [9]

Figure 4. Online sales as % of total retail sales.

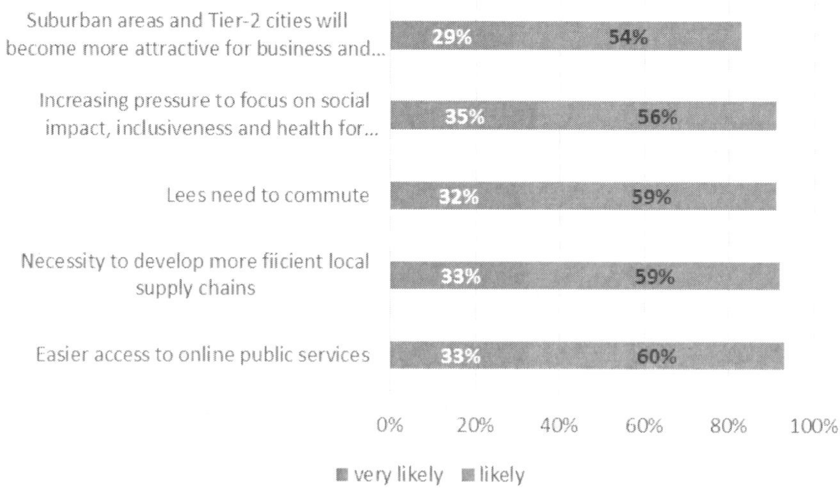

Source: ULI & EY Ernst & Young (2020)

Figure 5. Main changes initiated or accelerated by Covid-19.

Residential real estate will be affected as well. Although short term issues in the aftermath of Covid-19 such as a decline in rent collection rates and an increase in vacancy were almost not an issue in the residential market and affected mainly short-term rental and expat segments in the market, there will be long term complications. Though a re-emerging phase of suburbanisation is unlikely to happen, as the city remains the place for idea formation, career growth, and networking, consumers will look to places to live differently. Outdoor space, workspace in the dwelling, air circulation quality, and sound isolation will become more important.

Research conducted by JLL [11] in Summer 2020 showed how priorities have changed in the aftermath of work. Feeling that remote working could become the new reality, one was prepared to accept a longer distance to the office, as daily commuting could become something of the past.

Striking was the shift in priorities when it came to criteria the dwelling searched for had to fulfil. Reflecting the concerns for health and being able to work from home, personal outdoor space, natural light, fast broadband, and private workspace are among the key criteria the dwelling had to fulfil, and all experienced a substantial increase in the aftermath of Covid-19. It shows that differentiation in the residential market is likely to become more related to health concerns and ability to facilitate working from home. Space parameters and implementation of technology are key to improve the housing stock in the direction of post-Covid needs. For investors, this implies major long-term tasks to upgrade and adapt their housing stock.

Besides re-arrangement of space, technology plays an essential role in upgrading the real estate stock. The fall-out of Covid-19 has been an important accelerator for further integration of technology into real estate. Technology contributes to more healthy, efficient, and comfortable buildings. Examples of Covid-19 related implementations are quality of air circulation, automatic doors, touch free elevators and touch-free toilets and taps. And infrastructure supporting the possibilities to work from home, such as fast broadband will make dwellings more attractive for those who have a long-term prospect of full or partial remote working. This doesn't only include cable connections in the street, but the way the building is connected to and integrated with the network in particular.

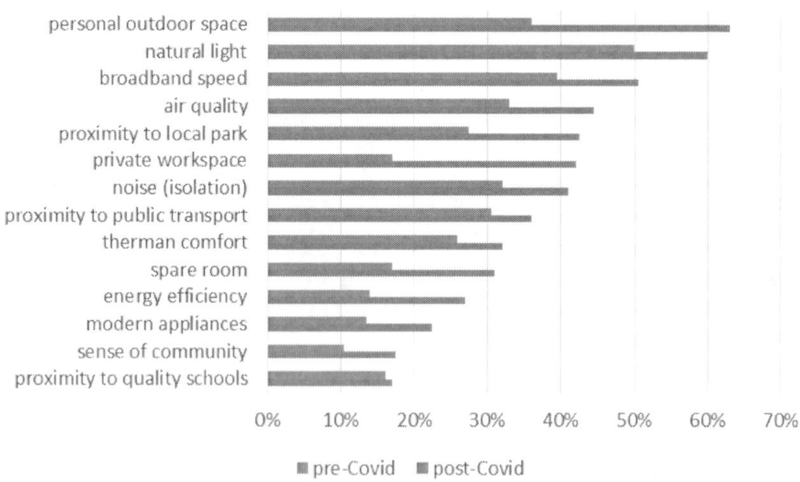

Source: JLL (2020)

Figure 6. Home location priorities.

3.3. Conclusion: Prospects for Urban Mixed Use

Large cities remain hubs of wealth, growth, and innovation. However, mixed-use real estate in central urban areas will have to be adapted to the post-Covid-19 period. Finding a new balance between urban clustering on the one hand and personal space on the other will be essential. This will require a higher degree of flexibility, a further shift to the service aspect of real estate, and an advanced integration of technology into real estate. A mutual task for investors, developers, and urban governments to be fulfilled for which cooperation between the stakeholders will be much needed.

Mixed-use environments are at their most efficient and most effective when they leverage a diversity of uses and users to create a balanced, dynamic, and integrated urban quarter. Urban mixed-use real estate has the potential to combine the needs of users in terms of health and wellbeing with the preferences of proximity of all functions, in an attractive walkable setting. This implies that both the physical construction, including infrastructure, systems, and the mix and partitioning of uses, and the public spaces both outdoor and indoor, create the kind sustainable and attractive places that provide a quality environment for people to live, work, and play, and a good return on capital and human investment. This placemaking happens when we can create or embrace mixed-use neighbourhoods. For municipal authorities, investors, and developers the task to work together to create and sustain viable neighbourhoods with an attractive and quality mixed-use building stock.

4. Cooperation in New Coalitons (by Joris Winters)

Real estate is, by definition, part of a larger (urban) spatial pattern and thus influenced by the facilities in and attractiveness of the immediate local area. Since the late 90s, due to global trends of urbanization and climate change, the planning, design and (re)development of these local areas is subject to an expanded range of forces. This creates a need to take a more integrated view on the real estate life cycle and, as the location of real estate is fixed and the most important factor in long term returns, the opportunities for cooperation with neighbors and various stakeholders in the immediate area. Apart from that, when the horizon of a 'future' is considered, these forces urge all real estate market participants to apply a longer-term horizon.

A typical challenge is that when long term investments in the improvement of a local area have to be made, there is a *common* interest by the real estate owners, but the *individual* appetite to contribute is often limited. Individual stakeholders tend to perceive such investments primarily in terms of (additional) costs, rather than returns from long term resilience. They often argue that others – such as the municipality or local utility companies – should invest in improvements of the area. This phenomenon is well known from biological science as the tragedy of the commons [12].

4.1. Dealing with Commons

A 'solution' to the challenge of the tragedy of the commons was developed by Elenor Ostrom, who was awarded the Nobel Memorial Prize in Economic Sciences for the underlying research in 2009 [13]. She argued that by pooling resources and forming coalitions, the likelihood to achieve effective long-term, collective governance of shared resources increased. Her work was based on the principle that common resources are well managed by those communities that benefit the most from them and that their regulation should be addressed at the local level, through the farmers, communities, local authorities and NGOs.

Can the Ostrom design principles be applied to cities to rethink the governance of cities and the management of their resources? Sheila Foster and Christian Laione (Georgetown University, Washington DC and

University of Rome) have argued [14] they cannot be simply adapted to the city context without significant modification.

They do find though that the concept of both economic and social "pooling" seems to capture the true essence of commons-based projects and policies in the urban environment. Another major pillar to govern urban commons is 'experimentalism': the presence of an adaptive and iterative approach to designing the legal processes and institutions. These notions of pooling and experimentalism might open opportunities to find solutions for common interest challenges – but then there is also the need to take a solid long term approach.

4.2. Dealing with Long Term

Vague risks in the distant future, as expressed in theories of the 'unknown unknowns', are often ignored by humans. American scientist, author, and entrepreneur Gary Marcus concluded that the roots of this is in the interplay of four psychological mechanisms [15]. First, concrete 'lively' information tends to have more impact than abstract information. Second, we do not calculate on (potential) benefits in the future and prefer one euro today rather that two over 12 months. Third, the reference-effect, in itself caused by 'priming': we are occupied by current topics, even if we see larger topics emerging later. Fourth: we tend to believe in a world of justice, where nature reaches its 'self-equilibrium'.

Another important observation, in 1972, was by the Club of Rome: a person's perspectives on time and space depend on his culture, his experience and the immediacy of the problems confronting him on each level. They pointed out that most people must have successfully solved the problems in a smaller area before they move their concerns to a larger one. And they observed that in general, the larger the space and the longer the time associated with a problem, the smaller the number of people who are concerned with its solution.

Richard Rumelt, the California-based thinker on strategy, has stressed the importance of proximate objectives [16]: one that is close enough at hand to be feasible, naming a target that the organization can reasonably be expected to hit, even overwhelm. Kennedy's 1961 speech on the US putting a man on the moon by the end of the '60s is perceived as an example of such a proximate objective. Rumelt does not specify what qualifies as 'proximate', but does observe that the more dynamic the situation, the poorer your foresight will be. Therefore: the more uncertain and dynamic the situation, the more proximate an objective must be. Assuming such proximate objectives to be feasible, they can generate a strong drive for teams and organizations at large to achieve targets.

These theories lead to the general phenomenon that both individual humans and companies tend to overestimate the short impact of crises - but underestimate the long-term impact. In the case of climate change adaptation this results in significant risks for the decades ahead.

In their book *Radical uncertainty*, John Kay and Melvin King note there is limited purpose in seeking to attach detailed estimates of probabilities to a range of potential future states of the world. This is also a conclusion of KPMG, having analysed annual reports of 25 listed companies on the Amsterdam stock exchange in 2020, they demonstrate it is important to address the potential impact of scenario's rather than trying to estimate probabilities, and to specify these in short, medium and long term. ABN Amro is mentioned as example of a company that has taken this approach in their 2019 report, where opportunities and risks of strategic differentiators are qualified within time horizons. Consequently, a 'long term' classification is applied for opportunities and risks that would materialize after 5 years, whereas the medium term is perceived as a 2 to 5 year timeframe – acknowledging though that 'often there is an effect over the short, medium and long term'.

It is important to realize that the notion of long term and the associated time horizon very much depends on the type of organization and its mission and objectives. For start-ups for example, a 5 year business plan to forecast cashflows is perceived as long: 'no one besides venture capitalists and the late Soviet Union requires five year plans to forecast complete unknowns'.

On the other hand, for established firms and governments the long term might imply a time horizon of up to 50 years, as exemplified by Shell's scenario's, which consider long-term trends in economics, energy supply and demand, geopolitical shifts and social change, as well as the motivating factors that drive change. The typical horizon for these scenario's is 20-25 years.

4.3. Long Term Perceptions in Real Estate and Finance

From a real estate investment perspective, what is typically considered as a long-term horizon for asset allocation? In the MSCI 2013 Global asset owner study, respondents were asked what they considered to be the appropriate time horizon for risk-forecasting in strategic asset allocation. The most common response was five years, although some thought that six months to a year was appropriate; others perceived the relevant horizon was ten years. This is a contrast to the nature of the future obligations of institutional investors, which can span 30 or 40 years ahead. In corporate and real estate finance, 'long term' can be up to 30 years: in 2019, Unibail Rodamco Westfield issued a bond due in 2049 [17]. Large, listed real estate investors often apply a 10 year objective to achieve sustainability targets – such as becoming carbon neutral [18].

4.4. The Road Ahead – Real Estate and Climate Adaption & Energy Transistion

A potential solution to address long term resilience in real estate at the level of district is in joint planning *and* participation in local entities by cooperation mechanisms, often structured in cooperatives or other special purpose vehicles (SPV's). These can effectively support transformations necessary to secure long term values for real estate, by enabling energy transition and climate change resilience.

Cooperation in new coalitions in joint ventures, also with parties from outside the traditional real estate domains, will be a crucial skill to remain competitive and adapt to new realities of climate change and energy transition. These are SPV's that integrate facilities to protect an area against the impact of climate change, typically in two domains:

- Adaptation measures: such as planning and co-investing in local infrastructure to protect area's against the future impact of climate change, improving resilience against flooding and/or urban heat islands
- Mitigation measures, focused on energy transition; generating and distributing renewable energy and/or by offering shared mobility solutions

Innovations to achieve such long term resilience and sustainability objectives are often subject to skepticism or threshold resistance. To demonstrate the viability and prospects of these cooperatives and SPV's, it I important to increase awareness of successful cases that have demonstrated that real estate can be 'protected' by preemptive planning and mobilizing (local) funding. We therefore now highlight a number of these in both domains.

4.4.1. Climate Adaption Cases

A classic, local government initiated case is the development of Hafencity – a large mixed use riverfront redevelopment district in the city of Hamburg (Germany), adjacent to the Elbe river, where the City developed a mix of innovative strategies to manage flood risk [19]. These enabled the area to be developed plot by plot, and that real estate development could start soon after the masterplan for Hafencity was approved by the Senat of the City of Hamburg in February 2000. The approach allows for some private responsibility for flood risk delegated to property owners and citizens. Nevertheless, the governance arrangement is dominated by the public parties involved. A local *verordnung* (law) forced property owners to implement and finance adaptive flood risk measures.

Property investors and developers were required to design and fund the elevation of the building plots, to take additional flood protection measures (such as flood doors), to reserve the ground floor for other activities than living/sleeping and establish 'safe' area's in case the protection system fails to prevent flooding. A considerable amount of the cost of flood risk management is thus borne by the private sector.

The idea of pooling money to fund climate adaptation is also applied in San Francisco's ongoing waterfront redevelopments of Mission Rock and Pier 70, where developers have already invested in climate change resilience by elevating the ground by 1, 5 to 3 meters. In 'Community facilities districts', fees ranging from $ 3,5 to 5 per square foot of property development are charged by the Port authorities to pay for adaptation work that it knows it will need as conditions change, but which cannot be planned 50 to 100 years out [20].

Another public-private case is Dutch developer BPD and the municipality of Kampen (Netherlands), who planned and developed a 'climate dike' with a length of 2 km and a width of 130 meters. This dike enables the development of 600 homes next to the IJssel river and protects the local area against potential flooding due to climate change.

Future models for long term real estate resilience are explored in the 7 Square endeavour program [21]. These include various partnerships models to achieve long term climate adaptation and energy transition at the local urban area level with solutions in several fields which include transport, environment, water supplies, urban planning, existing buildings and quality of life. Its focus is on integrated solutions for energy management, cyclical processes and green-blue designs. Initiatives to achieve these are smart grids (on site energy-generation, storage and exchange facilities), re-use of 'grey' water, implementation of green roofs and other new technologies that can be applied by and for all the people who live, work and undertake leisure activities in this area. Besides helping to create a better environment, participation also offers economic advantages, such as savings on energy costs as a result of using less energy. An example is Rotterdam's Schouwburgplein, where 'private-private' partnerships were structured to solutions mentioned above.

Square endeavour; artist impression Schouwburgplein, Rotterdam. © Vereniging Verenigd Schouwburgplein.

4.4.2. Energy Transitions Cases

The energy transition necessary to meet Paris climate agreement targets also offers future opportunities for real estate market players to cooperate in new coalitions, possibly by participating in joint ventures.

Significant prospects are in the emergence of renewable energy partnerships, where various public and private stakeholders create joint ventures to generate and distribute renewable energy for a local residential and/or commercial property district. An example is Etriplus, an energy company established in the Greenport area of Venlo (Netherlands), founded in 2013 by the area developer, the Development Company Greenport Venlo (DCGV), and the private companies Alliander, Arcadis, Greenchoice and Ekwadraat. Etriplus is engaged in energy production, infrastructure and energy savings with the aim of providing renewable energy and price continuity to companies - an attractive proposition that will strengthen the competitive position of companies in the area. The conceptual approach is based on the 'Quatras Energetica' [22] roadmap, delivering cost optimization, due to lower energy demands, price continuity and a lower carbon footprint.

In inner-cities and higher density residential environments, partnerships to enable the use of waste heat from supermarkets can be structured to improve sustainability of neighboring real estate. Examples are in Denmark where, since 2015, residents living near 20 of SuperBrugsen's supermarkets have their district heating supplied from the recovered surplus heat from the cooling system in the supermarket, reducing their CO2 emissions by 34%. This is the result of a cooperation between Danfoss heating systems, Sønderborg District Heating [23]

In more peripheral industrial and agricultural zones, cooperation to use waste heat from data centers offers opportunities – as long as the distance between the data center and properties to be heated is acceptable. An successful example is the Energy hub Aalsmeer (Netherlands): a unique energy exchange project by NorthC (data center) together with local greenhouse farming entrepreneurs and operators of nearby swimming pool and sports hall. These buildings use residual heat from the data center and are therefore completely free of natural gas. In exchange for the residual heat, the data center recovers cold and thus saves on its electricity consumption for cooling.

REFERENCES

[1] Wilson, B. (2020). *Metropolis*. London, Penguin Random House UK.

[2] Oxford Economics. (2020). *Data derived from Global Economic Database*, Jan 2021. Oxford, Oxford Economics.

[3] Jacobs, Jane. (1961). *The Death and Life of Great American Cities*. New York: Random House.

[4] BoC Business of Cities & Savills. (2019). *Europe's Core Cities: prospects for Mixed-Use Property Investment*. Report written for Meyer Bergman Ltd.

[5] Oldenburg, Ray. (1989). *The Great Good Place*. New York: Paragon House.

[6] Clark, G. (2020). *Reactivating Europe – The Role of Cities*. Key note presentation at ULI HSBC webinar 'Reactivating Europe – The Role of Cities', Dec 7th 2020. London, ULI, HSBC.

[7] Fabius, V., Kohli, S., Moulvad Veranen, S. & Timelin, B. (2020). *Meet the next-normal Consumer*. McKinsey & Company.

[8] Deana, K. (2020). Our Home is Our Castle. In Kok, H., P. Wessels. J. Veuger en K. Voolstra, eds: RICS white paper *'The Triple R of Covid-19: Reset, Recovery and Restructuring*, pp. 24-26. Deventer/ Enschede, Blockchain Saxion University of Applied Sciences (UAS).

[9] Mintel. (2020). O*nline Retailing: Inc Impact of COVID-19 – Europe, August 2020.* London, Mintel Group Ltd.

[10] ULI Urban Land Institute and Ernst & Young. (2020). *Future of Work*. Paris, Ernst & Young.

[11] JLL. (2020). *Housing needs and resident preferences across Europe during Covid-19*. London, JLL

[12] Hardin, G. (1968). *The Tragedy of the Commons*, *Science*, New Series, Vol. *162*, No. 3859, pp. 1243-1248.

[13] Olstrom, E. (1990). *Governing the Commons: The Evolution of Institutions for Collective Action.* Cambridge, UK: Cambridge University Press.

[14] https://www.thenatureofcities.com/2017/08/20/ostrom-city-design-principles-urban-commons/).

[15] Marcus, G. (2014). *Unknown unknowns, what should we be worried about? Real scenario's that keep up scientists at night*, Edge foundation.

[16] Rumelt, R. (2011). *Good strategy*, *bad strategy*, Profile books, London.

[17] Unibal Rodamco Westfield. (20 Nov. 2020) https://www.urw.com/-/media/Corporate~o~Sites/Unibail-Rodamco-Corporate/Files/Homepage/INVESTORS/Financing-Activity/Bond-Issues/EMTN-Senior-Bonds/FR0013431715-500Mn-30Y-EUR-July-2049-Final-Terms.ashx.

[18] Land Securities (20 Nov. 2020). https://landsec.com/sustainability/our-sustainability-strategy.

[19] Copernicus Institute of Sustainable Development, Utrecht University, the Netherlands. (2013). https://edepot.wur.nl/341526.

[20] Cohen, J. (2020). *Developing San Francisco's waterfront in the age of sea level rise*, Urban Land Magazine, fall 2020.

[21] *7 Square Endeavour* (22 Nov 2020). http://www.7square-endeavour.nl/EN/.

[22] Etriplus B. V. (21 dec 2020). http://www.etriplus.nl/english-summery/.

[23] Danfoss. (22 Nov. 2020). https://www.danfoss.com/en/service-and-support/case-studies/dcs/local-residents-stay-warm-thanks-to-supermarket-s-cooling-system/.

[24] Kok, H., Wessels, P., Veuger en K. J. & Voolstra, editors. (2020). *The Triple R of Covid-19: Reset, Recovery and Restructuring*. Essaybundel in E-book. RICS & Saxion University of Applied Sciences. https://bit.ly/2NZ5oTB.

About the Editor

Professor Dr. ing. Jan Veuger, MRE, FRICS is in 2019 appointed as professor Blockchain of the School of Finance & Accounting, School of Creative Technology and School of Governance, Law and Urban Development, Hospitality Business School and School of Commerce & Entrepreneurship of the Saxion University of Applied Sciences, The Netherlands. Therefore he was from 2012-2019 professor Real Estate at the Hanze University of Applied Sciences Groningen, Institute for Business. Jan graduated from the Erasmus University Rotterdam, one of Europe's top business schools for education and in the top three for research. Next to being a professor, Jan is co-promoter of several PhD candidates, Chairman of the Committee of quality certificates (CKV) at Quality Center Social Housing Corporations, member of Supervisory Board of Commissioners for four different organizations (to 2,000 employees) in the area of social housing and elderly care. Furthermore, Editorial Board Member Diponegoro International Journal of Busines (DIJB), member of the RICS Netherlands & Department Research and Innovation, Fellow of the RICS, President Academic Board FIBREE, Editor Real Estate Quarterly Research (REQR), member of the Academic Council Master Facility & Real Estate Management Saxion University, Editor & member of Scientific Editorial Board Conference of

Interdisciplinary Research on Real Estate (CIRRE), Board European Real Estate Society (ERES), author of many (e)book(chapters), international scientific and professional publications, research reports and has given many guest lectures.

https://www.linkedin.com/in/dr-ing-jan-veuger-mre-frics-11112617/

INDEX

E

F

G

H

I

J

K

Q

R

U

V

W

Z